LONG DRAWN OUT TRIP

GERALD SCARFE

LONG DRAWN OUT TRIP

Little, Brown

LITTLE, BROWN

First published in Great Britain in 2019 by Little, Brown

1 3 5 7 9 10 8 6 4 2

A CIP catalogue record for this book
is available from the British Library.

ISBN 978-1-4087-1155-2

Typeset in Perpetua by M Rules
Printed and bound in Great Britain by
Clays Ltd, Elcograf S.p.A.

Papers used by Little, Brown are from well-managed forests
and other responsible sources.

Little, Brown
An imprint of
Little, Brown Book Group
Carmelite House
50 Victoria Embankment
London EC4Y 0DZ

An Hachette UK Company
www.hachette.co.uk

www.littlebrown.co.uk

To my family

*What's your dream job? Mine would be to draw
cartoons. You have a life of complete freedom. You
work from home. You get started when you want to.
You have no boss, no irritating colleagues, no journey
to the office and back, and no timetable. You enjoy
all the creative independence of a film director, but
without the technical and financial constraints.*

I cut this quote out and had it pinned above my desk
for years. It's a nice sentiment but it's bollocks. I
don't know who the author was, but if they would
like to make themselves known, I would be very
happy to buy them a drink at Scarfes Bar and credit
them in the next printing of this book. I hope the
following pages will set the record straight.

Introduction

I was interviewing my friend Roger Waters for the Pink Floyd book I was writing when he suddenly rose from his chair and announced he had an appointment to play golf and had to go. I hadn't quite finished with the interview and, sensing this, Rog said, 'If you want any more memories . . . '

'Yes?' I said expectantly.

'Just fucking make it up.'

Well, I've not made up any of the following, but maybe it would have been more interesting if I had. History is bunk, they say. Depending on who wrote it and from what point of view, or what side. We all know if you have four people in a room together who witness a murder, when interviewed later individually they will probably give four differing accounts. So autobiographies are bound to be approximate, and the longer the time lapse the sketchier the memory.

I have written about my life and times as an artist and how I became what I am. I'm told that readers will be interested to know about my beginnings, what formed me. So this is an account of my childhood, where they say most people are formed – 'Give me a child until he is seven and I'll give you the man.' And what happened after. What in my childhood, background and environment turned me into the artist I have become? What has given me the reputation of a cruel, grotesque and satirical artist with a black view of life? Well, if one scientific theory is to be believed, none of the above. Environment, home life and schooling have had no effect. It's all in my DNA. It's entirely and totally that which decides what I am, absolutely nothing else. But I'm not so sure.

It's interesting which memories survive: in my case often because they are moments of extreme pain: watching boys pulling the legs off spiders in the school playground and cruelly trying to do it myself; slipping my hand into my father's on a family walk during a visit he made to see us and burning it on his cigarette; and, another time, walking home tearful and soggy in dripping grey flannel trousers after falling in the river while tadpoling. I made a bow and arrow. I shot it and hit a small boy in the eye. I was so scared – I thought I had blinded him. He was OK, but all these years later the feelings of guilt and fear come rushing back when I think of him.

Writing an autobiography and talking constantly about oneself can be tantamount to blowing one's own trumpet. In trying to give a correct history I have had to include the good times and the praise I've had. That can feel self-promoting and big-headed sometimes, whereas recounting the bad times can seem self-deprecating and honest. I've tried to ignore this and to put in facts that I think might be interesting, whether good or bad. It is, above all, an account of my professional life as an artist. My private life is shared with others, but I do not want to hurt my nearest and dearest by exposing them to scrutiny. I have a wonderful wife, Jane, and four children: two beautiful daughters, Katie and Araminta, and two handsome sons, Alexander and Rory. We devastatingly lost my third son, Rupert, to illness three years ago. I do not intend to invade their privacy by writing about them in this autobiography. Likewise, my six grandchildren – Ella, Iggy, Abel, May, Ava and Freddie – will not be appearing and I will also not be embarrassing any of my ex-partners.

Inevitably Jane's name appears from time to time in the book, but these minimal references in no way reflect the closeness we have shared in our nearly fifty years together, or the huge influence she has had and continues to have on my life and work.

So, this is a memoir of some of my childhood days, and my progress through the art, theatre and film world. To avoid disappointment, it's probably best for me to come clean at the beginning. I am not a recovering alcoholic, although I do have a bar named after me. I am not a drug addict, although I have dabbled in drugs recreationally – opium in Vietnam, coke in my rock and roll days. Drugs have a different connotation to me. They invoke memories of illness. So drugs I have had a-plenty – for the wretched asthma I have suffered from my whole life. I have been asked if the cocktail of drugs I have been taking for over eighty years – including the 'speed'-like ephedrine and adrenaline of my childhood (both of which made me feel unpleasantly 'high') and the powerful, effective and life-changing steroids of my adulthood) – could have affected my perceptions and distorted my vision either then or now. I have never asked a medical person. I'm not sure they would know anyway. But it's an interesting thought.

Why write an autobiography? I'm not sure. Sort of like a tidying up, putting it all together in one drawer. It's fascinating to look back and see how much one has done, and also how little. How lucky I have been and yet how many opportunities I have let slide by. How many wrong tributaries I have taken and how on other occasions I have landed on my feet by sheer serendipity. Very little of it has been planned. I have almost tumbled from one job to another.

I have never kept a diary. Many of the memories I have assembled here come from rifling through what press cuttings, articles and catalogues I have. But the strongest memories are brought back by looking at my drawings, most of which I have kept – each one triggers the memory of when it was drawn and why, and how I felt at that time.

Although an Englishman working in Britain, I have always felt an outsider, an onlooker, a recorder. As a child I was lonely and shy, perhaps even prudish. I found that I communicated with others better by drawing my pictures.

As you will notice, words are not my métier. My education was poor, if not non-existent, especially in my younger years, when asthma wrecked my schooling. I will try to put words together as I would a painting, to make a picture using adjectives as colours.

I have written all of this autobiography in longhand. Being something of a Luddite I have never mastered computers. I am computer illiterate. It is not a matter of principle, simply one of laziness. I never had to make the effort as Jane and my assistant, Julie, are both completely on top of the game and do it all for me.

This does not mean computers are not involved in my work. Many of my drawings are composed on the computer. On paper I may draw two figures, for instance, and Julie scans them separately into Photoshop and we put them into a scene together, perhaps also adding a sky I have painted earlier, or other elements.

Today the internet is incredibly useful for whizzing drawings around the globe. In 1966 I was in a chaotic post office in Saigon filling in barely understandable forms in an effort to get a large parcel of drawings back to England. Utter confusion – I thought I'd said goodbye to them for ever, but they made it. Now a press of a button and they are there in a flash.

But for this book it had to be all handwritten, which is limiting – words, sentences, have to be added by writing over the top of existing copy if I want to change anything. Tolstoy managed it (no comparison suggested), or rather Mrs Tolstoy did, and many writers still prefer to work in longhand, establishing a tactile contact with the page to help see where they have been and where they went wrong. The whole history of the piece is always there. So in my case it's very like drawing – battling through the mistakes and imposing the correct drawing on top, always aware of the path taken.

The process of drawing can be wonderful when it works, ideas flowing, an urgency and necessity to get them down before they evaporate. But beware those days when nothing, nothing, nothing will happen. No wonder we believe in the muse. I end up trying to trick myself into working: rushing it, sidling up to it, caressing it. But nothing happens. The pen won't work. The ink is too thick. My hand is like a steel claw or a mountainous piece of dough. There is no connection between my hand and my brain. The work stuttering and spluttering on to the paper. The nib snaps. It's hell! Damn! Where did it go? It was here a minute ago.

Incidentally, people often ask me if I think my drawings change anything. My answer is 'Not a jot'. So, why do I bother? I don't know. I feel I must cry out – perhaps it can raise the public conscience, prick the public nerve. But the poor public nerve is numb with bombardments from all quarters. We sit with great heaped plates of food in front of us, watch television pictures of the dying and the starving and feel a momentary pang of guilt which moves on when the pictures change. Then we go to the fridge to see what we can have for pudding.

I

I know so little about my parents; when they were alive I didn't think to ask. I recently found out that my mother was not Welsh as I had believed but had only been brought up in Wales, in Radnorshire, where her father was headmaster of New Radnor School. (I have a book, *Halifax Gentleman*, a prize given to my mother when she was at the school in 1913 as a five-year-old girl. An illuminated plate inside on the first page reads 'Second prize awarded to Edna Gardner for regular attendance' and was signed by 'John Gardner, Head Teacher'. A slight whiff of nepotism there perhaps?) I was told that every summer the girls of New Radnor looked forward with excitement to the arrival of the four Scarfe brothers, who regularly spent their summer holidays in that area. It was there one year that my father had met my mother after riding down from London on his motorbike. On one of these trips he lost control of the motorbike and knocked out his two front teeth on the New Radnor Bridge.

My family home was in Swiss Cottage, north London, at 57 Goldhurst Terrace to be precise. The house is still there today. (As always on revisiting a place you knew as a child, everything now seems so much smaller.) I was born not far away in a private nursing home in St John's Wood, a well-to-do area, on 1 June 1936. I suppose we were middle, middle class. My mother had been a schoolteacher before her marriage. My father, Reginald, a Londoner, spent all of his civilian life in banking. I was their first child and my brother would not be born until after the war nearly nine years later.

I was always told as a child that I had a 'weak chest'. From the age of one I suffered from chronic asthma. When I reached the age of about five I would try to pretend I didn't have asthma so that other children would not see me as different. I inevitably did feel very different, and it was a terrible strain – trying to look as if I were breathing normally. A severe asthma attack is a horrible thing to observe. The sufferer, his shoulders heaving, gasps for every breath as though it is his last. It is truly frightening, and as a child I would see the fear on other people's faces as they thought I was about to die.

The nights were the worst. I dreaded them. So many were spent dark-eyed and haunted, my dry chest heaving, propped up on rigid arms to ease my breathing. Waiting for the night to end, waiting for the blackbird to sing – she signalled the dawn. It was a relief when daylight crept through the window and, still gasping for breath, in the morning light I could draw and read, listen to the radio, or watch the occasional bird through the window.

During this period I became fascinated with puppets, toy theatres and Meccano working models. I made umpteen glove puppets, string puppets, figures out of Plasticine, with scenery, and gave shows for myself. One day I felt delirious with excitement and knew for sure I would be doing this type of thing in the grown-up world. But then it could have been the drugs. (I did do the same thing later in my career, but the puppets were thirty feet high and the theatres and actors real.)

One of my favourite books was *Winky-Pop the Gnome*. My father thought it was a huge joke and called me Winky-Pop. Perhaps I had a fixation on gnomes, but one day when we were out shopping, I saw a porcelain gnome, about two feet high, for sale – a garden ornament. I so desperately wanted to own this ghastly gnome with his shiny green coat and pointed red hat. My parents really didn't want to buy or own it but I pleaded and they gave in and bought it. We carried it home to Goldhurst Terrace. I was so excited. We were going to put it in the back garden on the flagstone terrace. I wanted to hold it but my parents said I would drop it and it would smash, then I would be sorry. But I begged, saying no, I wouldn't drop it. Eventually my father carefully put the gnome in my arms. I don't know exactly what came over me but I had this feeling of wondering what would happen if it did fall. I purposely opened my arms and let him slip. I know I did it on purpose – but why I don't know. He smashed into smithereens and I cried my eyes out. I had destroyed the very thing I desired.

Naturally the imminent prospect of war produced a great feeling of unease everywhere. My parents must have done what they could to hide their feelings of dread but I, as a small, anxious child, picked it up. We were still living in Goldhurst Terrace when war was declared in September 1939.

The German air raids on London began in 1940 – like wolves in the night, the eerie howling of the air-raid sirens struck fear into all stomachs, and citizens scurried to the shelters. The doodlebugs with their noisy engines whizzed overhead. When that engine cut out and stopped, as it was designed to do, the air was full of fear. Without the power of the engine it dropped earthwards, full of death and explosives, on to the roofs below.

Where would it land? Everyone held their breath. Whose lives would be finished? Whose would never be the same again?

We had a corrugated-iron air-raid shelter at the bottom of the garden. It was never used, often full of rainwater and, I can see now, completely useless. But it was a great place to play. Sweet are the uses of adversity.

Whenever the siren sounded and the bombs began to fall we went down and sat in the cellar. But I was more frightened of the wolf someone had told me lived and was hiding down there than I was of Hitler and his Luftwaffe. I was also terrified of the claustrophobic Mickey Mouse gas mask I sometimes had to wear in that cellar. The government had thought that by sticking a couple of Mickey Mouse ears on to a repellent rubber gas mask children would be tricked into enjoying it. Absolutely not. To a young asthmatic child who was short of breath it was a suffocating nightmare. I could not breathe. I thought I would die.

When I was a boy, Dad's lead soldiers would be brought out of large cardboard boxes on special occasions. They belonged to him and his three brothers but were always kept in our house – tanks, gun carriages, infantry, cavalry etc. We would set them out in ranks along the top of an old oak chest and then put them away again. I was far too young and they were far too precious for me to play with alone. Later I learned that lead is not good for you.

My father was called up and enlisted in the Royal Air Force. He wasn't Biggles. He didn't fly aircraft, but flew a desk, as they used to say. The RAF were the 'glamour boys' of the forces, also known, disparagingly, as 'Brylcreem Boys' after the glutinous hair cream that plastered the hair on to the scalp and gave the short back-and-sides hairstyle a slick look. In 1940 my father was posted to an RAF base in Cardiff, and my mother and I went with him.

Not long after the move to Cardiff it was to be my first day of school. On that day my mother woke me before dawn and, standing me on the kitchen table, dressed me in my new school uniform by flickering candlelight because of the black-out. I felt apprehensive. In the soft darkness I imagined what school would be like. There would be lots of new friends, I was told. Lots of games to play. It would be fun. Then my father took me on the crossbar of his bicycle downhill through the dark streets towards the school. I was miserable. It was horrible. I had not thought that I would ever have to leave home. I wet myself in assembly and felt horrific shame. My asthma was bad and my attendance worse. My one distinction at that school was that at the age of five I became renowned for drawing the Welsh dragon. I had already found that drawing made a difference – it lifted me and made me feel special. I had discovered something only I could do, something that others, including teachers, would praise me for.

Great excitement ran through the school one day. A Jerry had been shot down in Cardiff. We missed the plane crash itself but watched the pilot float silently and gently down, swinging from side to side under his white parachute. He landed in the allotments among the vegetables. Six or seven men ran forward wielding spades and gardening forks, but he stood up, offering no resistance, and was led silently away. He was very young, apparently. 'We shall fight them in the hills, on the beaches and among the runner beans . . . '

Occasionally other disasters of war touched our lives in Cardiff. One evening I heard my father tell my mother he had seen an airman cycling across the runway. Dad said that somehow he'd cycled into a taxiing plane's propeller and was chopped into bits. Naturally these stories stay in the mind.

Throughout this period I continued to suffer badly from asthma attacks and regularly had to go to hospital. 'There will be lots of toys,' coaxed my parents, but hospital was frightening and visiting hours were short. Sometimes my parents would walk across the fields at the back of the hospital to wave to me from behind a wire fence. Misery! I was in an adult ward. The cleaning lady looked like a witch; I had to humour her. The man in the bed opposite threw me a slab of toffee because I was crying. It missed the bed and slid into the fluff underneath. The witch gave it to me. I smiled at her. Better to keep in with her. You never know. By the way, the promised toys were not that great.

Perhaps because of these prolonged absences from school and my scant experience of socialising with other children, I was very shy, blushed easily, and found it almost impossible to talk in public. Through most of my early childhood I spent much time alone with my mother and was never really encouraged to make conversation. Adults tended to talk above me and over me. Sitting in the back seat of my father's car, I heard my grandfather say, 'The lad doesn't say much, Reg.' This stung me at the time, again making me feel not normal and cut off, but my father stoutly defended me, saying, 'No, but Gerald thinks a lot.' I did think a lot, and worry a lot. Dad was right.

There followed a succession of schools as we moved around the country. My parents put me into the nearest one regardless of quality so that, should I get an asthma attack, they'd be near at hand. At one school they started algebra while I was ill. When I returned I had no idea what the teacher was talking about and no one bothered to explain it to me.

When I was six, my father was posted to Ludlow in Shropshire, where we lived over a pub. The pub owned an Alsatian, who slept under my bed and scratched his back on the underside of the mattress – not great for my asthma, I learnt later.

Although I have memories of playing mothers and fathers with the girl who lived next door, and, afterwards, letting her have a go on my tricycle, I had few friends, and any I did make lost interest because I was never at school and they found it boring to visit someone who was bed-ridden, coughing and spluttering.

More often I was to be found in solitary pursuits. One day I tempted fate by walking under the belly of a grazing horse as a dare set by myself, fear and excitement pricking the back of my neck as I walked around behind his back legs, which could have kicked hell out of me; and then when I got away with it, walking under his belly to see if I could get away with it again, and then once more to make sure. That day I found a beautiful horseshoe, and had it taken away by a bigger boy.

I had always been 'good at drawing' so, in my isolation, I took to it more and more, and it became my method of communication with the world. It would exorcise bad thoughts and allowed me to make my own world. I could spend hours engrossed in a drawing and not notice the time pass by. I still can.

I remember everyone sang 'Bless them all, the long and the short and the tall' as my father, the only man in uniform, carried me on his shoulders into an air-raid shelter when the siren rang out. My mother and I felt very proud, sure that the song was sung for Dad.

I watched an army exercise on the wooded banks of the River Teme in the shadow of Ludlow Castle: a mock battle with Tommies versus Tommies dressed up as Germans. A German fell off the bridge into the water. The Tommies won. This made me and everyone around me happy – we had triumphed. All the 'Germans' were either captured or dead. This play-acting of victory over the enemy was the next best thing to the 'real thing'.

Around 1943 my father was sent on another posting, to Shaftesbury. My mother and I followed to the comparative safety and bliss of the Dorset countryside, where the two of us would walk down golden-brown country lanes in the autumn sunshine collecting acorns for pigs as part of the war effort and eating dried eggs and dried bananas. My mother saved all of the family's butter ration to 'build me up'. I hated it; I preferred margarine.

I watched my father playing the double bass in the RAF band at a Christmas dance at Motcombe House, a grand stately home in the park where he was stationed. Afterwards I waited for my turn to get a present from Father Christmas by the Christmas tree, watching the presents go, one by one, only to find I was the one child who had been forgotten. My father blamed the sergeant who he claimed didn't like him.

This was the last time we followed my father on one of his postings, as he then went up to Inverness in Scotland, I think around 1944. It was felt it was too far for my mother and I to travel to be with him so we went to live with my mother's parents who were now living in Kidderminster. I didn't see very much of my father during this period as it was difficult for him to get leave.

My grandparents' house was in St John's Street, a street of modest Victorian two-storey houses. But theirs was the 'big house' at the far end of the road. There was a large garden with a grand drive that opened through double gates on to the road. On the drive was a wrought-iron garden seat from which I had fallen at a very early age and gashed a hole in my cheek. I still bear the slight scar today. My mother was convinced the wrought-iron arm of the seat had pierced right through my cheek. It hadn't, but I can recall her panic. The house was large but not enormous. At the foot of the stairs in the hall was a series of bells set on curly springs, which had at one time been used to summon servants. Unfortunately we had none, so they lay silent. Years later I went back to look for the house for a TV programme but it was no longer there. A motorway runs straight through the living room.

My grandfather, white-haired, distant and stern, was now a retired headmaster and, apart from his weekly trips out to play billiards, seemed to spend most of the time in his study, which was a no-go area. He is a hazy figure in my memory, and had very little to do with me. He would not allow my grandmother to water the garden because it was a waste of water: he always stuck to the rules and there were wartime measures in place to save water at that time. She and my mother would do it anyway, during his afternoon nap.

I was woken up one night and taken to see my grandfather, who was very ill. There was a strange atmosphere in the room, people crying I think. I was taken back to my bed and, shortly afterwards, my mother came to tell me he had gone.

'Gone where?' I said.

She tried to explain.

There was no escaping the war, and many Americans were stationed in Kidderminster, which was exciting for us ten-year-olds – and, I started to understand, for the older girls, who found their uniforms attractive (among other things). These American soldiers were said to be 'overpaid, over-sexed and over here'. With a great effort I forced myself to pluck up the courage to ask a 'Yank', 'Have you got any gum, chum?' The boys at school had told me how they did it. He knew the drill, reached into his jacket pocket and handed me a pack of Wrigley's Spearmint.

At the end of St John's Street was a prisoner of war camp called Wolverley, a converted factory in which Italian prisoners of war were interred. Its large wooden double gate was permanently open. It was clear that none of the Italian POWs would try or even wanted to escape – they were quite happy working on the local farms. So much better than fighting for the deluded braggart Mussolini and his evil pal Hitler. One day I walked to the camp and plucked up even more courage to ask an Italian POW to give me a torch. All the other boys had. He told me to go to a side window and passed it through the wire mesh of his 'open prison'. '*Escapa, escapa,*' he said, and I ran for it with my prized torch.

My mother told me that as it was wartime toys were scarce and Father Christmas would not be leaving much that year. I was disappointed, but on Christmas morning I found Santa had left me a model farm with toy animals – cows, sheep and ducks, a little farmhouse, a pig sty – something I later learned my father had spent many long hours making out of discarded cardboard boxes. There was a mirror for a duck pond which I thought was very clever.

Paper was scarce during the war, so being a prolific artist, always drawing and hungry for something to draw on, I covered every scrap of paper on both sides with sketches. My father would bring me ruled accounts books with a red line down one side from his RAF barracks which I filled. I made a drawing of a house-wife at the sink washing the dishes while a louche-looking Yank lounged in the doorway casually smoking. Mainly I drew scenes from Disney films, but I don't think I had a sense at that early point that art would be my vocation. Everybody said I was a good artist but it didn't strike me as anything lasting or significant.

None of my drawings from that period have survived. I don't think my parents were sentimental about my work. Maybe because of our nomadic lifestyle, moving from one address to another, we had to travel light.

One thing I did cherish was my collection of cigarette cards. Some of the grown-ups in the family, including my father, smoked, and most packets of cigarettes in those days, far from carrying a 'death warning', enclosed a cigarette card – an encouragement to smoke on as heavily as possible. These would be pictures of famous sportsmen or film stars, and children found them highly collectable. They would be swapped by the boys at school. If you wanted a particular footballer to complete your set you might have to give three or more of your cards in exchange in order to get it.

My favourite cards were called 'Howlers': beautifully drawn, they dealt with popular misconceptions in terrible jokes which I thought were quite clever at the time: 'Julius Caesar was a very strong man and threw a bridge across the Rhine'; 'Queen Elizabeth I was thin and pale but she was a stout participant'; 'An artist is a man with long hair who can't sell anything'. At school there was a game we played with them. The cards were flicked towards a wall and the person whose card finished closest to the wall won all the flicked cards. I became quite good at this and amassed a vast collection of assorted cards.

The playing fields of the local grammar school were at the end of St John Street. Through the railings I could see the boys playing rugby. They seemed different creatures to those in my school: more confident, and with very loud voices. My mother told me that that school was where she would like me to go.

Mother had always put much emphasis on being well spoken and well brought up. My parents' efforts in this regard exhausted me. My father always raised his hat to ladies. I'm not sure whether that is politically incorrect these days. I don't wear a hat, but I no longer see those who do doffing theirs. I do still rise to my feet when a female comes into the room, and my mother always told me to hold the door open for ladies. The main problem was that I was speaking with what they perceived to be a 'terrible Brummie accent', which should have been of no surprise since I was going to school in Kidderminster where everyone spoke with a Midlands accent. I was trying to be like my friends and fit in. Even now my wife tells me I sometimes tend to imitate or adopt the accent of the person I'm talking to. I don't feel I'm being patronising – it is more an effort to communicate. I was quiet and shy, and, ironically, to my schoolmates I still sounded posh, and so felt even more like an outsider. I tended to befriend those who also felt themselves to be underdogs, and became close to two boys, Dharam Dass and Heinz Katchke. We were all outsiders for different reasons, which drew us together. I didn't even like the name Gerald. Most of my friends had much more down-to-earth Christian names and Gerald seemed to be 'toffee-nosed'. I still prefer Gerry today.

'I don't know what's the matter with you, Scarfe,' said one teacher when I was in my early teens, reinforcing this feeling of being different. 'Why are you always drawing disasters?' He was right – I *was* always drawing disasters. Trains crashing, native uprisings, volcanoes erupting, ships going down at sea – it was always disasters. Everything was a disaster. What had brought about these dark thoughts? But it was hardly surprising: we had just lived through six years of war, and disasters seemed to be everywhere, even in the relative calm of Kidderminster. One day a boy at school told me he had seen a woman being murdered at a second-floor window. I didn't believe him. He took me to see the exact window. I still didn't believe him, but such was his zeal and conviction in putting his story across, I wasn't entirely sure.

But I did see a poor man suffering an epileptic fit in an alleyway between gardens. As he shook and swayed he held on to the railings with one hand while the other let drop his morning's shopping – a paper packet from which a gleaming silver fish slipped on to the ground. I was too scared to help, but a kindly lady stepped in and picked up his fish. Around the same time I saw a cat dart across the road. There was a thump as it was run over by a passing car. I saw the poor cat with a broken back trying to run crookedly to the pavement. A man hit it on its head with a walking stick. It ran into a wall and died there with its pink tongue lolling out. I often wonder if I've logged these images and unconsciously allowed them to influence my work.

I suffered from the most horrific nightmares. Shouting and confused, half asleep and half awake, twisting and turning. My hands on the counterpane felt 'thick' and swollen to an enormous size. I thrashed around, the blankets sweaty and tangled. I struck out with my legs and once caught my grandmother, who was trying to quieten me, full in the chest. She reeled back and fell to the floor. I was at once asleep and awake at the same time. I was in a strange, heightened, lonely world. I could still see the room around me but everything seemed a long way away, sometimes as though down a never-ending tunnel. It was very frightening.

Could it have been the drugs? There is no record of what I was being prescribed at that time.

A very large picture that hung over the fireplace in the bedroom didn't help. It looked creepy. It showed three monks in aprons carrying a large table laden with plates of food. One of the monks had three legs. I don't think it was intentional: the artist had repainted the leg he didn't like in a new position and forgotten to take the old one out. I found it disturbing.

Lying alone in the dark one night I felt something walking across the counterpane. Panic swept over me – it felt like an animal. A cat? But we didn't have a cat, so it couldn't be. I shouted out in fear without daring to look. It was a witch's cat, I thought. Another nightmare? But no, it turned out it *was* a cat, looking up at me completely unaware of the terror it had inspired. How it got on to my bed and from where it came I never knew.

Probably because he was frequently away, when I saw him my father seemed 'new' to me. I didn't know him well. I think when he visited us in Kidderminster my mother urged him to try to get to know me. One day I walked shyly hand in hand with my dad to nearby Hadley Valley for a drink at the Fountain pub, where he had a half of bitter and I drank lemonade. It was slightly awkward, as though he didn't know what to say to me. Maybe being in the RAF had kept him away for a long time.

My father was a gentle, rather shy man and I was extremely fond of him. He was very kind to me. Some of my friends had pet white mice. They told me a shop in the Kidderminster Butts was selling them so I went down there on my own and made my first ever purchase, buying the last white mouse in the shop for a shilling. I took it home. My mother and grandmother were a little nonplussed and irritated at first, but my father got to work building it a little wooden cage with a door and a wire mesh front. There was a place for my mouse to sleep on one side and a place for her to walk about on the other. All went well for a while and

I would take out my little mouse with her pink eyes and let her explore my arm and the small area that was my room. We were both very happy.

I became convinced my mouse was going to have babies. She was tearing up bits of paper and making a snug nest in her home. My mother patiently explained to me that you need a father mouse and a mother mouse to make babies – my first proper lesson in this unbelievable and puzzling concept. Surely that couldn't be right? The boys had told me about it at school but I didn't believe it: too surreal. I knew my parents hadn't done that, it was unthinkable! And as my mouse was shut up in her cage all the time it was not possible anyway. But I remained convinced that my mouse was pregnant, and sure enough she had a litter of small blind mice. Incontrovertible proof that you did not need a father and mother to make a baby. I later learned that it had not been an immaculate conception, and that somehow my mouse had been receiving a gentleman caller. I think my father's carpentry skills must have been a tad shoddy and a common (but bold) brown house mouse had got into my pink-eyed lady's little house and had his wicked way with her. The next day, when I returned excitedly from school with friends to show off my baby mice, I found that my grandmother had drowned them all in a bucket of water. A cruel lesson in bereavement. I was devastated. She had been worried the house would be overrun with the creatures.

Asthma continued to plague and attack me, though as any person with a disability knows, one learns to live with it. Apart from crippling attacks I was able to make my way wheezily through the day. One of the more bizarre, almost medieval 'cures' was thought to be having a hot poultice applied to my chest. It was said to draw out the bacteria. It is still used for horses.

My parents announced that if I wished I could spend the summer holidays with my paternal grandmother and grandfather in Twyford, near Reading. Initially it was thought that getting away into the country air would do me and my asthma good, and indeed I think it did do me good, but not perhaps in that way. It was a relief to get away from my lonely life at home; it gave me a sense of freedom. My Aunt Mary and my cousins Susan, Monica, Tim and Dick would most likely be there and we could play in the garden, roam the fields, go for walks, climb trees and ride our bikes along the unmade dirt roads with their enormous brown puddles at will. I loved every moment of it.

Although Walt Disney was my biggest hero as a child and I waited with excitement for any of his films to appear, my first artistic influence was my paternal grandfather. He was a magician with wood – it seemed he could transform it into anything he wished. His workshop in the garage was a child's delight. Racks of chisels, bradawls, planes and saws. Shelves with brightly coloured pots of paint and half-finished toys, and the floor covered with ankle-deep wood shavings. The smell of those shavings stays with me even now. He made toys for all his grandchildren.

Most of all I admired his model soldiers. Some were mounted and some were on foot. Hussars, Lancers, Horse Guards and Coldstream Guards – every detail carved and painted to perfection. When I was about fifteen, I copied him and made some myself. I still have them. My grandfather had been in the army and appeared to know every regiment, every rank and every uniform. Even late in his life he had a military bearing with a very straight back and upright posture. He looked like the film star C. Aubrey Smith.

He made toys for us children throughout the war. One Christmas he made me a wooden machine gun with a metal attachment that made a 'chattering' sound when I turned a little handle. It might not stand comparison with the computer games of today but nevertheless it carried its element of violence.

My grandfather also kept chickens, and it was a treat to go down to the hen house at the bottom of the garden with him, open the lids of laying boxes at the back, put my hand into the deep straw inside and rummage around. The sensation of feeling warm, beautiful, brown or pearly white newly laid eggs nestled in the straw was wonderful. We would take them back to the house where my grandmother would prepare fresh boiled eggs with buttered toast for the breakfast table.

Much to my grandmother's distaste, my grandfather had a particular way of dealing with annoying flies. When one landed on the kitchen table his hand would hover over the unsuspecting insect merrily going about cleaning its black legs, then with a loud smack he would hit the table. End of fly. 'Gotcha!' he would say. My grandmother found this behaviour coarse and cruel. 'Oh, do stop that,' she used to say.

All the Scarfes had a great sense of humour. I asked my grandfather why the cockerel who serviced the hens ran in such a strange bandy-legged way, with his legs so far apart. 'Well,' he said, 'he used to run with them so close together that the friction caused them to catch fire, which he found uncomfortable, so now he runs like that to let the breeze blow through.' I believed him.

My grandfather worked in London, in the Commonwealth Bank of Australia. He would often bring me bundles of used envelopes that had been sent to the bank. I was an enthusiastic stamp collector and would steam the stamps from the envelopes and add them to my collection. They were often exotic and colourful, and took me to faraway lands with wonderful names – Tanganyika, Ceylon, Samoa, Abyssinia . . . I had some very rare and unusual examples: a couple of Penny Blacks, and others from Commonwealth countries with the King and Queen on that I was told were valuable. There is a great deal of money in stamps, but unfortunately I later left my collection in a house I owned which was torn down. So in my case philately didn't get me anywhere

I enjoyed digging holes, big deep holes. I would take a spade from the garage, go down to the bottom of the garden and dig a hole. I loved it – I'm not sure why. I told the adults I was digging for coal. They said they thought I was on my way to Australia. One day I did unearth some shiny black coal. Too shiny really. Something didn't seem quite right. I discovered later that one of my aunts had buried it there for me to find.

In general, life at Twyford was idyllic, but every silver lining has a cloud. That cloud was my uncle Bobby. I was about eight years old when, as I walked to the top of the stairs one morning in the house in Twyford, I heard the raised voices of Aunt Mary and her husband, Bobby, arguing in their bedroom. That morning there had been great excitement as Aunt Mary had suggested, as a rare treat, an outing to the cinema in Reading – me, my cousins Tim and Dick, and Uncle Bobby and Aunt Mary. I heard Uncle Bobby shout, 'We don't want that kid coming with us!' As I stood on the landing outside their bedroom I realised, with a frozen coldness creeping over me, 'that kid' was me. Choking back my tears I said, 'It's all right, Aunt Mary, I'd rather stay here – don't worry.' There was a prolonged silence from behind the door. I heard my aunt say, 'You wretch. You wretch!' Then, coming out on to the landing, 'Oh, darling, he didn't mean it.' She put her arm around me. 'Let's go downstairs.' In floods of tears I went downstairs.

To cut a long story short I did go to the pictures that afternoon to see Danny Kaye in *Up in Arms*, followed by tea and cakes. Looking back, it's hard to see how I could have gone anywhere with Uncle Bobby – but I was a young boy and was easily consoled and tricked by being given a real banana (a scarcity in those days), and also by the loving care of my aunt. But I never liked or trusted my uncle. He was, I learned later, generally disliked, and my aunt and he parted company some time later. By the way, I far preferred dried bananas to real ones, and dried eggs to real ones as well. After all, that's what I had been brought up on thanks to wartime shortages and rationing.

But mostly they were hot, sunny, happy days in Twyford. Ronald, my youngest uncle, who was an officer in the British Army in Africa and the most fun because he was the most irresponsible, visited often. He brought me presents of small ebony carved wooden figures of African women with pendulous breasts and silver metal necklaces and earrings made from fuse wire. One day he told me indiscreetly that African women were free and uninhibited. I didn't know quite what he meant but I knew it was something saucy. He would take me into Henley for an afternoon at the pictures, driving too fast through the leafy sunlit lanes around Marlow in his open Riley sports car. Once, Uncle Ron and his friend Joe had to leave the cinema halfway through *The Hound of the Baskervilles* because Basil Rathbone scared me stiff. Joe wasn't at all pleased. Other days we played darts on a dartboard behind the garage door.

Uncle Jimmy, Uncle Ron's brother-in-law, was an air force pilot. He told us to stand in the garden at twelve o'clock one hot summer's day. We did as we were told, stood in the garden and waited. Sure enough, at noon over the horizon came Uncle Jimmy's Spitfire at full throttle, missing our chimney pots by what seemed inches. Show-off. It seems unimaginable with today's regulations, but it was wartime – what the hell! Uncle Jimmy was later killed in action.

Life at Twyford seemed heavenly compared to London. I used to lie on my back in the long grass while butterflies danced around me and bees hummed, and watch biplanes drone overhead leaving trails in the summer sky. With my cousins Tim and Dick I made tunnels and pathways, crawling through the goldenrod, a perennial plant with bright yellow flowers which grew in profusion throughout the large garden. The air was clouded with pollen – I blamed the goldenrod for years, but I now know that it would have been the ragweed which frequently grows alongside it. Terrible asthma attacks followed but no one seemed to make the connection. My grandparents and aunt were at a loss what to do. They put me, coughing and choking, to bed in a dark back bedroom. My biggest fear at the house in Twyford was a grimacing stuffed Capuchin monkey who lived under a Victorian glass dome that stood on a dark brown chest of drawers in a corner. My uncle Ron took it away.

Happy summer holidays were also spent in Kington, Herefordshire, with my father's brother, Uncle Fred, and his wife, Aunt Clarice. I adored them both. They owned a riding school and I learned to ride. My uncle nicknamed me 'Horseman'. The horses were for hire and at the end of each day my older cousin Susan and I would ride the horses from the hotel, where the people who hired them were staying, back to the stables. Sue rode her horse, Sierra Sue, and I rode Ginger home at dusk along the lonely roads, between the hedges with their dark and mysterious shapes, and under the gaunt trees, their black, twisted arms with clutching fingers stretching over our heads in the darkness. Although I was scared, it was an honour and I felt grown up to be trusted to bring the horses back safely – but I was relieved when we reached the stables. My aunt, a countrywoman, told me she felt completely happy and safe walking through the country lanes after dark but wouldn't dream of doing the same on the streets of London.

I was also allowed to help shepherd sheep through the narrow lanes while standing on the running board of my uncle's old Austin 7. (Occasionally Uncle Fred would carry a couple of sheep inside the Austin 7 from one field he owned to another. They smelled a bit.) Fish and chips afterwards, bought from the local shop. I was allowed to stay up late. So exciting. There were visits to the local fleapit cinema: farm boys with their steaming boots up on the stove while Hopalong Cassidy galloped to the rescue. Then there was the Horse Show at the Recreation Ground; champion show-jumper Colonel Harry Llewellyn and his horse Foxhunter were coming. Good days.

Cyril, Aunt Clarice's Welsh brother-in-law, was a malicious little farmer who lived up in the Welsh hills. He didn't like me. I could feel it. When I was younger, he had menacingly suggested I go for a walk down by the river that ran through their land; I had a feeling he would like me to fall in. Another day, while he was up a ladder picking pears, he called me over and handed one down to me. As I grabbed it my fingers sank into its soft flesh and it seemed like a thousand electric shocks pierced my hand. I screamed. He had given me pear that had been half eaten away and was full of wasps. He grinned. Evil little Welsh bastard. I can still see that cruel grin today.

Much later I recall my mother saying, 'Oh you can't trust the Welsh.' This seemed a sweeping statement, even though she had spent much of her young life in Wales. My knowledge of my mother's family is very scant: only a few bits and pieces remain. Her brother, Douglas, had also been a teacher but had always harboured an ambition to be a farmer. He eventually moved to Wales, where he had a farm at Llandudno on the north coast, with fields that ended at the cliff edge with sheer drops down to the Irish Sea. He was a bluff, straightforward character. I didn't see him very often but I liked him. Notable for the amount of hair that came out of his ears. Uncle Doug also had the misfortune of backing his tractor and trailer over his wife, Dora, and disabling her for life. His son, my cousin Kenneth Gardner, was a great authority in the field of Japanese historical bibliography and a distinguished historical librarian at the British Museum, and later the British Library. My mother also had an older sister, Sibyl, who was a golf champion.

Life in Kington was pretty slow. Every evening there was a gaggle of depressed-looking youths hanging around outside the brightly lit windows of the gas showrooms in the centre of town. In the early post-war years there was no sign that they had any intention of building a New Britain. There was always a time lag between country and town. Twenty years after teddy boys had long since disappeared from London they still walked the streets of Kington like zombies. It was a time capsule.

At the end of the town where the road led to the next village was an ancient stone bridge. At one end of the bridge was a small hexagonal building with a conical roof, maybe once a toll gate. My uncle often said he would like to turn this little tower into an ice-cream kiosk. This was a very attractive idea to us children – we imagined how many free ice-creams we would eat – but it went the way of many of my uncle's good ideas: it didn't come to pass.

I spent many hours leaning over the parapet of the bridge with the warm sun on my back, gazing into the clear shallow water of the river running below. So crystal clear I could see the stony bottom, long, bright-green strands of weeds waving lazily in the current. Little silver fish lurked among those undulating fronds. They were my prey. I slowly lowered my primitive fishing tackle into the water near to where a small shoal of several dozen fish moved in unison. They flinched and darted away as one, in perfect formation. This was the general pattern. I had no success until one morning, at last, I caught one. I hauled it up to take out the hook and throw him back as I had been taught to do. The hook had gone into his mouth but had poked out through his eye. I was horrified. I made a mess of removing the hook. Poor fish – I threw him back all the same, and never went fishing again.

Uncle Fred had a down-to-earth, no-nonsense attitude. He couldn't stand people who 'put on airs'. He had been to Harrods where he thought he would buy a beautiful figurine for my aunt. When he examined it he discovered a small chip in the delicate porcelain. Because of this he asked if he could have a reduction in the price.

'Oh no, sir,' the snotty salesman snorted. 'This is Harrods. We don't do that sort of thing.'

'Why not?' said Fred. 'You're a bloody shop, aren't you?'

I liked that attitude.

Uncle Fred had many strings to his bow. He ran a small confectionery and tobacconist shop in Kington High Street, which had been left to him by his first wife. I loved this shop with its jars of boiled sweets, humbugs and jelly-babies, and the wonderful smell of tobacco – every type of cigarette and cigar that you could wish to kill yourself with. And best of all, I was allowed to serve the customers. It had an old-fashioned till with a little drawer that shot out – a drawer full of half-crowns, florins, shillings, farthings, sixpences and twelve-sided threepenny bits, all stacked in separate compartments. I whiled away the time making sure they were in the right ones. We weren't terribly busy.

I felt very grown up being trusted to take money and give change to the customers. It improved my mental arithmetic enormously. I knew where everything was. But there was one customer I became wary of. He was the local auctioneer – a very tall, pompous and self-important figure with a booming plummy accent. I couldn't understand a word he was saying so didn't know what he wanted. He once became so impatient and irritable that he thumped the little brass shop bell that stood on the counter while looking over my shoulder for my aunt. She put her head round the door at the back of the shop. 'Oh, he always has "Passing Cloud",' she told me. As an onlooker and watcher, I suppose subconsciously all of my life I have been collecting types to caricature. He was an early one.

Uncle Fred himself was another study. He was partial to a pinch of snuff. He habitually carried a silver snuff box in his waistcoat pocket which he refilled from his personal supply at the shop. 'Disgusting habit,' said Aunt Clarice.

He was very fond of clocks, from carriage clocks to grandfather clocks – all clocks were welcome. Uncle Fred loved tinkering with them, doing them up and getting them going. The house in Kington became loud with the sound of ticking as his collection grew and grew, and when they struck the hour the noise was insufferable. Inevitably the sad day came when Aunt Clarice, who could stand it no more, relegated them to the large shed at the bottom of the garden down by the river, where his beloved clocks ticked away in murky darkness telling the time to noone. One day the river flooded and my uncle, who was away, anxiously telephoned my aunt. 'Are my clocks all right?' he enquired. 'Oh, they're quite happy,' she said, 'all bobbing away down there in the shed.'

As well as the shop, Uncle Fred worked for the Ministry of Food and one of his tasks was to travel to various depots around the country where large stocks of food were stored by the ministry in case of an emergency. He would sometimes take me on these trips. The food stores were often on disused airfields and while I waited for him I made watercolour paintings of these romantic, weed-filled concrete runways, imagining the pilots running to their Spitfires as the order to scramble sounded. 'Chocks away!' and off into a trail-streaked Paul Nash sky.

I was an only child until my brother Gordon's birth when I was eight and a half. We were still living in Kidderminster at the time. My mother went away to hospital. I was not allowed to visit. Then one morning my mother arrived home with my new baby brother. I was fascinated. Gordon became the centre of interest. 'He's the one,' said Gladys, my barmy aunt. 'He's the one!' I was always wary of her thereafter. What she had said made me feel very sidelined, almost no longer necessary. It's extraordinary how some adults can say things within earshot of children as though they can't hear them. Anyway, it has stayed with me all these years. Walls have ears.

Gordon also suffered from asthma, and during our sick-bed years chamber pots were useful things. Gordon couldn't say 'chamber pot' and in his early years called them 'arkys'. This gave me the opportunity to call out 'arky' in crowded streets, while my brother died of shame and embarrassment.

Our age difference meant that we didn't have a lot in common to begin with. Gordon had a great sense of imagination and spent much of his time playing alone. I was the annoying older brother who couldn't resist teasing him. He would play cowboys and Indians with his small metal figures on the drawing-room carpet. At the height of the battle I'd come along with a Dinky Toy van and start selling ice-cream to the Indians. He complained I was spoiling his game – but that's what older brothers do.

As time went on, we became closer: it was just the two of us. Throughout his life, Gordon regarded me as 'big brother', and I know he relied on me emotionally. He told me later in life that he was devastated when I left home at the age of nineteen and he was ten. As we grew older and the age difference grew less and less significant, Gordon became my friend and supporter. As I was his. Over time we developed an almost telepathic understanding. We had these little catchphrases that grow up between people of close acquaintance. I once took Gordon with me when I went to buy a motorbike. We looked at several models, and while explaining the merits of the BSA bike the salesman turned to me and asked, 'How old are you?' At least that's what I thought I heard. 'Thirty-three,' I answered confidently. My brother immediately crumpled up in a fit of giggles. The salesman looked confused. He had actually asked me if I wanted to pay in instalments. I had misheard. Thereafter I could make Gordon double up with laughter simply by saying 'thirty-three' at any random point. It was one of the many tiny things that bound us together. I never felt Gordon was jealous of my success – quite the opposite in fact. He seemed very proud to be my brother. We had daily telephone calls and exchanged family jokes for the rest of his life, which was tragically cut short when he died of Parkinson's disease in 2018. I miss him.

In May 1945, when I was nine and Gordon was still a baby,

the war ended. I remember the VE day celebrations: long tables with cakes and jellies down the centre of streets, Union Jacks and bunting flying in the sunshine. We returned to London, back to 57 Goldhurst Terrace, which was still there, untouched by Hitler's bombs. There were one or two houses at the bottom of the road which had been bombed and flattened. A large concrete water tank had later been built in the middle of the rubble to service fire engines. I found bomb-ruined houses fascinating. Roofless homes with fireplaces that the residents had once warmed themselves around, now just gaping holes in the adjoining wall, still with the mantelpiece and the tattered floral wallpaper. A staircase clinging to the wall climbing to nowhere and ending suddenly in space three floors up with a terrifying drop to the smashed concrete and brick floor below. An eerie emptiness. In this hole someone had once lived and perhaps died. Now it was a playground for local children who played dangerous games of tag and hide and seek among the broken, fire-blackened chunks of masonry, in and out of the lonely rooms, up and down the hanging staircases. There was no health and safety legislation then.

Recalling these chaotic scenes reminds me that my paternal grandfather used to call our house in London – ironically, I think, looking back – 'Buckingham Palace' as it was so spick and span. We had a perfectly kept drawing room with a chandelier and French furniture. Traditionally it was only used on special occasions. It was opened every Christmas with a fire and egg flip. It gave out through French windows on to a small lawned garden with apple trees and a shed at the far end. My mother would gaze out of the window and say, 'Oh look, there's a blackbird on the lawn.' I used to think, Yes, so what? Now I have got to that point in life where my garden is important so I understand.

My father was demobbed, he returned to work, and I began to see more of him. We always had books in the house, as my father was fond of reading. He adored Dickens and from time to time would read aloud to me passages of *The Pickwick Papers*, chuckling as he read. To be frank I was bored stiff, but I appreciated the fact that he was involving me in his enjoyment. Today I am myself a Dickens fan – he is a caricaturist, after all – but guiltily I feel I don't read enough. Often when reading my mind will skid off and drift across to an idea I could draw. I imagine scenes and interpret them in my own style. I'm illustrating the book mentally even as I read it.

My father's favourites were the diaries of Samuel Pepys and John Evelyn, and occasionally he'd tell me how 'naughty' Pepys was with his dillying and dallying. Perhaps he envied him. He encouraged me to read *Tom Brown's Schooldays* by Thomas Hughes, the story of Rugby School and the horrific treatment of Tom by Flashman, the bully who roasted him in front of an open fire. Was he hinting that I was lucky not to go to public school? He would also read military history with titles such as *Foch in Flanders*, biographies of Napoleon, Wellington, Cromwell, the Sun King and so on. All of my uncles and grandfather on the Scarfe side had a romance with the military.

My very first literary experience had been *Gulliver's Travels*, which my mother read to me when I was four. I still have the book, with the inscription 'To Dear Little Gerald, from Mummy, 1940' on the frontispiece. I also became entranced by everybody in Nutwood, home of Rupert Bear, Algy Pug and Bill Badger, and every year a new Rupert annual would be in my Christmas stocking. Anna Sewell's *Black Beauty* was the first book I read all the way through. Later I read Richmal Crompton's *Just William* and admired the exploits of William, Ginger and the Outlaws. As I reached my teens I must have read every Tarzan book by Edgar Rice Burroughs in picture comic form. I was so keen I stole one from a stand outside a shop in Eastbourne. My parents were in the shop at the time, so it was a double rush.

As I said, when I read I conjured up pictures of the people and scenes I was reading about. Often my mind would spin off into a reverie and I would find I had left the book behind and was in my own world. I have wondered if illustrated books spoil our imagination. Do they stunt children's natural interpretations? Can we imagine Pooh and Piglet without seeing E. H. Shepard's illustrations? Would Alice and the Red Queen exist so definitively without Tenniel? Would it be better for children's books to be unillustrated to allow their imagination full rein? What do I think as an illustrator? I am agnostic. Some books cry out for it, others less so – *The Very Hungry Caterpillar*, for example, would be nothing without its illustrations. My Pink Floyd designs definitely added another dimension, a not-too-literal interpretation, to the music. I am told that the marching hammers and the 'loving' flowers remain in people's imagination. But music is not so explicit in its meaning, and interpreting it in visual form adds another experience. They seem to love vision with sound in the rock world.

I was introduced to *Swallows and Amazons* when I was about fourteen by the mother of a friend of mine, David Jobson, who lived in Goldhurst Terrace. His father owned a building firm and his mother was a teacher. She changed my life radically. Looking back, I feel she set out to help educate me. Not only did she recommend books, she also taught me how to play Monopoly and Mahjong. I remember setting out the tiles: Pongs, Kongs, Chows; East is the prevailing wind.

One day my friend Heinz Katchke announced that he and his family were leaving soon to live in America. On the day of Heinz's departure I went round to his house as we had arranged to say goodbye. His parents and aunts stood around sympathetically and watched us. I hadn't realised it would be quite so emotional, and we both did our best to hold back the tears, but unsuccessfully. Once in America, Heinz would send me parcels of American comics. My excitement was intense whenever a package arrived marked with American stamps, and when I opened it, inside would be Superman, Batman, Blondie and Dagwood, and also pictorial comics of famous classics such as *Ivanhoe*, *The Hunchback of Notre Dame* and *A Tale of Two Cities*. That was my first introduction to many of the great works – not exactly a classical education but better than nothing.

Radio featured heavily in my childhood. I adored the surreal world of *The Goon Show*, its anarchic humour, and I'm sure it affected my sense of humour. *Journey Into Space* and *Dick Barton Special Agent* were also great favourites of mine, a serial on every evening. Would Dick escape yet again? The only radio was in the sitting room, and I had to have it on quietly. My mother read the newspaper every evening when I was trying to listen, so I often missed Eccles's punchlines or Dick's dramatic climax because of the rustling and crackling of that bloody *Telegraph*.

My father's association with culture and the arts didn't end in the library. He, his three brothers and his sister had all been taught an instrument – my father played the violin – and they would have musical evenings together. There came a time when my parents thought I should learn an instrument, although I wasn't keen at the prospect of all those tedious lessons. But they continued with their quest and said I should think about it seriously, so I thought about it in an off-hand way until one day I was listening to *Variety Bandbox* on the BBC Light Programme and heard Eddie Calvert playing *Cherry Pink and Apple Blossom White* on his trumpet. It all became clear. That was it! A trumpet, of course! It was so obvious as I heard Eddie's trumpet dipping and soaring. I felt truly excited. At the end of his solo the *Variety Bandbox* audience clapped and cheered. I imagined myself in Eddie's shoes, bowing to an ecstatic audience. Famous! I couldn't wait to tell my parents. I rushed downstairs and passed on the good news.

'A trumpet? Don't be ridiculous! Think of the neighbours.'

So the neighbours won, and high-end entertainment today was

robbed of a second Eddie Calvert. The trumpet would have been wonderful for my asthmatic lungs, too.

So I didn't become a prodigious young trumpeter. All I had was my art. I drew constantly, though paper remained scarce. Uncle Ronald was incensed when I didn't win first prize – any prize – in an art competition for schoolchildren held at Finchley Road Baths. He went in and complained to the organisers, who agreed. 'Yes, his drawing was the best, but the judges just didn't believe that a nine-year-old could have drawn it.'

It was a defining moment for me when I was given a book based on the Walt Disney film of *Pinocchio* and read,

One night, long, long ago, the Evening Star shone down across a dark sky. Its beams formed a shimmering pathway to a tiny village and painted its humble roofs with stardust. But the silent little town was deep in sleep. The only witness to the beauty of the night was a weary wayfarer who chanced to be passing through. His clothes were grey with dust, his well-worn shoes pinched his feet. His back ached from the weight of the carpet bag slung over his shabby shoulder. To be sure it was only a small carpet bag. As a matter of fact he was an exceedingly small wayfarer. His name was Cricket – Jiminy Cricket.

I was instantly absorbed and obsessed by the world of Jiminy, Geppetto, Pinocchio, Honest John the Thespian Fox and his dim sidekick Gideon the Cat, Stromboli the wicked puppet master and Monstro the Whale. That Christmas Eve, I could not sleep. I was electric with excitement knowing that Santa might bring me the LP soundtrack of *Pinocchio* that I had asked for. Eventually, my parents relented and got me up and took me in to the drawing room. Sure enough, there was the LP wrapped in shiny red paper. My father put the disc on the turntable in the huge mahogany radio-gramme that stood in the corner and lowered the needle

on to the slowly revolving grooves. Immediately, the room was
filled with *Pinocchio* and I fell in love with 'When You Wish Upon
a Star' for the rest of my life.

And so, when I was ten, with my excitement at fever pitch, I
made my way with my father to the Regent Cinema in Regent
Street to see Walt Disney's film of *Pinocchio*. A huge event for me.
For months I had been anticipating seeing the film. It had had a
limited release during the war but it was rereleased in London in
1946. When we arrived at the box office Dad found that the only
tickets left were 7/6d – expensive in those days. So expensive, in
fact, that he decided it was too much and we left. My disappointment was enormous. We had not taken many steps up Regent
Street before my tears welled up and I began to cry. We stopped,
and Dad relented. We returned to the cinema, handed over the
money and I had one of the most memorable days of my young
life. When the cigar-smoking braggart Lampwick's coarse, cocky
voice turns to a bray, his hands become hooves and he transforms
into a long-eared donkey calling for his mama, it is one of the
most frightening moments in cinema.

Pinocchio had a huge effect on me. I copied and drew all the
characters; I was especially fond of Honest John, the scheming
fox. To this day I draw eyebrows with the flourish I first saw on
Honest John's face. Later I read the original story of Pinocchio by
Carlo Collodi, in which Pinocchio is burned, hanged and chopped
up. Even more terrifying. Equally scary was the cackling witch in
Snow White and the death of Bambi's mother, although my mother
put her hands over my eyes at that moment.

It was a golden age of Disney animation: *Snow White*, *Bambi* and
Pinocchio. Without knowing it, seeing these films stirred thoughts
and feelings that would inspire me much later in life. I could never
have imagined that I would one day be the only outside artist to
be production designer on a Disney movie.

2

I DON'T GET NO EDUCATION

Another bad asthma attack. My father rang Harley Street.

'Put him in a taxi and bring him here,' the specialist said.

'But he can barely breathe, let alone move,' said my father.

'He'll manage it,' the specialist told him.

We arrived in Harley Street to find that the doctor had moved on purpose to the top floor. I struggled upstairs and was near to collapse at the top.

'Lie down,' said the doctor.

I was fighting for every breath. I lay down with difficulty.

'In a minute you'll feel better,' he said.

He put his hands on my naked chest and mystically and miraculously the asthma began to lift almost immediately. No drugs were involved, and he was not Jesus. Maybe he hypnotised me, but fifteen minutes later I walked easily downstairs and left his house feeling perfectly normal. No sign of asthma. It's a strange disease. But it never stayed away long.

At its worst, that dry cough. It was wheezing and choking. Unable to breathe.

I saw so many doctors with so many different theories. One thought I wasn't swallowing properly and fitted me with a plastic mouth-plate. It was no good: I hated it. Another, an osteopath in Redcliffe Gardens, rabbit-punched me on the neck, knocking me unconscious, until my father intervened: 'Hey hey hey! That's enough of that,' he said. Dangerous. During one bad attack my parents, on doctor's orders, thrust a walking stick between my elbows and my back to make me sit up straight. It was unbelievable torture. The next day the doctor said, 'Oh my God, not *during* an attack!'

I didn't ever smoke apart from a very quick teenage experiment at the age of sixteen. Luckily, for obvious reasons, I didn't like it. But the thirties, forties and fifties were wreathed in smoke. If it wasn't the fog and the smog that often hung in the air it was people smoking. In old black and white films of that period, nobody is without a cigarette. It was thought sophisticated to hold a cigarette. Even doctors were always smoking in films (and in real life), and they would even offer their patients a cigarette to 'calm the nerves'. Cigarette smoke was everywhere – on the buses and trains, in the pubs, cinemas and bars, on the streets and in the shops. Everywhere. Not good for asthmatics. Not good for anyone. Asthma attacks so distorted my body that I developed a concave chest and a hunchback.

My condition continually hampered my enjoyment of life. I had joined a Scout group in Belsize Park, and became obsessed, as many other boys did, with obtaining badges. I was able to sew on to my uniform my trees, knots and birds badges. All of which have been very useful since.

On the weekend of the Scout outing. I so desperately wanted to be at Box Hill with my friends, sitting around a camp fire and spending the night in a tent. But my parents deemed that it would be 'bad for my chest' to spend a night under canvas, so at five o'clock I took the train back to London. The following morning, as early as I could, I took the train back to Box Hill and joined my friends. They had exciting tales to tell, and once again I felt left out of it, coddled and always wearing my thick under-vest. It's quite understandable that even when I was fifteen my mother continued to worry about my chest, but at the time it was a source of great frustration.

I was the last boy in the class still to be in short trousers – a terrible sense of shame and arrested manhood, and it made me a laughing stock. I pleaded with my mother for some long flannel trousers but all in vain. I continued with red chapped legs and derision for some time. 'Appearance' was important, if not paramount, in our house. There seemed to be an ongoing issue about my hair. It was too long by my mother's standards. 'Get your hair cut,' was a frequent order. 'You look a sight.' Really my hair was not long by any standards, just slightly longer than my father's. His hair was always a neat 'short back and sides' and he occasionally joined in the 'hair police' when urged to. 'Your mother says you should get your hair cut, lad,' he would say. Ever since, I have tried not to judge people by their appearance. My sons have had by turn extremely long hair and brutally short hair. It doesn't worry me.

When I was fifteen my father began to talk about sending me to the Haberdashers' Aske's public school in Elstree, Hertfordshire. I'm not sure why – perhaps my parents were anxious about the fact I might leave school with absolutely no qualifications or prospects. How would I earn a living? The emphasis was very much on me being self-sufficient and not relying on them. So I was to take the entrance exam for Haberdashers' Aske's. When I mentioned this to one or two close friends at my school, Haverstock Comprehensive in Chalk Farm, one in particular seemed jealous. 'Why should you go there? Do they all drink from golden goblets there?' Thereafter, day after day, he chanted, 'Ooh, golden goblet school, going to a golden goblet school.' I became upset with this and feared my friends would all think I felt I was better than them. So when I took the exam I didn't try. I threw away that chance on purpose. But I didn't want to go to that school. It felt very alien, and even if I had tried harder I doubt, with my lack of education, I would have got in.

By this time I had passed into that difficult period in a child's artistic development when he wants to draw 'properly' or realistically and scorns the charming, naive and direct drawings of early childhood, the simplicity of which so many artists try to recapture in later life. I taught myself to do realistic watercolours and shaded drawings by looking at 'real' fine artists. My headmaster thought that I was exceptional and should start at St Martin's School of Art in London. I was just fifteen – a year before the normal entrance date – but they agreed to see me, so I duly went with my father for an interview.

'Where are your drawings?' asked the principal of St Martin's.

'I haven't brought any,' I replied.

'Ah! Remember, you are an artist. You should never go anywhere from now on without your portfolio.' 'Anyway,' he added disappointingly, 'as you know, the official age of acceptance is sixteen, so I think you're too young at fifteen.'

Of course, I feel that if he had seen my drawings, I would have become a student at St Martin's – he had granted me the interview knowing my age.

Thereafter, I never went anywhere without my portfolio.

But St Martin's was a fork in the road I failed to take and there was no going back. University and further education were not to come my way. I'm glad to say that now many people, including my own children and grandchildren, go to university, but for me it was not to be.

Untutored, I really didn't know how to draw or in which

direction to push my work. I have a drawing that shows a small hotel I stayed in while having asthma treatment. It is a watercolour and perfectly respectable in that the hotel itself is drawn architecturally correct with perspective. Little green shutters on the windows and surrounded by trees, not so well painted. It's OK, but I was coming to understand (and it worried me) that this was really just a sub-photographic image and that an artist's job was to offer something more. Another vision. More information than in my artwork's rendering of buildings and trees. What was that something more? I knew it was there but didn't know how to find it – and I had no one to ask. All I knew was that my work was boring and not good enough. How did you get from there to Picasso?

Determined to find out, I persevered. Drawing continued to be a compulsion for me, something I couldn't put aside, and it helped me enormously during my periods of illness. I am now a patron of Campaign for Drawing, which encourages people to continue with art or to return to it if not as a job then as a hobby. It doesn't matter if you feel you can't draw 'properly'; just putting anything down – lines, colours, shapes on paper or canvas – is satisfying and therapeutic. Winston Churchill tells us that it was his painting that saved him from even worse 'Black Dog', as he called his sporadic depression. Even if we only produce daubs and keep them private, I believe there is some ancient instinct in our make-up that gives us satisfaction in making these marks.

I was never quite sure whether my father understood or approved of me being an artist – after all, he had hoped that I would go into banking. Strangely, in his old age my father told me that he had always wanted to be an artist when he was young. And years after his death, my uncle Ron recalled an occasion when a mutual friend had asked my father, 'What became of your boy Gerald?' My uncle told me, 'Without a word your dad went across to the bookshelf, took down *Who's Who*, opened it and pointed proudly at your entry.' Many years later when I was telling this story to a journalist I choked on my words and tears welled up. I suppose I hadn't realised it meant so much to me.

But life in London in the late forties and early fifties was dull. I argued with my mother. School was impossible and my asthma was bad. The teachers knew it wasn't worth bothering to coach me: I would be absent again in another week. I was dismayed when I unearthed my school reports recently to read that even as late as 1948–52, when I was between twelve and sixteen years old, asthma was still crippling me severely. Each report ends with the master's comments:

July 1948 (age 12)
Gerald's progress has suffered a great deal from unavoidable absence. He is a willing worker.

December 1949 (age 13)
Gerald is a sound and careful worker. It is a pity that absence (through illness) has impeded his progress. I hope he will be more fortunate next term and do very well indeed.

21 December 1950 – Form 4A (age 14)
Despite unavoidable absence Gerald has done very well indeed. He is a reliable and sometimes gifted worker and is always willing to do a job. I am pleased with him.

19 December 1951 – Form 5A (age 15)
Despite his unfortunate absence due to illness Gerald has tried <u>very</u> hard to keep up with the class. I think he has done surprisingly well. A very commendable result indeed!

25 July 1952 – Form 5A (age 16)
Gerald has tried very hard during the year – often despite severe setbacks. He is of good intelligence, has real determination and

an ability to turn out work of a worthy standard. His general standard is good. In art he is outstanding.

Playing tag at school one day with three of my friends we ran into the school lavatories, which were in the playground, to hide. Playing around the area of the lavatories was forbidden – possibly because many of the boys tried to pee over the very high urinal wall into the next playground. Unfortunately, we were caught by Mr Needham, the caretaker, and marched before the headmaster, Mr King. He duly administered six of the best with the cane to each of us, three on each outstretched hand. It stung but was bearable. Then, as we stood in a line, he singled me out. 'I am particularly surprised at you, Scarfe, coming from a good family as you do.' The shame. I had held back the tears during the caning but when he said that they flooded down my cheeks. The terrible shame. I had let my family down.

But perhaps because of this sense of being 'secondary', I took more and more to expressing my hopes and fears through my drawings, where I could work alone.

In 1950 a new comic, the *Eagle*, was born. Founded and edited by a clergyman, Marcus Morris, it was a more educational publication than most other comics. I bought it every week. I admired the accomplished, precise drawings of Dan Dare by Frank Hampson and the centrefold, which always showed a fascinating 'exploded' diagram of the workings of a ship, the *Queen Elizabeth*, or an aeroplane, the Comet – all technically well drawn.

There was a call for examples of readers' work. At the age of sixteen I sent in a drawing called 'Eagle Artists Nightmare', which showed the bodies of well-known *Eagle* comic characters on to which I had supplanted the heads of other *Eagle* characters. To my excitement they used it. I loved seeing my work in print. I knew there was something here, but I had no idea how I could make a living by selling my drawings.

Shortly afterwards *Eagle* ran a competition inviting readers to 'draw an advertisement for Ingersoll watches and win a grand prize'. So I did, and came first. I felt my first glow of recognition. And it was a very grand prize – a sweater, a shirt, a Dan Dare watch and a boomerang. I thought I'd like to carry on winning grand prizes – it felt good. When the results of the competition appeared under the picture of my winning drawing, the text read 'This design has won Gerald Scarfe 1st Prize. Hearty congratulations also to the following consolation prize winners . . . ' And at the bottom of the list was 'David Hockney, Bradford'. Years later David pointed this out to me, and said that his mother had drawn his attention to it. He also told me from memory he thought he had come second. Ever since then David has been getting first prize. In 2018 one of his paintings, *Portrait of an Artist (Pool with Two Figures)*, sold at auction for ninety million dollars.

A few decades later, while I was working in LA on *The Magic Flute* (more on that in a later chapter), David and I were standing on the deck at the back of his beach house, a cottage overlooking the Pacific Ocean. An outdoor open fireplace smouldered behind us and the pounding surf crashed before us. 'Oh,' said David, after a period of silence and contemplation, 'it's grand to be an artist, isn't it?' I had to agree that it was, especially in his case. David also had a place up in the hills with his famous wiggly-lined swimming pool. He told me he was planning to design Wagner's *Ring* cycle for LA Opera and that he was going to set it in the Hollywood Hills. He had prepared a tape of Wagner's music and said we should take a drive up into the hills and play the tape which had been edited to be in sync with the changing scenery throughout the drive. We made our way to Pacific Highway which runs alongside the ocean in his open-top red Mercedes. As soon as we hit the highway David pressed the button and the music of Sousa blared out – one of his marches. *Pom pom te pom pom te pom pom pom pom.* 'This is just to get us going,' he said. We eventually turned off the highway and climbed into the hills.

Immediately the music changed to Wagner. As we drove steadily along at thirty miles an hour the music did indeed match the scenery perfectly. We rounded a corner, and as the vista opened before us, the 'Ride of the Valkyries' pumped out of David's speakers. It was magnificent. We turned another corner and just ahead of us appeared a blue Volkswagen driven by a little old lady. She was doing twenty miles an hour so David had to brake. 'Come on! Come on!' he shouted. The delay was buggering up the synchronisation. 'Come on! Come on!' There was nowhere to overtake so David desperately tried to rewind the tape to get the music back in sync. 'Oh come *on!*' But the little old lady took no notice. It's very difficult to get old ladies in sync. 'Oh well, never mind,' said David eventually.

That experience was a long way from lying in my bed at sixteen, Dr Fraser standing over me looking anxious. Through my half-closed eyes he went in and out of focus. 'He'll be all right,' he said. He had just given me an adrenaline injection and my heart was going like a trip hammer. He picked up my hands – the fingernails were blue. Maybe he had given me too much. 'Perhaps we'd better get him to hospital.'

My parents called the ambulance. I could tell they were panicking. It was a long time coming. For some reason they didn't come with me. My doctor gave the ambulance man a letter to pass on carrying the strict instructions 'On no account give this boy any more adrenaline'.

At the hospital I was shown into an arrival room. The nurse asked me umpteen questions. I could hardly breathe. 'How old is your father?' I couldn't answer. 'Then let me give you something to help you.' She came towards me with a hypodermic syringe. 'I'm just going to give you an injection,' she said.

'What is it?' I wheezed.

'Adrenaline,' she replied.

'I mustn't have it!' I gasped. 'Didn't you get the doctor's note the ambulance man brought?'

'No,' she told me, 'he didn't give me anything.'

I've always been frightened by and intolerant of incompetence since then and have a terrible fear of being out of control.

I had only recently been sent to the French spa town of La Bourboule in the Auvergne. The water there had arsenical qualities that were reputedly good for asthmatics. I drank the water, bathed in the water, and shivered in the water. As part of the 'cure' I was subjected to a questionable ritual. Asked to undress and stand naked in the corner of a white-tiled windowless room, I was 'douched' by needle-sharp jets of cold water through a hose pipe wielded by a sadistic attendant nurse. My God, it hurt. It was as though I was being sliced by an open razor as the laser-like jet traced down my back on to my buttocks. I thought at the time that my naked vulnerability and pain was giving him pleasure. It was daily abuse, and medically worthless.

In a dark-brown consulting room behind heavy net curtains, through which no French sunlight ever penetrated, I sat on a stool between the legs of an enormously fat and pompous French doctor. He whirled me around on the stool and put the fear of God into me by telling me I had a weak heart, that I needed 'cupping', and that on no account should I go out into the sunlight. Cupping is the almost medieval French custom of placing glass jars with burning candles in them on the skin of the back while the patient lies face down on a bed. As the candle burned up the oxygen, my flesh was drawn by suction up into the glass jar. There I lay with great red mounds of sucked-up flesh all over my body. Fortunately, he had given up the use of leeches and blood-letting.

The main benefit of these visits to France (I went twice) was the wonderful feeling of freedom and independence. It released me from the claustrophobic tension at home. This, in its turn, benefited my asthma. There should have been a third visit but the organisation that ran the trips said I was a disruptive influence on the other boys and that I thought of it as more of a holiday than a cure. I have to admit I did enjoy a mild flirtation with a pretty French girl in the town and I am ashamed to say I stole some sweets from a stall overnight. But my worst crime was sunbathing – strictly against Dr Pierre's orders. Miss Spinster, as I called her, one of the minders, entered my room one day without knocking and found me, shirt off, lying full length on the floor in front of the french windows, sunbathing in the baking sunlight. So I was banned from making the third visit that was part of the course. My father was furious with them, having invested on the understanding the course was to be three trips. I'm glad to say he was not at all cross with me.

Now Dr Fraser said, 'Send the boy to Switzerland. Let him work as a waiter in a Swiss hotel. The mountain air will do him good.' Everybody laughed. It sounded like a crazy idea at the time but in reality it would have without doubt improved my asthma, and maybe the tips would have been good too.

In my late thirties and early forties I took up skiing. My wife, children and I, together with a group of friends, enjoyed many holidays in the French Alps in Courchevel and Méribel. Those were the times in my life when I felt at my most healthy. It was exhilarating. I'd thunder and tumble down mountains in flurries of powder snow and, apart from breaking my leg one year, I came to no harm. I discovered, not for the first time, that my cosseted body could take much more than I had been led in my childhood to believe. The high altitude and crisp cool air, apart from making me breathless like anyone else, made me feel wonderful. And no doubt that glass or possibly bottle of crisp white wine at the top of the mountain with the magnificent Alps spread around me helped as well.

A longer-standing love of mine is the cinema. Perhaps it is the memory of those wonderful free days in Twyford when the cinema was a special treat. Driving into Reading to see classic movies such as *The Secret Life of Walter Mitty*, with Danny Kaye dropping into daydreams and imagining himself as various brave swashbuckling characters. I thought Kaye very funny then but not now. Interesting how tastes in humour change.

The Odeon Swiss Cottage played a significant part in my early life. It was there I first went to the Mickey Mouse Club and grew to love films and the cinema. Later I went to 'Saturday Morning Pictures' where, after a morning of Hopalong Cassidy, hundreds of would-be cowboys galloped out into the Finchley Road at the end of the film whoopin' and a-hollerin' – 'Yee-hah!'

Later, when I moved to Parliament Hill, I went frequently to the Everyman Theatre in Hampstead, which specialised in foreign films. There I saw *Bicycle Thieves*, *The Cranes Are Flying*, *Rififi*, *Jules et Jim* and many others. I loved the surreal films of Federico Fellini, in particular *8½* and *La Dolce Vita*. The films' stars – Yves Montand, Gérard Philipe, Fernandel, Jeanne Moreau, Jean-Paul Belmondo – were my heroes. It was there that I first saw the brilliant films of Jacques Tati: *Jour de Fête*, *Mon Oncle*, *Les Vacances de Monsieur Hulot*. I liked that the jokes were mainly visual and in a Chaplinesque way would be understandable to most people around the world. They were kind and fond observations on people dealing with the confusion of the modern world.

The telling of stories with pictures and words was what I wanted to do. I thought it would be the most wonderful thing in the world to be a film director. I can see now that I was very much influenced by comics and cinema –mainly visual story-telling.

My mother never went to the cinema, and for some reason I never quite fathomed she didn't want me to go 'to the pictures' either. 'Pictures, pictures,' she would say, 'that's all you think about.' Pictures, pictures I suppose did become my life. Annoyingly, she always seemed to find some job I had to do for her half an hour before the film programme was about to start. She would announce that I must help with the shopping but could not seem to come up with a list until it was too late for me to get to the cinema in time. It was usually six pounds of potatoes nearly every day. 'Why can't we have eighteen pounds of potatoes every three days?' I reasoned. But that was never possible. I loved films, perhaps partly because they were discouraged, and I suppose they were an escape to other worlds, too.

It was in the back row of the Odeon Swiss Cottage that I finally got my first kiss. A girl I liked who lived in Fairhazel Gardens, Pat, took me to ballroom dancing lessons, which I hated. But for our second date we went to see *White Christmas*, and that day I plucked up the courage. It was something of an anti-climax I must say, but at least I'd done it. I think Bing Crosby must have pulled Pat more than I did. Shortly afterwards she left for pastures new, and we lost touch.

Sex was really hard to come by in the 1950s and, unlike today's shockingly easy access to it on the internet, pornography was hard to come across too (if you'll excuse the pun). The most risqué material that was available were the works of Hank Jansen who wrote about dangerous redheads and men with guns, with titles like *Her Weapon is Passion*, *Baby Don't Dare Squeal* and *The Sexy Vixen*. Boys at school had told me about *Health & Efficiency*, a naturist magazine featuring naked women in athletic poses, exercising, throwing beach balls, playing tennis etc. In *Health & Efficiency* the women were naked, yes, but the photographs were in a dull, smooth grey and they had been airbrushed and 'cleaned up' so that any element of sex was almost eliminated – all nipples were removed, no titillation there. It came as a shock to me many years later when I discovered women had pubic hair. In my manual they were as bald as a coot.

After a night at the cinema I would walk home through the dark and silent streets in smoggy night air lit by pools of light from the sentinel lampposts. I would look up at the bedroom windows and imagine what girls were letting men do to them.

Off screen, the person I most lionised was Ronald Searle, who first came to my attention when I was about fourteen. My grandmother took the *News Chronicle* and I very soon became aware of this outstanding and different artist. He could really draw. He had a huge effect on me. I wanted to draw like him. His pen was always searching, exploring and recording every nook and cranny of his subject. His exciting, electric style fascinated me. I still have memories of a wonderfully detailed drawing of Shepherd Market in London showing the cafés and fruit stalls, with the added frisson for a teenage boy of prostitutes waiting on corners for trade. I also admired the stunning immediacy of his huge Lemon Hart rum billboards. I discovered St Trinian's in the magazine *Lilliput* and his *Rake's Progress* in *Punch*. His accurate theatrical caricatures of Donald Wolfit, John Gielgud and Fernandel, his drawing of a gerund in the *Molesworth* books, Molesworth himself and Fotherington-Tomas ('he are a weed') and many, many more — they were all brilliant.

I admired him so much I became a stalker. I found out where he lived – 32 Newton Road, Bayswater – and I cycled there from my home in Hampstead on many occasions. On the journey I would rehearse all the many things I wanted to ask him. How could I become a successful cartoonist like him? There are no schools that teach cartooning. His house was set back from the road behind a high brick wall and in the wall was an arched doorway with a brass doorbell. I would park my bike and approach the door. But my finger would not, could not, press that doorbell. There was a psychological barrier. I always lost courage, and after cycling in circles in the road for some time I'd go home, mission unaccomplished and feeling a dismal failure. I never did ring that doorbell.

Fifty years later Jane took me for a surprise birthday lunch to a small restaurant in the Provençal village of Tourtour in the south of France. To my delight, sitting at a table for four in a corner of the otherwise empty restaurant were Monica and Ronald Searle, and on my place setting was a beautifully wrapped parcel about four inches square tied with blue ribbon.

'Is this for me?' I asked.

'Yes, yes,' he said. 'It's nothing.'

'May I open it now?'

'Yes, of course.'

I carefully untied the ribbon and undid the wrapping. There inside, lo and behold, was a doorbell – a brass doorbell with a message attached in Ronald's neat, minuscule handwriting that read 'Please ring any time'. That doorbell has sat on my desk in my studio to inspire me ever since.

For many summers following that memorable day Jane and I would go back to that same wonderful restaurant, Les Chênes Verts, to lunch with Ronald and Monica. Monica was a delight. Whenever we visited she would have had her hair done the day before and then slept bolt upright all night so as not to mess it up. Monica was very fond of truffles. She once ordered some for me and for herself, and kept giving me more from her own plate. Well, I like truffles too, but enough is enough. As they kept coming I began to secrete them in my napkin while she wasn't looking. Later in the meal, during pudding, I forgot and dabbed my mouth with my napkin. Several truffles bounced merrily across the white-tiled floor. Everyone pretended not to notice.

The walls of the room in which we dined were peppered with drawings Ronald gave to the owner every year, and one could see that, even into his nineties, the quality of his draughtsmanship and ideas had never dipped.

After lunch we always returned to his house to talk and talk, lubricated by more 'engine oil' (his favourite pink champagne, Billecart-Salmon Rosé), about art and this and that. His house was a labyrinth of small passages and short staircases leading to rooms stocked with books, prints, drawings, paintings and sculptures, all in very orderly chaos. He had a wonderful library, mainly on comic art, from Gillray and Cruikshank, Hogarth and Rowlandson, to artists of today. Ronald's knowledge of art was extensive. He had a valuable collection of prints and books which he donated to the Museum Wilhelm Busch in Hanover. Such was his enthusiasm for the art we shared, he sent me a book, *Mein Vorurteil gegen diese Zeit*, about an artist called Karl Rössing who was a contemporary of George Grosz. I took a copy of my book *Drawing Blood* to Provence as a present for him, and he later sent me a fulsome two-page critique of the collection in his tiny handwriting. Ronald's enthusiasm burned bright and his ideas kept flowing. He talked frankly and freely about other artists, praising some and others not. Like many artists, he would often agitate about where the next commission would come from. He told me he had earned very little from the films that were made from his creations of St Trinian's girls; in fact he felt they were a curse from which he could not escape. He felt England had ignored him. He talked occasionally about his horrific experiences in Burma during the war. It was hard to believe that this frail, gentle man had once been a prisoner of the Japanese. There was no bridge over the River Kwai, he told me – it was purely invented for the film. The railway ran alongside the Kwai and never crossed it. They built one later for the tourists.

Ronald's great friend in Paris in earlier years had been the Hungarian-born artist André François. His work also had a big influence on me. He drew like no other cartoonist. To some his work may appear childish and naive but it is wittily subtle. His line may seem as though scratched on to the paper with a pen that has a broken nib but I found it very expressive. He loved to draw knights in armour, tattooists, artists and models.

Given all this, you can only imagine how delighted I was to read in an article about Searle in the *Sunday Times* in 1982 that 'Among younger contemporaries, he most admires Gerald Scarfe, in Searle's opinion a more direct descendant than himself from the bloody quilled age of Cruikshank.'

And what did one of Britain's great artists do in the evenings? I once asked Ronald. 'Oh,' he replied, 'we have an early supper, watch something on television we don't like, and then go to bed.'

3

Scartes' Studios

When I left school at sixteen, the idea of my going to art school seems to have been dismissed. There was no talk of my going to university either. When I did bring up the issue of university at a later age my mother said that children who go to university often turn on their parents in a snobbish manner and look down on them, thinking themselves better. My parents were convinced that I would be dependent on them for the rest of their lives, and my mother told me so. But I had other ideas.

The time came for me to find a job. A proper job. My parents sent me for an interview at the Commonwealth Bank of Australia where my grandfather had worked. I didn't like the idea of this at all, figures and mathematics being far from my strong point. It sounded incredibly dull, too. I went, if only to show willing, but I must admit that during the interview I didn't try very hard

and they decided that with my record of ill health and absentee-
ism I was not worth training. I must be the only person to fail a
bank interview on medical grounds. I didn't care. (My mother
always used to say 'Don't care was hanged', an expression I never
understood.)

Fortunately there was one other artist in the family: my
father's brother, Uncle Cyril, who ran an advertising studio at the
Elephant & Castle in south London. He agreed to take this bank
reject on at thirty shillings (£1.50) a week as a junior. It wasn't
my dream job, but I was proud that I would no longer be relying
on my parents. I insisted that I did not want any special favours. I
wanted to be treated the same as any other junior. No nepotism.
That was a mistake.

This studio was just yards away from the black and grimed
wall that was all that remained of the Marshalsea Prison. I'd read
about the Marshalsea in *The Pickwick Papers*: it was there that Mr
Pickwick was unjustly imprisoned. I had a fellow feeling with Mr
Pickwick because Scarfe's Studios itself was an old Dickensian
building and my first chore at 8.30 in the morning was to bring
buckets of coal from a filthy shed up the threadbare linoleum
stairs with their brass edges and light the antiquated stoves with
newspaper and wood. Then, to further my talent, I had to clean
the artists' water-pots, sweep the floor and make the morning
tea. I also had to run errands and make deliveries all over London.
When I got home at night I would wash my coal-stained shirts
ready for the next morning. Taking the overcrowded Bakerloo
Line from Swiss Cottage to Elephant & Castle I used to think
that if I ever made it from here it would be the perfect traditional
deprived Dickensian beginning, and I would never travel on the
Bakerloo Line again. But I feared I would never escape. It would
have been unthinkable to me then that sixty years later I would
receive an email from a hyperbolic fan that said: 'Dear Gerald
Scarfe, You have lived the greatest life to me. You married the

most beautiful actress of all time, your artistic talent is above everyone else, and you lived the life with rock stars. But I love all of the simple works you have done, the ones that don't get all the fame, because they are the ones to me that come from your heart and mind.'

Mr Alfrey from 'up north' was the studio manager, in line to take over when my uncle retired. I think my arrival at the firm made him worry I was a contender. He needn't have been concerned – that was the last thing I wanted. Nevertheless, Mr Alfrey taught me how to draw an ellipse correctly and apply a clean watercolour wash – both very handy skills in a commercial art studio. All of which was very easy for me. Once I had been told the method I picked it up immediately and became proficient very quickly.

As time went on and I proved that I could draw, my uncle realised I would be more useful inside the studio than outside and I spent more and more time at the drawing board and less time running errands. Before long I was doing some of the main work in the studio. It was excruciatingly tedious. Some artists spent all day painting stitching, one stitch at a time, on to photographs of shoes. Retouchers spent hours putting highlights on to photographs of saucepans, sometimes adding unnecessary work so that the client would think he had got his money's worth. The airbrush was king. I can still hear the thumping sound of the pump that supplied it, as it added glints and sparkles to the dullness of life.

Thankfully, I was given some of the relatively freer work and was able, in a limited way, to invest some feeling in the drawing. I might have to make flat pieces of flannel look like deep fluffy sleep-enticing blankets, sad pieces of rag like crisp linen tea towels; glasses sparkled, furniture gleamed, shoes shone. The world was one wonderful big highlight, and it was all for sale. And I was bored stiff. I could not stand it. I was convinced there must be more than this. I could not wait to get out. And here's the shameful thing: I knew I was misusing my talent, prostituting my ability. I already felt that the whole point of being an artist was to use my craft to tell what I saw as the truth. This advertising was lies – attempts to hoodwink the public. I am sure my later work was a strong reaction to all this. An effort to put down on paper what I really felt in a truthful way. The uber truth.

I believe the great artists Francis Bacon, Andy Warhol and Jeff Koons started out as commercial artists. Bacon, who began by designing rugs is another great hero of mine. He could rip the flesh of a person apart, disassemble and tear their very being into fragments and then reassemble that person in a different form with brush strokes and turbulent oil paint on canvas. But even he had to earn his crust through less inspiring work at the beginning: many artists have commercial origins. The only positive outcome of all this tedium was that it taught me to draw faithfully and representationally. I could draw most objects put in front of me. I drew everything from bedroom suites and bicycles to Humpty Dumpty. Incidentally, it's quite difficult to draw a bicycle. Even Toulouse-Lautrec found it difficult; he wasn't much good at them. I have in mind the poster he designed for La Chaîne Simpson to advertise their bicycle chains. So, I can draw bicycles correctly and Toulouse-Lautrec can't. But as Spike Milligan famously said, 'Just because I cut my legs off it doesn't mean I'm Toulouse-Lautrec.' The French painter's wonky bikes were more expressive than any of my journeyman diagrams. The constraints of commercial art cramped my natural longing to draw freely and I'm sure that is why when I did break free I distorted, elongated, destroyed and remade people and objects in my later work.

I shared my room with Len, who was a chain smoker. The room was blue and foggy with smoke. Needless to say, that, together with the coal fires, did not help my asthma. He was a very interesting man and I think he sensed my eagerness to learn. He would talk to me at length about ancient civilisations, and recommended books like *Ur of the Chaldees* and *Digging Up the Past* by the British archaeologist Leonard Woolley, which I still have, and also a book on the Hittites by O. R. Gurney. This led to me buying many more Pelican and Penguin books and I turned to Dostoevsky and Stendhal to stimulate myself and catch up on the education I felt I had missed. Len was fascinated by Tibet, and encouraged me to read *Seven Years in Tibet*. He made me think. Forgoing small talk, Len might greet me in the morning with, 'Did you know a Buddhist can see the whole world in a blade of grass?'

Mr Wills was my room's third occupant. A nervous middle-aged bachelor, he was very shy – you couldn't really hear what he was saying. He wasn't able to draw anything unless it was by tracing an existing example by another artist. Consequently he had the most voluminous files, labelled 'Hands', 'Feet' or whatever, filled with cuttings from magazines and newspapers. He would have to find the right hand in the right position. It took hours. I liked Mr Wills. Most days he and I would go for lunch at Lyons' Corner House at London Bridge. There we would partake in a fine plate of baked beans on toast and cup of watery tea.

London Bridge, although pretty grubby and grotty in those days, has since gone up in the world and is a trendy district, housing the famous Borough Market. My brother Gordon was the first in our family to discover Borough Market and brought us some sausages from the Ginger Pig. Jane wrote about the Ginger Pig in an article, and when he next visited Gordon saw a notice on a blackboard written in chalk – 'Will Jane Asher's brother-in-law please make himself known to the management'. As a thank you, the butcher gave Gordon a string of sausages.

The Scarfe's Studios staff made for an eccentric bunch. There was Mr Polly, a cheerful, good-looking man with an Errol Flynn moustache who would breeze in occasionally to pick up work. My closest chum was Bob, the other junior in the studio, and the only other person around my age. He lived in Dagenham and invited me one day to meet his family. They were all gathered in his tiny house – mother, father and two siblings. His mother asked me if I would like something to eat – bacon and eggs? To be friendly I said yes and she cooked me two fried eggs, bacon and fried bread. I was puzzled by why I was the only one eating but they said they were all going to eat later. The mother then asked if I would like some more, and in order to compliment her food I said yes please and polished off another plateful. It was about a year later, when I knew Bob better, that he told me I had eaten all their food that day and none of them had had any supper that night. Awful! I felt ashamed: I was completely out of touch in my privileged middle-class world.

Any opportunity I had, I dropped my mindless commercial work and drew whatever I could see outside the studio window in Newington Butts. I filled sketch books with people, animals and buildings. At weekends and evenings I had taken to sketching in Hampstead coffee bars and on Hampstead Heath, as I thought an artist should do. I entered several of my paintings of the Heath in the open-air exhibition in Heath Street near Whitestone Pond, but nobody bought them. Nonetheless I felt it was my first stab at the world of 'fine' art.

It was decided at the studio that I would make a good fashion artist – the gifted elite in advertising at the time, earning big fees – but that required figure drawing. So, to this end, I was sent to St Martin's School of Art in Charing Cross Road for life drawing classes one evening a week. It was the first time I had seen a live naked woman, which was exciting at first, but the nakedness soon gave way to the very demanding task of drawing the human figure – how to depict bones, muscles, foreshortening, a feeling for flesh and blood on paper. It seemed at first that the demands were very much the same as translating the image of an inanimate object on to paper – a question of looking and portraying what I saw before me correctly. But this was quite different; this was a soft, flesh-and-blood living human being and a much more complex emotional task.

At St Martin's it was a different world, and I felt at home at last. Here I was mixing with other artists but, paradoxically, their aims seemed to be totally different to mine. They had all the time in the world and produced very messy drawings covered in charcoal smudges and fingerprints. In the studio I had been taught to clean up every drawing and to do it quickly, against a deadline. If the students had a new folder they would drop it in the mud on a rainy day and jump on it until it looked old and used. Instant experience was what they sought. Instant knowledge. Instant gravitas. I could have done with some instant gravitas myself.

With my scattered education I also sought instant experiences, academic as well as artistic. Despite that newfound sense of belonging at St Martin's, I felt a tremendous lack of academic achievement, completely uneducated. I improved my school French and started teaching myself German. I got as far as learning one of Hamlet's soliloquies in German, which hasn't proved very useful to date. *Sein oder Nicht Sein. Das ist hier die Frage.* I went to the theatre and struggled with Shakespeare, though I enjoyed sitting in the gods at the Old Vic and watching the charismatic Richard Burton proclaiming in *Richard III*. I devoured books. When I first read Dostoevsky's *Crime and Punishment* I felt rather like Alan Bennett, who wrote about his excitement at the prospect of reading a classic and enjoying it when he first got to university: 'Ooh, look at me'. I read Hemingway. I even read *Le soleil se lève aussi* in French, looking up every word I didn't understand. I became better read, but I never did cure my insecurity over my lack of formal education. I still felt very angry about that.

The Ancient Greeks truly inspired me. I became obsessed with Greek art and the beautiful simplicity of archaic sculpture. I spent hours at the British Museum. The first coffee-table book I bought was on Greek art. I bought art books from Zwemmer's book shop on Charing Cross Road. Beautiful big books, books with gorgeous plates in full colour. I thought these were wonderful things to own. It was my attempt to surround myself with 'true' art. Looking back, I can see I was flirting with the 'real' fine art world all along, rather like a little boy with his nose pressed up against a sweet shop window. I made notes at the time of all the books I bought. They clearly excited me. One note read: 'Zwemmer's book shop – I bought Flemish Painting, Paul Klee and Egyptian Art. Yippee!' Another note later: 'Zwemmer's – bought Jules Pascin, Michelangelo drawings, Raphael and Leonardo.' I must have kept Zwemmer's going for years. I was turning the money I earned from my commercial work into 'real' art.

I still have these books in my library, old favourites. Several years ago I thought I should organise them, put them into their correct sections: Impressionists, German Art, Italian Art etc. I asked a young girl who was cataloguing some of my drawings for me if she knew enough about art to do the job for me. 'Oh yes,' she said. 'Well,' I asked, 'for instance, where would you put this book of Tintoretto?' After a moment of deep thought she said, 'Was he the one that cut his ear off?'

During this period I even flirted with facial hair. After several weeks trying to grow a moustache, Uncle Cyril said to me, 'Who do you think you are, Ronald Colman?' My mother would also tell me to 'shave that ridiculous moustache off'.

I made a good friend at St Martin's. His name was Michel Atkinson – his attractive mother was French and his father English. I liked his father: he was a bit of a ne'er-do-well with a large handlebar moustache and he liked his drink rather too much, but he had a certain charm. He reminded me of a major who had been drummed out of his regiment and thrown out of the army. The family didn't have a great deal of money and lived in a flat off Finchley Road. In that small, sparse home with hardly any furniture, his mother's one treasured possession was a walnut wardrobe, in which she kept all her clothes – everything she had. One day Michel's father, who didn't seem to have a regular job, had a brainwave, a brilliant idea to improve the flat. With some effort he sawed his wife's wardrobe in half and screwed it together to fashion a corner bar for the living room. Very chic, very stylish, he thought. He went out and bought a few beers to give it a sophisticated finish and was admiring and leaning on his new creation, lager in hand, when his wife came home after a hard day's work as a courier. I learned some handy French swear words that day.

Michel used his artistic prowess to earn beer money by drawing passers-by on the pier at Brighton from time to time. I was impressed by Michel. He led what seemed to be a carefree, vagabond's life; he had many pretty girlfriends but very rarely had any money, and if he did it was soon gone. Occasionally when he was hungry he would walk into a restaurant and order a slap-up meal of steak and chips, and when the bill came he'd tell the manager that he had no money. What did they do? What could they do? He had no money so he washed up in the restaurant kitchen for several hours. I felt he was behaving like a proper artist.

Humour had become the mainstay of my life. From an early age I had listened to every radio comedy programme on my crystal set: not just the Goons and *Variety Bandbox*, but *Educating Archie* and *It's That Man Again*. Certainly, making jokes about the unsayable seemed to dispel my anxiety, and getting it down on paper helped too. I had always made little cartoon drawings to amuse myself, so cartooning still seemed like a possible way out – rather like boxing and football are to other prisoners of life. In 1956, while still working in the studio, I sent my first cartoons to the *Daily Sketch*, and to my excitement they accepted one and paid me three guineas. It seemed like money for old rope, so I became a joke factory, churning out batch after batch every week, sending them to the *Evening Standard*, *Daily Mirror* and *Daily Sketch*. I was soon selling a great quantity. Many were based on the macabre, which continued to come easily to me.

This success gave me the confidence to leave home. I was nineteen, and I should have left long before that. Life at home had become stifling. I argued with my mother constantly and it seemed everything I did was wrong. I was getting too old to be a typical teenager. I would go straight from work to Swiss Cottage arcade, where night after night I would order four hefty sausages with chips at the local café and then hang around the streets until it was time for bed. When my good school friend Remo Tamburini suggested we share an apartment I jumped at it.

We moved into No. 6 Parliament Hill, a road in north London leading to the Parliament Hill part of Hampstead Heath. The house was owned by Miss Murray, an Irish spinster who lived on the ground floor, from where she kept a watchful eye on all her lodgers through a crack in her door, which was left slightly ajar for eternal vigilance. We had one room, two beds, a table and two chairs, and a small kitchenette behind a partition. We shared the loo on the landing with other tenants, and there was a strong whiff of cabbage permanently about the house. It wasn't much, but it symbolised freedom.

On the top floor lived a real artist . . . well, a real art student. David Goulash was a painter – he painted in oils. The real McCoy. One morning just after ten there was a surreptitious knock on the door of my room. Paintbrush in hand, I opened it. There stood Miss Murray in a great state of excitement. Without a word she beckoned me in a conspiratorial way to follow her up the winding stairs to David's room. What was she doing? David was out. She was giggling in a skittish, schoolgirlish way. When we reached David's room she took out her pass key and let us in. It was a typical art student's messy room, a jumble of half-finished canvases covered in dark chocolate brown and green. Paint pots were propped around the walls. Barely containing her excitement, Miss

Murray led me towards a large finished canvas leaning against the filthy paint-spattered sink. It showed a full-length self-portrait of David lying naked on his bed, legs apart, masturbating. It was entitled, in large black capital letters, MIDNIGHT MADNESS. It was an awkward moment. Was Miss Murray getting a vicarious rush? I made my excuses and left.

Remo and I got on pretty well. We had been friends for a while and had got into the usual scrapes together. When I was around sixteen he and I had decided to go to London Zoo. Instead of doing the conventional thing – pay at the turnstile – we thought we would climb over the spiked railings to add a little excitement and to get in free. We found a quiet spot down by the canal and Remo climbed first. I don't know how he did this but I can still picture him crouched on top of the two-metre-high railings, gripping the spikes on either side of his feet which were on the top rail. He stayed there for a bit, then teetered, and with a shout fell backwards. The spikes pierced the palms of his hands. He hung there impaled on the zoo railings. He didn't complain but I realised it was my job to get him down. I crouched under his backside and heaved him up so that he could pull his hands off the spikes. There was not much blood and he told me that, surprisingly, it didn't hurt that much. He must have been in shock. We walked to the nearest hospital and made up some cock and bull story about falling over. 'Oh yes,' said the doctor wryly, not believing a word of it.

Remo and I happily spent our flat-sharing evenings going to the cartoon cinemas in Soho and Baker Street, watching Mr Magoo, Tom and Jerry, Road Runner and Woody Woodpecker – all possible influences on my future style. But now I think, What a waste of life. Other evenings and weekends we would chat at the recreation ground on Parliament Hill, where we mucked about on the swings, parallel bars and rings. Over the months that certainly improved my physique.

Remo's parents were separated. His mother was an English

actress, his amiable father an Italian sculptor and a staunch communist. He told me once he had remained seated during the National Anthem at the end of a film showing at the Odeon Swiss Cottage and was walloped over the head with an umbrella by the gentleman behind. 'Stand up, sir!' bellowed the umbrella owner. 'Stand up for the King!' That's what it was like in the forties and early fifties. At the end of the film you either had to make a bolt for the exit before the first chords of 'God Save the King' struck up or stand to attention, trapped in an apparent display of loyalty. As though some gigantic pause button had been pressed, we would stand motionless, some caught in mid-flight.

We would linger over coffee at the Prompt Corner coffee bar – a misnomer if ever there was one. Nobody was prompt. There would be bearded writers in polo necks (intellectuals) lounging on cushions, expounding on Sartre and Proust. Others explained to black-eyed girls with long straight hair the meaning of life (which usually involved getting them into bed). Many who went for breakfast and a game of chess were still there at ten o'clock at night, moving rooks to King Four and trying to checkmate. It was Hampstead's stab at an artsy-craftsy, Left Bank lifestyle.

On the subject of getting girls into bed, I admired my cartoonist friend Fotis Georgulakis. He seemed to have no trouble at all. Fotis was Greek. Very Greek. Charmingly Greek. I met him on an outing to Woburn Abbey with the Cartoonists' Club that I was a member of for a short time, and he asked if I could give him a lift back to London. He became a very good friend of mine, and when he later moved to America, I would often go to stay with him in Jackson Heights. Naturally I had a keen interest in sex, and I asked about his success with women. 'How do you do it, Fotis?'

'Purely advertising,' he told me. 'If you let yourself be known as a womaniser your reputation goes before you and the job is half done. Girls expect you to bed them.'

I tried this but it didn't work.

I tried being a knight in shining armour, too. One evening in Hampstead I was passing the Playhouse Cinema at the bottom of Pond Street. I saw two girls with beehive hairdos fighting. One was trying, viciously, to gouge holes in the other's legs with her stiletto heels. Foolishly I jumped between them to stop her getting hurt, holding them apart at arm's length. They both immediately turned on me. At the same moment I was knocked backwards on to the ground by one of the girls' boyfriends. The other boyfriend sat astride my chest and, in a well-practised manoeuvre, tightened the tie I was wearing around my neck, choking me as I lay gasping and helpless on my back, fighting for air while being punched. Passers-by told my assailants to 'pack it in' and dragged them off. After that I thought less about demonstrations of heroism and more about minding my own business.

Once a week I would gather with Fotis, Frank Dickens – creator of Bristow in the *Evening Standard*, Rovi – a 'gag artist' and other cartoonists in a Hampstead coffee bar for an ideas session – a kind of lukewarm Bohemia. We would sit over cups of espresso discussing desert islands with shipwrecked mariners putting messages into bottles while sitting under a single palm tree from which flew a tattered shirt; mothers-in-law armed with dangerously large rolling pins waiting behind doors for their errant drunken sons-in-law to come home from the pub; burglars in masks and striped jerseys with bulging bags marked SWAG; magicians producing rabbits from top hats; policemen with trousers down; drunks clinging to lampposts. And so on. Such was the stuff of cartoons. It became routine and tedious. Surely, I thought, there must be more. Once again I felt I was treading water and really wanted to move on now that I had discovered I could express my thoughts and feelings through my drawings. My black humour had begun to creep into my work and my natural approach to life was showing in my drawings. Even in those early days they were dark and surreal. A soldier building a snowman at the bleak and bitingly cold snowy roadside during Napoleon's retreat from Moscow. A prisoner hanging by his manacled hands in the salt mines, saying 'pass the salt'.

It felt momentous when I finally left Scarfe's Studios after five years. When I announced I was leaving to become a freelancer there was a slight sense of resentment from my uncle, who – perhaps understandably – felt he had nursed me as a family member. I didn't feel that. I felt I'd been held back. I had done much of the major work in the studio and had been meanly rewarded. I think I was earning £8 a week when I left. Mr Alfrey on the other hand was delighted to get rid of what he thought was a future rival for the running of the firm and encouraged me to go. 'I know you, Gerald. When you've made your mind up there's no stopping you.' Well, there wasn't, and off I went. It was the first good career move I made.

I had to start again. Most of my work came from Hugh White Studios in Warren Street. I would fill the car up with goods, then drive back to the flat where I would set to work drawing each object, making them look sexy and desirable – and, above all, saleable. When I'd completed the job I'd drive everything back from Parliament Hill. As I became more successful and began to be sought after, I found I had much more work than I could handle. I'd be up much of the night in our tiny kitchenette drawing prams, blankets, eiderdowns, tricycles and other 'crap' for Selfridges and Gorringes catalogues or suchlike. But I was making a fair amount of money. Remo got fed up with me working into the early hours of the morning and disturbing him. Things also became difficult because my making money divided our lifestyles. When Remo announced he was leaving, I was sad but I understood: success can separate people, as I would come to learn.

I drew catalogues for a shady man in the rag trade, Mr

Corbluth. He often wouldn't pay me and before long owed me hundreds of pounds. I was forced to hunt him down to get my cash and would chase him around a musty, cavernous room in his clothing warehouse off Warren Street, packed with hundreds of frocks. I knew he was in there somewhere – I could hear him scuttling around like a giant rat. We'd play a mad kind of hide and seek. I could find him only by dropping to my knees and looking under the hems of the frocks hanging on the racks. If or when I caught him he would reluctantly give me a cheque for £20 'on account', suggesting I return the following week for the balance, telling me as he made the cheque out how poor he was, how times were hard. I told him times were hard for me too. But that didn't seem to move him quite so much and I had to repeat this performance week after week. I never got the full amount.

I worked night and day, non-stop, as a freelancer, and made a great deal of money. I bought a car, an Austin Sprite, and with this new feeling of confidence my asthma began to improve. Meanwhile, the cartooning took off. I was making a very good living for a bachelor, selling five or six jokes a week to the *Daily Sketch*, *Daily Mirror* and *Evening Standard* at five to seven guineas a drawing – about £150 in today's money, which isn't bad.

I still admired Frank Hampson of Dan Dare fame. He was an English artist who drew in the American style. I'm sure the American comics that Heinz had sent over had also had an influence on me, with their dramatic and economical drawings of Superman and Batman, so I thought I might become a comic book artist. I contacted a publisher near High Holborn who said they would try me out and gave me a Robin Hood story to illustrate. For some months I drew Robin and his merry men in a realistic style, which wasn't easy. I worked hard and long into the nights. Whenever I returned to the publisher, they told me my drawings were almost there, but not quite a bullseye. I would try again with the same results. I became fed up with Friar Tuck, Little John

and boring Alan A'Dale. I wasn't feeling particularly merry about
it all anyway so I abandoned Sherwood Forest and made my way
back to cartooning.

I also took lessons in 'General Drawing' at the London School
of Printing where I met the only man who ever taught me anything about art. His name was Leslie Richardson, and I owe him
a great debt of thanks. Once a week I would meet Leslie with a
group of other students. He simply showed me how to think of
myself as an artist by encouraging and bringing out what I had to
offer. He didn't give me examples, he didn't show me his work;
he just talked to me.

Leslie gave me the groundwork and legitimacy to become an
artist. He made art a viable pursuit, something I could do as a
career. In the arts, I believe, teachers have to inspire, orchestrate
or manage their pupils, and not necessarily be able to excel themselves in the subjects they teach. I wanted desperately to know
the secrets of art and Leslie brought the best out of me, teaching
me specifically how to use colour and how to use different imple-
ments. But what he did so well was talk about the theory of art:
what I should be doing and looking at. He never once corrected or
altered my drawings with a pencil – an excellent policy, because
once you do you are interfering with that person's method. Every
explanation he gave was done with words rather than actions.

Leslie's constructive way of teaching was so beneficial that I
felt encouraged enough to apply to the prestigious Royal College
of Art, where David Hockney – my fellow *Eagle* winner – was
studying at that time. My first day at the college made me feel
as though I had received a card saying 'Return to Go'. My tutor
made me carry his books upstairs for him; he was going to show
me that I might have made my name in the outside world but in
the RCA I was just another student. That was bearable, but when
he talked about the world outside the Royal College I knew he'd
never been there. He seemed to be a student who had become a

teacher and never applied a theory in his life. 'When you leave here and receive your first commission,' he told me, 'it won't be easy. You may have to finish the rough design in two weeks and may not get more than another two weeks for the finished artwork.' I knew from experience that this was nonsense. Two hours was more probable.

Sadly, the Royal College of Art came too late for me. I was twenty-seven and earning a healthy living, I was already out there. Money and greed won, and three weeks after I started, I left. I now wonder where I would be had I stayed. An oil painter, an architect? Or a down-and-out? Some say it's a good thing I didn't go to art school. They can be places of laziness. I might have turned out like a pea in a pod.

David Hockney eventually dropped out too, leaving a year early. He has made a gigantic success of his work. I always admired him and he certainly capitalised on his considerable talent. He realised there is a certain amount of showbiz in the art world, and even at the Royal College he dyed his hair blond – 'Blonds have more fun,' he'd say – and took to wearing a gold lamé jacket. He made himself noticeable. I, on the other hand, always thought I was a bit of a disappointment as an artist at that time. I think people expect artists to have beards, get drunk and piss on people (or is that a cartoon idea?). I couldn't wear a gold lamé jacket. It didn't suit me.

Many years later I was asked to deliver a lecture on my work at the Royal College of Art. After I had finished and was tidying up my things at the front of the stage I heard the eminent sculptor Eduardo Paolozzi, who was passing behind me, say in a loud, booming voice, 'Well! That was disappointing, wasn't it?'

As my career developed, Leslie and I drifted apart, losing contact. I remain grateful for his teaching. I am so lucky to do what I do. It is tough making a living as an artist – but at that time of my life I really wanted it. Art was the subsistence I needed, having

been practically bedridden for the first sixteen years of my life,
and Leslie certainly helped to feed that urge. Up to that point
I'd thought of myself as a failed banker. Although I had drawn
all my life, I was still not convinced that it was my vocation. It
took Leslie's kind wisdom to give me the confidence to say: I am
an artist.

4

Private Eye and the Explosion

'How did you get your style?' people often ask. My style, like handwriting, arrived on its own, in its own time, as a direct result of my experiences and feelings, which were aching for an outlet. My cynical attitude to life, which was to fuel this style, had evolved over the years, and is more or less the same today as it was then.

In 1960 *Punch* magazine accepted one of my cartoons, a simple drawing of a club type sporting a blazer and a handlebar moustache (I don't get it now, but they bought it). In the early sixties *Punch* was *the* magazine for written and graphic humour. To appear in it was a great honour. It's hard to imagine now how important it was. Sadly it fell on hard times when the much more hard-line satirical magazine *Private Eye* was born. *Punch* appeared tame by comparison. It fell into decline and closed in 1992, and despite an attempt by Harrods owner Mohamed Al-Fayed to relaunch it a few years later (after he was criticised in *Private Eye*), it never regained its status.

Punch jokes came easily to me, and I was soon a regular contributor, but I began to tire of churning them out. I wanted to draw something with more point than shipwrecked mariners putting messages into bottles on desert islands, because they were not 'real' situations. They seemed as endless and meaningless as the blankets and shoes I had drawn in the commercial art studio and I had the continual feeling that I was a late beginner who had taken a seriously wrong turning and had to make up for acres of wasted time. I wanted to move on and felt an urgent need to make drawings that had some purpose, that expressed my hopes and fears about life around me: above all the need to capture on paper some sort of social comment. I wanted to use my pen to speak. The pressure was enormous. I knew there was more in me.

In 1963 the dam broke. I found a way of expressing myself. I made a series of drawings which I named *The Pleasure Seekers*, depicting the various weird and wonderful ways humans seek pleasure – by hurling themselves down fairground roller-coasters, or roasting themselves on crowded beaches and turning purple with sunburn. One shows a father holding his little son on his shoulders to get a better view of a fatal road traffic accident; another, an ambulance standing nearby as punters blithely scare themselves to death on the Big Dipper. Simple though the drawings were, it was a bridge. I was expressing people's emotions – pleasure, pain and terror – and I realised that humour, properly used, is a devastating weapon. I had found a new direction.

My great champion at *Punch* was Kenneth Mahood, the deputy

art editor, a charming, softly spoken Irishman who went out of his way to promote me and my work. He encouraged me, and I produced a long series of double-page spreads with satirical undertones: stories about human nature with cynical and ironic twists, like 'Miss Public Taste' and 'The Fad'. Sometimes I took directly from my experiences in life and produced drawings such as 'The Officials', 'The Vigil' and 'The Bandwagon'. *Punch* had also sent me on my first assignment as a visual reporter, in May 1962, to draw three pages on the newly built Coventry Cathedral. Many of my drawings from this period were destroyed in a fire at Liverpool Street station while being returned from an exhibition.

I was just twenty-seven when Punch produced an advertisement proclaiming me 'The New Face of *Punch*'. I was flattered, but in the early days I was continually getting notes from the art editor saying 'this nose is too big' or 'those feet are too large'. I think in those days *Punch* thought of itself as the ultimate arbiter of humour. *King* magazine printed a conversation between me and Bernard Hollowood, my editor at *Punch*, about political cartoons which gives some idea of *Punch*'s feudal attitude to its artists:

SCARFE: Couldn't you have a cartoonist with a view of his own?

HOLLOWOOD: I don't see much point in letting a cartoonist have his own say if one doesn't think much of his views anyway. Obviously people buy a newspaper or magazine because they find its views stimulating. And the best way we can guarantee interest among our readers is by recruiting a group of competent artists who can translate ideas into drawings under editorial guidance.

What a pompous bugger!

I can count myself lucky that apart from the noses being too big I didn't get any of this 'editorial guidance'. I continued commenting on things in general – education, architecture, health care etc. – all the while feeling I had more to offer. And I certainly never allowed any editor to dictate what my work should say, especially politically. I have never, in any of my national newspaper jobs, had any political guidance or interference. A cartoonist's job is to give their own point of view, not to support the paper's political line. I have often had a cartoon appear on the same page as an editorial touting the opposite political view to mine. Freedom of speech allows for the right to argue, and it's quite correct that conflicting viewpoints are printed alongside one another.

By now I was living in Rosecroft Avenue in Hampstead. It was an architecturally interesting Edwardian house on a hill leading to Hampstead Heath with towers and sloping roofs. I lived in the top attic flat under those roofs. A real artist's atelier. Below, the second floor was occupied by Arnost and Eva Vokalek, a charming bohemian couple. I believe he was an architect. On the ground floor lived the famous Marxist author Ralph Miliband and his wife Marion. Occasionally I would bump into Ralph in the hall. He was a serious, stern, gruff but kindly man. He had seen my work in *Private Eye* and seemed to approve. We chatted, but never got to know each other well. In the summer of 1965 David Miliband was born, and a few years later Ed. The Ed who couldn't successfully lead the Labour Party or eat a bacon sandwich, after he infamously stabbed his brother in the back when he won a fight for the party leadership in 2010. I've never met him, but if I ever did, because I have drawn him many times, I would tell him I was the bastard who lived in his attic. (Ed and I not only shared a house, we also shared the school on Haverstock Hill, which was known as the 'Eton of the left', though of course Ed went many years after me. As those reports showed earlier, still struggling with asthma, I'm not sure it did me much good, but look what happened to him.)

I continued my self-education by visiting record shops and

picking whatever took my fancy – Bach Cello Suites, Brahms Symphonies. I chose things at random from the Deutsche Grammophon label before returning home to play them on my old turntable as I was working. But I found my true release among the seedy sex shops of Soho. In very small premises over a strip joint and betting shop at 22 Greek Street, *Private Eye* was born.

Private Eye was the biggest turning point of my young career. I was launched into a totally new and exciting world. I can't emphasise how my life was changed. *Punch* was a big step but to be working with *Private Eye* brought me into contact with people of my own age who were putting the magazine together as though they were still at university – the university life I had missed but could now live vicariously. It was an outrageous publication that was constantly in the news and adored by many. I felt included and involved. They accepted and applauded everything I did, pushing me on to new excesses. I loved every moment of it. It was a breath of fresh air for me; *Private Eye* radically and thrillingly transformed my world. The bottled-up feelings of my frustrated, bedridden childhood found the perfect outlet. *Private Eye* was the ideal compost for my particular talents, and I very quickly began to flower. They encouraged me to develop and push my drawings even further. They suggested subjects and accepted everything that I drew. I was no longer drawing blankets, I was producing satirical social comment, and I was so very much happier. I was never told that my noses were too big.

It was my friend, the cartoonist and entertainer William Rushton, one of the founder members of *Private Eye*, who had urged me to try political cartooning during a party at my Rosecroft Avenue flat. That conversation changed everything for me. I finally got going, having wasted all those early years.

The Profumo scandal was in full flight so I took off after it. I was able to attack the sources of so many troubles: the powerful, the leaders, the politicians who think they know what is best for us all, the misuse of power. I focused my attention away from the victims of society on to those who created and ran it.

The Prime Minister, Harold 'you've never had it so good' Macmillan ('Donkey Head' my father called him), was my first political target. He seemed like a bumbling old fool to me at the time, a figure from another and now-dead society (although I did like it when Russian leader Nikita Khrushchev banged his desk in fury at the United Nations with the heel of his shoe and Macmillan stood up and drawled in his very English voice, 'I wonder if I might have that translated?'). It's difficult today to describe the repressive moral climate of the early sixties. The Lord Chancellor had to scrutinise the script of every play before it could be put before the public. The publisher of D. H. Lawrence's novel *Lady Chatterley's Lover* was prosecuted for obscenity. So the world was shocked by the revelations of Christine Keeler and Mandy Rice-Davies. When I drew Macmillan as Christine Keeler seated naked on that famous chair for the cover of the *Private Eye* annual, WHSmith, Menzies and other bookshops refused to stock it. They returned every copy to the warehouse. An academic later wrote that I was the first artist since the eighteenth century to draw a politician naked. If any one drawing ever changed my life it was that one of Mac on the chair. Everyone seemed to mention it.

I continued to lash out in every direction, sometimes flailing wildly and hitting my targets by a combination of luck and instinct. I drew every politician under the sun – as libertines, vultures, philanderers, dogs and pigs. It tumbled out, spilled and oozed. I was accused of using a sledgehammer to crack a nut. I really enjoyed myself. As Mandy Rice-Davies might have put it, Well, I would, wouldn't I?

Because of my lack of training in art, I taught myself anatomy from medical books. My efforts to represent faithfully the human body led to caricatures that showed its workings, the bones, sinews, muscles, skin, bulging flesh and veins and sometimes the

innards: the intestines, the heart, the lungs. Through these drawings perhaps I unconsciously expressed the frailty of life which
had been instilled in me by my hospitalised childhood. On the
lighter side I found I could draw whom I liked and what I liked,
warts, nipples and pubic hair. I had not known I had wanted to
draw such things but I experienced a great feeling of childish
release when I did, like shouting 'bum' out loud at the vicar's tea
party. I'm not sure I ever got it out of my system. I have always
had an urge to mention the unmentionable, to make jokes about
the taboo. Nothing was sacred for me – I had no heroes. All was
grist to the mill.

Richard Ingrams, the editor, and I would meet in the tiny
Private Eye office to discuss ideas. Sometimes he would phone
and say, 'We'd love a portrait of the frightful Wislon [*sic*] as a
toad.' Or, on another occasion, 'We want a cover for tomorrow
of Wislon kneeling behind Lyndon Johnson and licking his arse,
saying, "I've heard of special relationships but this is ridiculous!"'
When I showed him this particular drawing even Richard thought
I had gone too far. I had Harold Wilson's tongue actually in LBJ's
arsehole. I had to quickly redraw it and withdraw . . . the tongue
I mean. Richard later wrote that he enjoyed those sessions – but
also said in an interview with the *London Review of Books* that I 'got
very grand and didn't like being given ideas'. I don't remember
feeling that, but I expect he is right.

The *Private Eye* founders – Ingrams, Rushton, Christopher
Booker, Paul Foot and John Wells – were like old men. All
about forty-five even in their twenties. The dress style was
Oxford – baggy tweed with leather patches on elbows. My
fellow cartoonist Barry Fantoni told me they were pretty snide
about one another and about me when the victim was absent.
But it went both ways: for the glossy, hip *Queen* magazine I drew
Richard as a gossip peering from behind his lace net curtains
in his semi-detached house. Although I was known as a *Private*

Eye-man, I felt an outsider. I *was* an outsider. They all seemed to come from a different world.

Some misunderstood my motives. One of the *Private Eye* wives, when I went down for lunch at her country cottage, took me to the pub and snobbishly showed me the locals in the public bar. 'Just have a look,' she said. 'Aren't they a hoot?' But I did enjoy drawing some characters in Soho; at lunchtime we would wander down the street to the Coach & Horses for a pint or two and a bite to eat, where Norman Balon, 'the rudest landlord in London', who was fond of saying, 'If you don't like my food, fuck off!', was mine jovial host. Our other eating place was Jimmy's on Frith Street. On Sunday lunchtimes we would go down to the basement of Jimmy's and have great doorstep slabs of bread and butter with enormous plates of heaped food and a mug of tea, all for a very reasonable sum.

Private Eye scorned Macmillan's successor, the Right Honourable Sir Alec Douglas-Home, as a relic of the past and a dinosaur. They called him Baillie Vass after the Scottish news-paper the *Aberdeen Evening Express* accidentally used a photograph of Douglas-Home to illustrate a story about a Scottish baillie named Vass. During a meeting at the offices in the late autumn of 1963 it was decided that for a jape Willie Rushton would stand against Lord Douglas-Home for the seat of Kinross in Scotland in the upcoming by-election. I designed a poster showing a skull-like Douglas-Home saying 'Death of the Conservative Party'. We flew up to John Calder's mansion in Kinross. He was the Canadian-born writer and publisher who had inherited a beautiful nineteenth-century baronial house in Kinross-shire from an uncle and begun to use it as a centre for the arts. He was passionately against censorship of any kind and not a fan of Douglas-Home. I spent the night in a huge bed in a vast room.

The following morning when I went down for breakfast, I found the most extensive feast laid before me on the sideboard: eggs, bacon, kedgeree, sausages, kidneys – a stately home breakfast. John Wells and I walked off this banquet through the Scottish heather in the cold morning air. John became very morose and said that he would never make anything of himself, that it was OK for me, I would be remembered but he had nothing to be remembered for.

We all drove through the streets of Kinross with Paul Foot on a loud hailer with his head out of the sunroof, imploring every passer-by to vote – 'Postman, vote Rushton!' Taking my turn at the wheel of the Land Rover, I drove them back to Calder's mansion, bumping over the rough tracks and narrowly missing a large white cow that loomed up through the thick Scottish mist.

In order to gain a measure of credibility, the aristocratic Lord Douglas-Home said, 'I've lived amongst miners all of my life.' I made another drawing of him for the magazine showing him on the moors shooting grouse, while under his feet miners toiled at the coal face a mile below ground.

It was a good, if chaotic, time. While the strippers scurried business-like from club to club to take off their clothes, upstairs in the tiny *Private Eye* office I struggled to finish my work on a tiny desk, Peter Cook pushing past, knocking over the ink, while tea-making debutantes showered my drawing with sugar. I always thought that when I got a proper job in Fleet Street it would be different; things would be organised, not so haphazard. I was wrong. The only difference was it was not so much fun.

My work in *Private Eye* was often perceived as cruel and grotesque. I was genuinely surprised by this, since it was the way I drew naturally. I became known not for inventing a cartoon character like Mickey Mouse or Charlie Brown but for a view of life and attitude of mind. I was flattered by imitators. 'I'd always wanted to do that,' said one fellow cartoonist, 'it's just that you showed me the way.' But I couldn't shake off that lack of confidence, never having passed any exams or received any diplomas. Although I had been successful in the commercial art world, I still didn't know if I was any good as an artist. Being a real artist, I felt, had different rules, though I wasn't sure what they were.

But then John Berger, the renowned critic and expert on art, wrote favourably about my work and commissioned me to design and draw the cover of his book *Corker's Freedom*. John was the first person of any respected artistic authority to give me some sense of my place and possibilities in the mysterious world of art. He praised my work when I dined with him, but even then I was uncertain and made him and his companion glance at one another and smile when I asked, 'But is it Art?' That age-old question.

Berger asked if he could write an article about my work in his paper, the *Observer*, and did I have a drawing to accompany it? I gave him a drawing of two figures – a naked male and female. The female had propped-up breasts and looked into a hand mirror with a totally blank face, worms spilling from her trepanned skull. The man's belly spilled entrails in defiance. The *Observer* didn't like this drawing. 'Scarfe is that very rare thing, a natural satirical draughtsman,' Berger wrote. 'Gillray was one, Rowlandson wasn't. George Grosz was one but Low isn't. The supreme examples are Goya and Daumier . . . what is essential to them is that they draw faithfully – and with pain – the ghosts that crowd in upon them. He seems to me to belong to the proper and rare tradition. Certainly I can think of no other draughtsman in Britain who, since the war, has shown more promise in this genre.'

I have much to thank *Private Eye* for. I really found my feet there. For the first time I knew what I had to do – I knew the way. One particular moment remains in my mind. I was working on a series of drawings of the leaders of the social scene – Mick Jagger, David Frost, David Bailey, Jean Shrimpton – for a page of what *Private Eye* called Gerald Scarfe's *Box of Throwups* (a pastiche of Bailey's

Box of Pin-Ups) and they just seemed to flow, the drawings coming out of me so easily and successfully, as though I was some sort of conduit through which preconceived ideas from somewhere were arriving ready-made.

What effect have my drawings had? Alan Coren, the editor of *Punch* from 1977 to 1987, told me he couldn't recall what Jean Shrimpton looked like but he could remember my drawing of her. So it is certainly possible to create images that stay in people's minds. I left the hair in poor Jean's armpits, which seemed to shock and made the drawing memorable in those more innocent days.

Through *Private Eye* I met a successful entrepreneur, Gareth Powell, who had made a fortune in publishing. He asked me how much I made. I exaggerated a little and said £3,000 a year. 'That's peanuts,' he scoffed. Riled by this and being young I told him at least I was doing something that would last. 'Oh, great,' he said. 'Do you think Hieronymus Bosch gets a fucking erection every time someone looks at his drawings?' I took his point. He probably doesn't.

Reactions to my drawings could be flattering or levelling but also amusing. One in particular provoked an outcry: 114 schoolgirls wrote to say that they were appalled by my depiction of their sex-god Mick Jagger. 'Dear Mr Scarfe,' they said. 'For what you done [sic] to our Mick we are going to get you and cut your balls off. Yours sincerely, Angela Bunton, Jane Baxter, Pat Holland . . . ' Sweethearts. And so on – a petition signed by all 114. They haven't caught me so far. They had better get a move on. One of those girls wrote to me many years later:

Dear Mr Scarfe,

    I was one of the schoolgirls who signed that letter to you! . . . My classmate was obsessed with Mick Jagger – the wrath of a fourteen-year-old teenager is not to be taken lightly.

She was so outraged that she made us all sign the letter. Truth be told, I don't really care for Mick but Carol was insistent.

With warmest wishes,

Ruth

Another admirer wrote:

Dear Mr Scarfe,

For years your ugly and horrific caricatures have disturbed me. While I appreciate the fact that you must have talent to arouse one to this extent, I also object to being subjected to the horrors of your mind while reading a paper of my choice. Today I can no longer contain myself. I cannot send you a drawing to upset you. But I can tell you how sorry I feel for you. I can simply tear up the paper. But you have to live with your warped images for ever. Poor you.

Yours sincerely . . .

Once again, 'Yours sincerely'. Very civil.

Private Eye brought me to prominence – I was deluged with commissions, offered books, interviewed on television, given exhibitions, won awards, and critics took me seriously. It was bewildering. I almost began to believe it when the *Sunday Times* called me the only real satirist to appear from the whole move-ment. All of this seemed to result in a great well of sullen jealousy among some colleagues. Richard Ingrams said, 'Scarfe has begun to believe his own publicity.' Ingrams also disliked artists signing their own work. 'Personality cult', he'd observe. This didn't deter him from becoming a 'personality'.

I made large charcoal drawings from life of the Conservative politicians Enoch Powell and Iain Macleod for the magazine that Michael Heseltine's company owned, *About Town*. It is common practice that the rights to publish belong to the publisher and the original drawing belongs to the artist. However, Heseltine kept my drawings, framed them and hung them in his mansion. Some years later at a Tory Party Conference in Blackpool I confronted him and asked for them back. 'I think you'll find there was a clause printed on the back of your cheque which said the originals belong to me,' he said. I was pretty convinced this was nonsense, but since I had cashed the cheque I had no proof. I found it extraordinary that this high-profile politician should refuse to return an artist's work when the artist was so obviously upset about it. The journalist and broadcaster Anthony Howard told me years later that the drawings still hang on the staircase of his country house in Oxfordshire. When I told Peter Cook, he suggested, 'Well let's break into the bugger's house and steal them back.' When I drew Heseltine thereafter he didn't come out too well. I still call him 'Heselswine'.

In 1964 *The Times* commissioned me to draw Winston Churchill on his last day in the House of Commons. With special dispensation from the Serjeant at Arms I was allowed to sketch him from the Public Gallery. As I waited for Churchill to appear in the crowded chamber I imagined the Churchill I knew of old – the iconic British bulldog standing on the white cliffs of Dover, cigar clenched between his teeth, his two-fingered victory salute defying the Hun, possibly with Vera Lynn singing 'We'll Meet Again' in the background. Eventually he arrived – a shambling figure supported on both sides by two young attendants who carefully eased him on to his usual seat at the end of the row. And there he sat, apparently unaware of his surroundings. A senile old man. It was shocking. I made a number of detailed pencil sketches to use in the final portrait, which I made later in charcoal.

My drawing had to show the truth. I would have to convey the ravages of time, the difference the years had made to this once brilliant man. The absence of hope or ambition in those rheumy eyes, the sagging face and body. A shell. A husk. I couldn't draw the icon. He did not exist any more. It's important to draw honestly.

When I delivered it to *The Times* they loved it but refused to print it, saying that Churchill's wife Clemmie would be very upset when the newspaper dropped through the letterbox the next morning. She was trying to preserve the icon. When Churchill died the following year, *Private Eye* used it at Peter Cook's behest on one of its covers. No sentiment there.

Many years later, in 2008, it was suggested to me that this drawing should hang in the dining room at the Houses of Parliament. But when, eventually, I lent it to the Parliamentary Art Collection it ended up on the walls of Portcullis House. The Churchill drawing led to a commission from the *Sunday Times*. Once again I was given special dispensation by the Serjeant at Arms of the Houses of Parliament to sketch from the Public Gallery, so long as I was discreet. I went day after day and drew every member of the House present during those weeks. I learned to sketch on my knee without looking down and, using those hundreds of drawings, made an eight-by-four-foot oil painting, which at present also hangs in Portcullis House.

The mid-sixties was an explosion for me. What happened I still don't understand but it had an extreme effect on my life. I came out of the dark and was exposed. Against the bland background of the early sixties, although I didn't know it at the time, my work was a departure.

After several years of drawing for *Private Eye*, when I joined the *Daily Mail* in 1966 Richard Ingrams no longer asked for my work. Perhaps I had joined the enemy. I missed them. And I have so much to thank them for; not least for the invitation to travel down to Brighton on the last trip of the *Brighton Belle* for a party to celebrate *Private Eye*'s tenth anniversary in 1971. There I met Jane Asher, who became my wife. A few years ago, after I had done a lot of press interviews to promote publication of a new book, there was a small piece about me in *Private Eye* in which they summed me up thus:

That All Purpose Gerald Scarfe Interview:

Acid pen . . . biting satire . . . sixties . . . Private Eye . . . asthmatic childhood . . . Jane Asher . . . cakes . . . vitriol . . . Cheyne Walk . . . intensely private . . . marked contrast . . . sixties . . . Jane Asher . . . cakes . . .

When I left Rosecroft Avenue I tore up most of my early drawings – I didn't like them – and burned them in a dustbin. My brother Gordon, who was helping, said, 'Are you sure we should be doing this?'

5

Elvis and the Glittering Snake

As a child growing up in dull Britain in the fifties, America defined glamour. Oh my God was Britain drab! It was post-war, and fun was banned. Streets were grey, people were grey. Sundays were leaden with the false pretence in most quarters that the Sacred Day was still alive and well, not as dead as a dodo. Shops, cinemas and places of entertainment were closed on Sundays. You would enjoy yourself under pain of death. So America appeared to be the golden dream. Everything exciting was there – movies, Cadillacs, Elvis, sex, drugs and rock 'n' roll.

I got the chance to visit this exciting new planet in 1964 when I was twenty-eight years old. The phone rang one night: it was Peter Crookston, deputy editor of the *Sunday Times*. Could I leave tomorrow for New York and send back some drawings of the American elections by the end of the week? 'Certainly,' I burbled deliriously. 'No problem.' Well, there was a problem – I was naive. Peter assured me that the American correspondent Henry Brandon would set everything up for me, gave me his telephone number, and told me to call him when I arrived. And, oh, could I draw portraits of President Lyndon B. Johnson and his opponent Barry Goldwater and get them signed? 'Sure,' I said, with all the confidence of a twenty-eight-year-old offered a free trip to experience his wildest dreams. And off I went.

When I got to New York I called Brandon and explained what I wanted. He laughed. 'Forget it. You haven't got a hope in hell. These campaign planes have been booked up for months. You'll never get on.' He gave me the name and number of the press agent and rang off.

If I heard that today I would think, 'Mission impossible – can't be done' and would return to the hotel for a sleep, take a short holiday, then fly home. But in 1964 I was fired up, young, desperate and zealous. The *Sunday Times* had spent money on a first-class fare because economy was full. I mustn't fail them. So I rang the press agent and pleaded.

'Not a chance, buddy,' he said.

I had their schedule, and asked, 'What if I fly to Peoria in Illinois, maybe someone will get off?'

'Not a chance!' he repeated.

I continued to plead – it's my first assignment etc. Suddenly he took pity.

'Listen,' he said, 'fly to O'Hare airport and meet me tomorrow at two o'clock in the lobby of the O'Hare Inn. I'm promising you nothing.'

And he rang off.

The next day I flew to Chicago and found him. I was in luck. Again he took pity on me and let me board the reporters' press jet to Indiana. Suddenly I found myself in the thick of the impossible hurly-burly of an American election campaign. We travelled through Washington, Cleveland, Louisville, Nashville and Atlantic City. I had never seen or been involved in anything like it. As reporters scrambled to their seats, the jet was already taxiing down the grey runway, with its engines screaming, silencers removed for extra power. It took off at an impossibly steep angle. I clung to my seat as a typewriter and briefcases bounced down the gangway. We were on our way to Indianapolis on a whistle-stop tour following President Johnson. Our jet had to overtake Air Force One and land first, to enable the reporters to take pictures of him arriving.

I wrote at the time, 'The President's jet climbed into the sky, levelled out and dived to the next town, Indianapolis. It disgorged President, aides, reporters, et al at top speed. Pom pom girls twirl and the band plays "Hello Lyndon" to the tune of "Hello Dolly". Motorcade to town, speech, place name, back in the cars, airfield, take off, climb, dive, motorcade, same speech, different place name, Cleveland, motorcade, airfield, climb, dive, motorcade, same speech, Louisville, motorcade, airfield, plane, climb, dive, motorcade, same speech, Nashville . . . ' It was exhausting and exhilarating.

The further south we went, the deeper became the President's drawl, although the words of the speech remained the same. Lyndon Johnson was a swaggering Texan with a big personality. A crude back-slapper, a good old boy. He kept us reporters waiting at one press conference. 'Sorry, boys,' he drawled, 'sorry to be late, but I've just been giving Lady Bird one' (his wife). On another occasion he reportedly undid his flies and took out his penis: 'Look, boys, I bet Mao hasn't got one as big as this.' I drew him while he drawled, and decided to ask him to sign the drawing at a press conference later that day. I rolled up my drawing, which was about two feet long, and waited for him to enter the press conference room. Immediately he came in I took

In Provence with Ronald Searle, after a bottle of 'engine oil' – Billecart-Salmon Rosé champagne

Gerry Scarfe

Please ring —
— anytime

M & RS

Ronald gave me a doorbell with this note – it has sat on my desk ever since

My father, Reginald Scarfe

My mother, Dorothy Scarfe

Gordon and me, playing in the garden at
Goldhurst Terrace, London

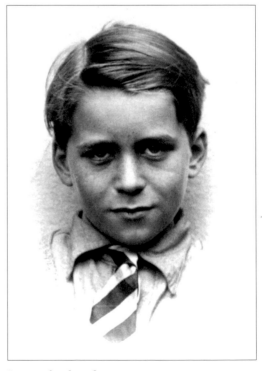

In my school uniform

The Ingersoll *Eagle* competition – look carefully to see a well-known consolation prize winner from Bradford

A catalogue layout I drew at Scarfe's Studios

EAGLE ARTIST'S NIGHTMARE, drawn by GERALD SCARFE (*aged 16*), 160 Goldhurst Terrace, Hampstead, N.W.6.

My first published drawing, which won a competition in the *Eagle* magazine

This drawing of Winston Churchill in his last days in Parliament was commissioned by *The Times* but not published until after his death when *Private Eye* published it as a cover

Drawing Buddhists at the Ấn Quang Pagoda, 1966

Gerald Scarfe: War Artist – reporting on the war in Vietnam, 1966

Sketching at the Republican Convention in Miami, 1968

Peter Cook, me, Richard Ingrams and Willie Rushton on our way to the Coach and Horses in Soho for the filming of *Scarfe on Scarfe*

The *Private Eye* team, from left: Christopher Booker, Richard Ingrams, Nigel Dempster, Peter Cook, Auberon Waugh, Peter McKay, Paul Foot [property of the National Portrait Gallery]

In my attic studio in Rosecroft Avenue, Hampstead, 1964

Making my film *Will the Real Mr Hogarth Please Stand Up*, 1969

In Los Angeles in 1973, making my film *Long Drawn-Out Trip*, which was drawn directly on to 70mm film

of the nostril to the corner of the mouth on my drawing: 'That is definitely an anti-Goldwater line!' The Senator was much more forgiving. 'Sure, I'll sign it,' he said. 'I've got a sense of humour.'

Against all odds I had accomplished my *Sunday Times* brief.

New York fascinated and hypnotised me like a great, glittering snake. Through some of my pals in the *Sunday Times* New York office I learned about all the 'in' places to visit. Max's Kansas City, a diner and bar near Union Square, was a constant haunt. Everything was so new and exciting – I had never seen so much excess, such violence, rudeness and inhumanity, such vulgarity, such energy, such riches, such poverty, and such a voracious appetite for getting to the top of the heap. Endless channels on TV spewing out endless opinions on endless disasters interrupted only by endless commercials. I was frightened and horrified the first day I switched on the multi-channel television in my hotel room: it told me of a human head that had been found wrapped in newspaper in a trash can. I wondered if this was the norm. Were people chopped up frequently in America? The answer was, I later found, yes – more or less. If not, they shot one another. Gun control was a big issue then as it still is today.

After the disruptive realistic nature of my reportage drawings I felt a strong need to draw what I saw and felt expressively. I made drawing after drawing of the American way of life. My first was 'Gorillas in the Streets', which told of the menace and fear I felt on the streets of New York at that time. It showed shambling, monstrous beasts lumbering menacingly, knuckles on the sidewalk, through the bleak canyons of New York City. For my own satisfaction I made a host of symbolic semi-surreal drawings of rampant controlling American females neutering over-developed muscular males. The males were all brawn and no brain, small insignificant heads on towering masses of muscle. The female was the dominant animal. Some were like Amazons, others were what Tom Wolfe described as social X-rays, skeletal women. And the voices! The bellowing, loud men and the painfully thin women, their voices with that particular piercing note that cuts the brain in half, like ice. I was scared but I drew them all.

My reputation had reached America and *Time* magazine commissioned me to draw the Beatles for their front cover. I had sketched them when they were filming *Help!* at Twickenham Studios and visited their homes. Now I followed John, Paul, George and Ringo around for a week or more. 'You're like me, Gerald,' said John Lennon while I was at his house in Weybridge. 'A cynic.' Ringo's house featured a psychedelic light show and bar. Many of the other rooms in his mansion were empty. I thought that coming from a two-up-two-down house he didn't know what to do with them. I liked Ringo. He wanted me to do a drawing of him on the wall, which I did while he posed. Paul was very nice and polite, proudly giving me a tour around his new house in St John's Wood. He introduced me to the dog, Martha, and explained how the secret of life was like a rose. I've forgotten how it goes now. It was in the days of Maharishi Mahesh Yogi's spiritual guidance. All four of these young men, suddenly thrust into global superstardom, were very polite and respectful.

I returned home with my pile of sketches, spread them around the walls and translated them into larger-than-life sculptural caricatures made of papier-mâché by dipping small pieces of torn-up newspaper in a flour-and-water paste and applying them in layer after layer on to a wire armature, which was then photographed for the cover. Many years later the sculptures made a dream home for the biscuit beetle: the fate of my Beatles was to be eaten by beetles.

When I had visited them when they were filming *Help!* I sketched them between takes. They were filming the scene which shows that all four of the Beatles have adjoining houses in one street. They each enter their individual front doors but when we cut to the interior of the houses, we see that all four doors open into one large communal room. While on the set I also made sketches of Richard Lester, the director, who thought I had over-elongated his face. 'Not bad, El Greco,' he remarked.

Given the immense fame of the band I had made a large colour drawing of them from my sketches. They all signed it, although George thought it was a doubtful likeness for he put a large question mark after his signature.

Because of the *Time* cover I was interviewed on the radio news programme *The World at One*. I was miffed because the interviewer only wanted to ask me about the Beatles – what were they like? What were they doing? He didn't seem the least interested in me and my work. The Beatles had been missing from the news recently and the world wanted to know.

Time was delighted with the Beatles cover. They flew me over straight away and, when I arrived in New York, Henry Grunwald, the editor, enthused and gave me many more commissions. The first of these was John Kenneth Galbraith, the economist. I flew to Boston to draw him. Galbraith was charming and asked if I had brought black tie with me. He was going to a dinner party – would I like to come? He later changed his mind and we ate in for dinner.

Armed with my sketches of Galbraith I moved into the Algonquin Hotel in New York and bought flour, wire mesh and all the newspapers I could carry, and smuggled them into the elevator and up to my room. I shut myself in there for days and had food sent up. The maid regarded me with suspicion. God knows what she thought, but evidently I wasn't one of the Algonquin's intellectuals, one of the Dorothy Parker set. I bent the wire into a linear caricature of Galbraith and covered it with strips of newspaper soaked in flour and water. Slowly, over the days, I built up a likeness of Galbraith – a three foot sculpture of his head and shoulders.

When I had painted the head it suddenly didn't look like him any more. My work has a habit of doing this. I'm convinced it's a real humdinger, I go for a pee, and when I come back it's a different person entirely. However, it was too late. The work had taken me about a week. *Time* was champing at the bit – the cover must be printed so I had to deliver it immediately. I washed, shaved, dressed and, gathering up the three-foot-high head, staggered out into the corridor and made my way to the elevator. The doors opened. Six frightened pairs of eyes stared at me and my creation. In silence I got into the lift among them. I pressed ground floor. The doors closed and we descended. Not a sound. Silence. The model smelled of stale flour and damp newspaper. 'Excuse me,' said the lady on my left. 'Isn't that John Kenneth Galbraith?' I was delighted – she'd recognised it. The doors opened, I stepped into the Algonquin's lobby. Success!

Soon after I'd finished Galbraith the management at the Algonquin asked me to leave my suite and move to another. I was embarrassed, certain that the maids had complained about my tiny bits of torn-up *New York Times* and the flour and water paste which had stuck to the carpet and furniture here and there. But no, it turned out that I had Ella Fitzgerald's room and she was back in town. She always stayed in the same room. I'd been sleeping in Ella's bed.

My next cover assignment was of the sketch comedians Rowan and Martin of *Laugh-In* fame. I spent a wonderful week with them in Hollywood, sailing on Dan Rowan's yacht on the Pacific and watching stars at play before going back to *Time*'s office in New York with another pile of sketches. This time my construction was so big that I built it in the *Time* magazine conference room. I had the place full of wood, plaster, wire, paint and all manner of assorted junk. I worked, watched by the baleful eyes of grim *Time* cover portraits of disapproving past presidents that lined the walls. I occasionally noticed the sliding doors opening a few inches and eyes peering at me. When I looked up they disappeared. The next time it happened I leapt up and slid back the doors. There, rather sheepishly, stood an editor I knew and several visitors to the building. 'Oh, hi, Gerry,' he said. 'Just showing the folks where you work.' I had become *Time* magazine's resident tame artist on the sixth floor.

In 1968 Richard Nixon was running for president; not many thought he'd make it. *Time* asked me to do a cover of him. His team had researched what kind of artist I was and refused outright to see me. Omnipotent *Time* was furious – no one told them what to do, let alone who would complete their covers. 'We'll send you on his campaign plane as a reporter; he can't stop that.' So, feeling rather unwanted and embarrassed, I travelled with Nixon through North Dakota, Montana and Nevada. Everywhere we stopped I would be in the front row drawing the 'expletive deleted'. He seemed uncomfortable too. Eventually he must have thought, if you can't beat them better join them, and he would throw me a sweaty smile. 'Hi, Gerry! Are your pencils sharp today? Ha, ha!' Once again I went back to New York, booked into the Hilton this time and completed a large papier-mâché head and shoulders of the Republican nominee. When it was dry I carried him in the bright sunshine across Sixth Avenue to the Time Life Building and proudly presented it to the editor in charge of covers.

'Um . . . it's a little extreme for us, Gerry. Could you try again?'

I did try again, but even that Nixon didn't make the cover. I later found out that in the meantime Nixon had come to look like a real contender for the presidency, and what's more the covers editor had joined his staff. What's sauce for the Beatles and show-biz is not sauce for powerful politicians.

I found America to be astoundingly insular. I travelled with Robert Kennedy in his small private jet. He was charming and friendly, with great – indeed legendary – charisma. He sat opposite me and asked what I was doing. I was working for *Fortune* magazine. Kennedy and I discussed Harold Wilson and how most people in the USA would not know who he was. Big fish in our

English pond look extremely small from other parts of the world. He felt sorry, he told me, for the girls – the 'bobby soxers' who faithfully waited for him on the wet and windswept tarmac at every airport we visited, though he would often invite them on to his jet during the stop. The thrill of a lifetime for them. I was in Los Angeles when he was assassinated. The writer and journalist David Leitch and I were staying at the Ambassador Hotel where he was shot, but that evening we had gone for dinner a short walk away. During the meal a reporter rushed over to our table and gasped, 'Robert Kennedy has been shot!' We raced to the Good Samaritan Hospital, where he later died. I then flew to New York for his lying in state in St Patrick's Cathedral and from there to Arlington Cemetery. I could not believe he was dead.

I had just stepped off the plane from New York to London when I received a telephone call asking me to report on the Republican Convention in Florida. Exhausted though I was, the next day I flew to Miami and booked in at the Fontainebleau Hotel (pronounced locally 'Fountain Blow'), then made my way to the convention hall where blue-rinsed, vulture-necked ladies and turtle-faced, wrinkled old men took part in a grotesque, over-sized children's party, with banners, bands, rattles, whistles and balloons. The cheering was deafening, shaking the foundations. The hall became one great monstrous beast bellowing its approval of America's greatness. An unhealthy mixture of mawkish sentimentality and thuggish bullying. The whole thing was like a bad movie.

A couple of years earlier, in 1966, Mel Lasky, the editor of *Encounter* magazine, had asked me to make portraits of a number of prominent American intellectuals while I was in New York. Within a few days I found myself sitting with the poet Stephen Spender on a bed in the Iroquois Hotel while he wrote letters to his intellectual friends: 'This is to introduce a young artist friend of mine from *Encounter*. Please allow him to sketch you.'

I found it very difficult to know how to approach these drawings. I certainly didn't feel I could make simple caricatures of
these illustrious geniuses and celebrities. So I decided to make
more realistic drawings and to work in charcoal, a forgiving
medium because the lines do not have to be as precise as a pen
line but I could put down what I saw as faithfully as I could

It takes time to make and distil a caricature, time to get to
know a person well enough to boil down their looks and personality to essentials, to a few lines that sum them up. Another
inhibiting fact is that when I am drawing someone from life I
know that when I have finished my drawing the sitter will want
to see it and I don't feel I can show them a distorted portrait.
Nevertheless, my style inevitably means that there is a slight element of caricature about them.

While I sketched him, the charming Arthur Miller sat patiently
reading a book. I was a long time; he could have read the whole
book while I scratched away. Although I chatted to him, in general
I find it difficult to talk while I work. I can't concentrate fully on
the drawing when making conversation. He did say at one point,
'A pity Marilyn isn't here, you could have sketched her.'

I sketched Stravinsky rehearsing his orchestra at the Met.

'Would you sign it?' I asked.

'Why should I?' he said. 'I did not draw it.'

'Please sign it for Stephen Spender,' I said.

He did, and added 'A good drawing by Gerald Scarfe'. I later
showed it to Stephen. 'Wonderful,' he said. 'He's signed it to me.
It's mine.' Reluctantly I had to give it to him, but he gave me a
beautiful Walter Sickert print, *Ennui*, in return.

Late one night I drove through the near-deserted dark streets
of New York on my way to draw the beat poet Allen Ginsberg,
who lived in a very poor area. While waiting at a red light a tattered drunk lurched out of the darkness and fell across the car
bonnet. What could I do? If I got out he might attack me. He was

very, very drunk. Slowly I backed up and he slid gently on to the tarmac, got up and tottered away. Drama over, but very New York. Ginsberg lived in a beaten-up house. He opened the door himself and took me upstairs to his hippy apartment. There, while I was sketching, he propositioned me.

'I'm not that way,' I said.

'That's OK, man,' he replied. 'Let's just carry on.' So I carried on, and when the drawing was finished he signed it and added a little symbol of three entwined fish.

Robert Oppenheimer, the man who developed the bomb in Los Alamos, sat staring into space while I drew. He didn't approve of my drawing and wouldn't sign it. His wife told me he was upset by it. Mel Lasky liked it and said, 'He looks like a man who's wondering what he has done.' Indeed!

I drew Leonard Bernstein during rehearsals. I was astounded when the orchestra suddenly broke for lunch. 'Please, gentlemen,' said Bernstein, 'we are almost there – give me five more minutes to finish the movement.' They ignored him and walked out.

When I'd finished drawing the painter Robert Motherwell, he asked if I would be interested in sketching Mark Rothko. 'Yes, that would be great,' I said, and he telephoned Rothko to ask if I could come over. 'Yes,' he said and I went to his studio and made several large charcoal sketches. When I'd finished I showed them to Rothko and asked if he would sign them to give them authenticity. 'No,' he said, 'I don't like them.' Awkward! Off into the streets of New York with my tail between my legs. The great Rothko didn't like my work.

The next day I called on Norman Mailer, the author, who lived on the top floor of a magnificent building in Columbia Heights in Brooklyn with a stunning view of the harbour and docks. Like most of my other sitters he was charming. I tried to work in my usual medium, pen and ink, for his portrait but that was a mistake – it didn't work. It didn't have the loose quality of charcoal.

It was too restrictive, and I ended up with some pretty poor drawings. Disappointing and embarrassing. He said he looked like 'a punched-up Beethoven'. He only had an hour to spare. He signed my copy of *The Naked and the Dead*, 'To Gerald after the rush hour'. It was an intense period.

Over the next days I made drawings of the poet Robert Lowell and the artists Adolph Gottlieb, Barnett Newman and Larry Rivers. Larry wasn't happy with the nose I had given him. It was too big, he thought. He redrew it and signed it 'Nose by Rivers and Scarfe'.

When I was in New York in 1970 I stayed with Clay Felker, the charismatic owner of *New York*, a hip magazine employing Tom Wolfe and Gloria Steinem. David Frost had been staying with him but was returning to London so I took his room. Clay was very generous and complimentary about my work, and wanted me to draw for his magazine. He wanted me to work with Jimmy Breslin, a witty satirical writer of the New York scene, so we all met in a bar and talked about the misdeeds of the rich and powerful. One weekend Clay and I went to Tower Records and he bought two dozen LPs of the latest music – José Feliciano etc. – and we sat for a whole Sunday listening to them. He really tried to introduce me to the New York scene. He threw a party for me in his elegant mid-town apartment so I could meet some of the movers and shakers in that town. Dick Waddell, owner of the Waddell Gallery where I was exhibiting, was a likeable rich guy who really yearned to be in the art world. At the party he and his colleagues overstayed their welcome and were still there, over-excited to be in Clay's presence, long after all the other guests had left. Clay lost patience, took me aside and said, 'Why should I waste my evening talking to these people? Can you get rid of them?' I did. But Clay was a great host, tall with a booming voice, and he knew everybody. That evening he seemed lonely and morose, however, and talked to me about his ex-wife, the actress

Pamela Tiffin, from whom he had recently divorced. He showed me pictures of her in some film magazine. She was an extremely pretty blonde. I think he was still very much in love with her.

The only drawing I made for *New York* magazine was one of Richard Nixon. Looking back, I see that on various occasions I was unable to seize the moment. This was one of them.

While drawing the New York intellectuals, I felt I dearly wanted to work for the *New Yorker*. Kenneth Mahood had put me in touch with a famous New York-based cartoonist called Charles Saxon, who took me to meet Jim Geraghty, the all-powerful art editor of the *New Yorker*. Lolling back in a chair behind his desk Geraghty said to Saxon, 'Well, do you think we can find something for Gerald to do?'

To say I felt patronised is putting it mildly. 'Oh no, I'm not begging for work,' I blurted out. 'Look, I don't want to work for the *New Yorker*,' I said with youthful arrogance. That was that.

However, many years on, in 1991, I found myself sitting opposite Tina Brown, editor of the *New Yorker*, in her booth at the Royalton Hotel in Manhattan. Tina had flown me to New York to discuss working regularly with the magazine, which I subsequently did, very happily, for the next fifteen years. Chris Curry, the art editor, was continually kind, sending me thank-you faxes saying 'You're a genius – we can't get enough of you.' The editor, David Remnick, was encouraging too; he sent a note saying 'When you appear, the whole magazine lights up.' Although my studio was three thousand miles away from the *New Yorker*'s offices I could still get my drawings there on time. A piece required for the next day could be worked on until five o'clock in the morning if necessary. A courier would then come to my house and take it to Heathrow. Concorde left at nine a.m. and arrived in New York four hours later, at eight a.m. local time, and the drawing would get to the magazine by ten. Now my drawings are sent electronically but in the days before the world of the internet they flew by Concorde.

In general I found the Americans more prudish than the British when it came to sex. Rather like the Victorians, everything is very correct on the surface but all sorts of shenanigans go on out of public view. Different countries have different senses of humour and prudishness. I use sex in my drawings because it shows us at one of our most vulnerable animal states in life. Likewise naked-ness. Depicting world leaders, dictators, in all their nakedness shows their fallibility, that they are not gods. I made a drawing for the *New Yorker* of Jack Kennedy surrounded by naked female breasts. I called it 'Jack at Play'. They refused to print it – but they did pin it up on the office wall.

6

10. Cheyne Walk

The 'swinging sixties' did not begin on the last strike of midnight with the chimes of Big Ben and the singing of 'Auld Lang Syne'. In Britain, the early sixties had been as dull as the fifties as far as I was concerned. But by 1966 things were definitely swinging a bit more. The Beatles and the Stones, Terence Stamp and Jean Shrimpton, Twiggy and Justin de Villeneuve. David Bailey and David Hockney. All appeared during that decade.

I was still working for *Private Eye* at the time, and every fortnight I would illustrate the poet Christopher Logue's column in the magazine. Christopher would pick up bizarre stories from newspapers and rewrite them in a witty manner. They triggered many surreal drawings from me. I was lunching at the Ark restaurant in Notting Hill Gate with him one day and Christopher suggested we order some asparagus, which had just come into season. This was the first time I had eaten it. Seeing my struggles, Christopher said kindly, 'I should eat the other end if I were you.' I felt abashed. (I am now a huge fan of asparagus – during the season in May I tend to OD on it.)

Christopher asked me to make a caricature of him to frame, hang and show off on the wall of his Notting Hill flat, which I did, but he admitted some time later that he dared not display the 'grotesque' in case it put his girlfriends off.

He also told me that the last time he'd dined in the Ark it was with Peter Cook. After a while the two of them became aware of a group of rowdy 'Tory Boys' at a nearby table laughing and talking about Christopher and Peter. They heard the word 'poofters'.

'You're a couple of queers, aren't you?' they jeered.

'Yes,' Peter replied, 'we are. Would you like to come and suck my cock?'

Apparently this shut them up.

Peter's humour was a surreal stream of consciousness. I would shake with laughter until I couldn't breathe and my stomach would truly hurt. He would go on and on telling his inventive stories, always in a voice other than his own, joke upon joke, giving me no time to get my breath.

Peter once turned up at my house in Cheyne Walk clutching a tape of his new record. He wanted me to draw the cover. It was the time when newspapers were full of the Jeremy Thorpe trial. Thorpe, the leader of the Liberal Party had been in a homosexual relationship with a man called Norman Scott. Scott was pestering Thorpe and it was alleged Thorpe had ordered his murder. But the gunman had cocked it up, shooting Scott's dog Rinka instead. There had been a trial during which the judge was grotesquely biased against Norman Scott: Thorpe was let off. Peter had made a brilliant parody of the judge's outrageously biased summing up and that was what he wanted to play me. He started the tape running and watched as I listened like a hawk. Would I laugh? I was this genius's only audience. It was very funny, but under Peter's piercing scrutiny I couldn't laugh. Bizarrely, I began to pretend to laugh. I drew the cover.

Peter asked me to make four sculptures of the Rolling Stones to accompany him and Dudley Moore on the end revolve on *Sunday Night at the London Palladium*. The Stones had performed in the show, but thought themselves too cool to appear at the end when stars would traditionally wave to the audience as the credits rolled, so they used my models instead.

One sunny summer afternoon in Hampstead's Church Row I was sitting with Peter in his garden talking about this and that when Peter became transfixed by a bee. 'Look out! Look out! It's a bee!' It turned out that Peter had a fear of bees. 'Ugh! I can't stand the little buggers.' Interesting, because I noticed that some of his surreal sketches involved bees. Like most creative folk, myself included, he was putting his life into his work, especially his fears.

My childhood passion for collecting things never abated. I swapped a drawing of a Puritan tickling his nether regions I'd made for Logue's *True Stories* for a couple of medieval spurs and an eleventh-century sword found in the Thames mud, and began to collect spurs as a hobby. An article about my work in the *Ham & High* thought it a suitable pastime for a 'cruel artist' (medieval weapons). As the collection grew, one by one, I made contact with an expert at the Tower of London. She told me of a man who wanted to get rid of his comprehensive collection of spurs. I bought it for £35 – dozens of spurs of all types. And immediately lost interest. There was nothing more to collect. It was done.

The jazz singer, critic and writer George Melly was to write a piece about me for the *Sunday Times*. We met at a restaurant, and George was charming. One of the questions he asked was if I was disgusted by the flesh, by sex in fact. I said, perhaps trying to be helpful to his theory, Yes, maybe I was – actually I am not.

He ended his piece, 'politely and correctly Gerald finished his lunch'. When my mother read the article she was perturbed by the sex revelation. 'Well, you don't have to tell them everything, you know!' She was right.

On a visit to George's house in Gloucester Crescent I was impressed to see that hanging over the fireplace was Magritte's *Rape*, a painting of a naked woman's torso which the artist had turned into a face. He told me he had picked it up relatively cheaply.

George told me the story that he had been walking home at night after a very heavy evening of drinking when he felt the need to relieve himself. Wandering unsteadily to a nearby wall, he let fly.

'Excuse me, sir,' said a voice behind him, 'are you aware it is an offence to urinate in public?'

George turned to see a policeman who had emerged from the darkness.

'Oh, have a heart, constable,' said George. 'I'm an old man and I got caught short. Have a heart.'

'All right,' said the copper, 'I'll let you off this time, but next time try not to do it against the wall of a police station.'

Another George, the journalist George Gale, had asked me to have a small exhibition at his club in Wivenhoe where he lived. Locals Peregrine Worsthorne and Kingsley Amis were present, and much drinking was in progress – it was that sort of club. One day he came for a few drinks with me and several friends at Cheyne Walk. George was partial to a jar or two – he was known at *Private Eye* as George G. Ale. After some time he announced he needed to relieve himself. I showed him the loo and left him to his business while I returned to chat to the others. After three or four minutes from behind the closed lavatory door there came the thunderous noise of what sounded like a thousand coins of the realm showering on to the floor, followed by an almighty crash – the frightening and unmistakable noise of a heavy body hitting the floor. Ominous silence. We all looked at one another.

'Are you all right, George?'

Silence.

I tried the door. It was locked.

'George, are you all right?'

Silence.

What should we do? Break the door down? While we were making moves to do this, the door silently opened. There stood a slightly abashed and dishevelled George, steadying himself on the door frame with both hands. 'Sorry,' he said, 'had a bit of an incident.' No more was said. When I went into the loo much later I discovered the floor was covered in loose change, which must have come from his lowered trousers, over which he had tripped.

In 1966 the *Daily Express* had run an article on me. 'Just you wait,' said a Fleet Street friend. 'They'll all start trying to buy you up now.' Sure enough, the *Express* editor rang. Would I like to come for lunch on Tuesday? 'Wonderful, yes please,' I said. The next day the *Daily Mail* rang. Would I like to have lunch on Thursday? 'Wonderful, yes please.'

I was determined to go to these meetings and make it clear that I wanted assurance of political freedom in my forthcoming cartoons. First I went for my lunch with the editor of the *Express*, Derek Marks. 'Well,' he said, 'you won't want a big lunch today. What say we pop over to El Vino's for a sandwich? They do a damned good sandwich over there!' He offered me £5,000 a year and a Rover. I forgot to mention political freedom.

The *Mail* did better. The editor, Mike Randall, and the owner, Vere Harmsworth, took me to the Caprice for lunch.

'Now, what car have you offered Gerald?' said Vere after a couple of glasses of white wine.

'Well,' said Mike, 'we thought of giving him £5,000 a year and a Rover 2000.'

I tried to explain about the political freedom I had hoped for.

'Nonsense,' said Harmsworth, who wasn't listening. 'Give him £6,000 a year and an E-Type. Ha!' He slapped the table. 'Let him have a short life and a merry one.'

They all thought this was a huge joke.

'It's not really the issue,' I said lamely. 'I've already got a car. I was wondering . . . ' But too late – they were busy paying the bill. Even so I hesitated.

Vere noticed, then in a moment of inspiration he said, 'Petrol! Free petrol! You can fill up at the *Daily Mail* garage across the river.'

Thoughts of political freedom faded. Free petrol? Wow! 'OK,' I said, 'I'll join the *Mail*.'

Later I thought, This is very, very good, this Fleet Street lark. They up your money and then insist on giving you a car as well. Fantastic! It never happened again. Not once.

They had to urge me several times to pick up my E-Type. I owned a Triumph TR4 which was fine. Eventually I collected it and discovered it was an exciting car. 'You never had it so good,' as Harold Macmillan said.

But I was lost at the *Daily Mail* and missed the camaraderie of *Private Eye*. One summer evening I drove to a *Private Eye* benefit theatre performance in Charing Cross Road, in which the jazz musician John Dankworth and his wife, singer Cleo Laine, were appearing. I parked my silver E-Type directly outside the theatre – you could do that in those days: no yellow lines. Leaving after the show with some of the *Private Eye* gang and John and his wife, I saw John pause by my car. 'I wouldn't be seen dead in one of those things,' he remarked. Ashamed, I walked past my car, denying it. I said goodnight to the others and hung back round a corner nearby until he and the group had all gone and then snuck back and drove it home.

Soon after I arrived at the *Mail*, Mike Randall cornered me and pointed out, 'Now you are working in the national press you will have requests from people who would like to buy your work. Will you sell the original drawings?'

I explained that many drawings were made against a deadline and therefore not always quite as perfect as I would like them to be and I wouldn't want bad examples of my work hanging on people's walls. 'So in that case I would sell if I thought it good enough, but otherwise not.'

'No, no,' said Mike, 'that won't work. People won't understand if you sell to one and not another. It's either sell or not sell.'

In that case I decided I would not sell, and I did not for many years.

Bernard Levin, the star writer on the paper, sought me out and gave me a really great piece of advice: to invent a character like Disney's Mickey Mouse or Schultz's Charlie Brown, or Snoopy – a character that would become part of British folklore and carry me through in years to come. Easier said than done I'm afraid. I did not take his advice.

However, in 1970, he wrote in his book *The Pendulum Years*:

For the true spirit of the decade in drawing we had to wait a little longer, when it blossomed forth in the *fleurs du mal* of Gerald Scarfe, whose caricatures, so far from turning their subjects into lovable figures with enduing foibles, must make him a reasonably likely candidate for the position of the first man to be prosecuted simultaneously for obscenity, blasphemy and criminal libel. If Timothy Birdsall had Swift's holy rage, Scarfe appears to have inherited his disgust with the flesh, to judge from some of his monstrous, dropsical faces and bodies, the products of a deadly, though still undisciplined genius. If, then, we could see a future Hogarth in Birdsall, it may be that in Scarfe we can recognize the heir of Hieronymus Bosch, and a Bosch, moreover, without the didacticism, which only makes the prospect more disquieting.

Life at the *Daily Mail* wasn't a merry one. In fact I loathed my time there. After *Private Eye* I felt restricted on subject matter. I had an office in a forgotten corner of the *Mail* building in Bouverie Street. I didn't know anyone. From the *Mail*'s point of view, they didn't know what to do with me. My detailed, spidery drawings did not look good on newsprint amid clamouring headlines and advertisements, and I found thinking up and drawing a daily cartoon difficult. The drawings I had been given the freedom to do for *Private Eye* were not possible in a 'family newspaper'. The *Mail* wouldn't print the type of explicit material I'd been producing for *Private Eye*. They had signed me up because of my notoriety at *Private Eye*, but, as another journalist explained, when the readers opened their familiar *Daily Mail* in the morning and saw a Scarfe drawing, it was as though the family dog had just shat on the breakfast table.

One day Mike took me with him to lunch at a hotel just off St James's with Edward Heath. I can't recall what was discussed but it was of a very high order. At one point I nodded my head.

'Ah,' said Heath, 'you're nodding. What do you think?'

I was truly stumped.

'Oh, Gerald is here only as an observer,' said Mike, gallantly coming to my rescue.

I disliked Heath for maliciously putting me on the spot and making me look foolish, and for his prissy, snotty attitude towards me. I'm afraid whenever I drew him thereafter it was with a flavour of that snotty snob. Since then I have tried to avoid meeting my victims. It would be even worse if I liked them.

The *Daily Mail* was, and is, a traditionally right-wing Conservative organ but during my period with them under Mike Randall's editorship they endeavoured to move towards the left. It didn't work. Mike fell ill with a bad back and while he was away convalescing he was sacked – stabbed in the back in time-honoured Fleet Street fashion. I decided to leave, and in a meeting with Duke Hussey, the managing director, managed to persuade him to give me a year's salary and let me keep the E-Type. Not bad. I recently met his wife at a dinner party and told her this story. 'Oh,' she said, 'he wouldn't have known what an E-Type was.'

On 2 July 1968 I received a letter from an enthusiastic young man telling me he was starting a magazine for students, and that being a student himself he didn't have much money. He was hoping I would make some drawings for his new publication, but he could not pay me. Of course I did and over a period of time I made several drawings for different issues of the magazine. One comes to mind in particular, of Spain's despotic leader General Franco as a piece of shit. The other day I came across a letter from that young man, saying, 'Dear Gerald, thank you for the drawing which has been acclaimed by everybody who has read *Student* as excellent. I should have liked to run it over two pages which would have done it more justice . . . ' He ended the letter by saying 'Should you be around this way perhaps you would like to drop in for a drink sometime. Best wishes, Richard.' That young man was Richard Branson, the Virgin Group entrepreneur.

I didn't reply at the time, but thought I should do so now and sent him a copy of the letter with a covering note:

Dear Richard, Sorry to have been so long answering your letter. I hope it's not too late? I would be delighted to drop in for a drink. Best wishes, Gerald Scarfe.

A couple of days later I received an email from Richard:

Dear Gerald, Thanks so much for sending this. Happy memories! It is the longest time anyone has taken to accept a drink offer (50 years). But it has made it all the more enjoyable. Any time you are in the Caribbean do let me know and we would welcome you to Necker Island. Thanks for all your help all those years ago. I definitely owe you a drink. All the best, Richard.

I don't know whether we will ever make that drink on Necker Island, but I have invited him to a drink in Scarfes Bar any time he is in London.

Right at the end of the sixties I had the most incredible stroke of luck. While still living in Rosecroft Avenue in Hampstead but looking for a place to work, I took rooms at number 10 Cheyne Walk in Chelsea. I rented a second-floor flat with the most wonderful views over the River Thames and the Albert Bridge, with Battersea Park opposite on the other side of the river. It was built on the grounds that housed Henry VIII's hunting lodge. The King's Road was a short stroll away. It was idyllic.

I have a sepia photograph taken around 1890 which shows Cheyne Walk before the Embankment was built. Several hackney carriages are trotting past, and it can clearly be seen that the River Thames is lapping the other side of the road that runs past the house only twenty yards away. A number of magnificent river barges with enormous folded sails are moored opposite the site of my house, together with a collection of smaller vessels jostling alongside.

When I first moved into Cheyne Walk in 1969, Battersea Park was a no-go area after darkness fell and the whole other side of the river was regarded as 'rough'. To cross the Albert Bridge was to take your life in your hands. You might meet some dodgy fellows. Now it has been gentrified and has become known as 'South

Chelsea'. In fact, the whole of the south side of the Thames has changed radically. We on the north side now gaze across in horror at the hotch-potch of architectural follies that form that side of the river. When an artist makes a drawing it can be torn up. When an architect puts up a rotten building it invariably stays there offending the eye for a lifetime or more. There is one building on the south side that resembles a ghetto blaster, and from inside that hideous building the residents can gaze at the wonderful view of our side with its elegant houses of old Chelsea.

Soon after moving in I began work on a show I was preparing for the Grosvenor Galleries in London, making wire-cloth and papier-mâché figures of the great and good – Charles de Gaulle, Enoch Powell, Ted Heath, Nixon, General Montgomery and a pregnant Pope. The living room began to fill up with twisted and contorted figures, but Mrs Hartley, my wonderful gentle landlady, was most understanding and didn't object in any way to my strange nocturnal behaviour.

Mrs Hartley, who came from a very good family, announced after some time that she was putting the house on the market – it was too big for her – and moving to a far more manageable bungalow in Bognor. I pleaded with her to sell it to me, which she agreed to do.

So, I found myself the owner of 10 Cheyne Walk and a certain amount of good furniture and oil paintings that would not fit into her new bungalow. I took out a new fifty-year lease from the landlord. And there I lived for fifty years, and between the River Thames and the parade ground that was and is the King's Road Jane and I raised our family. I slowly put the house back together as a single home by cannibalising a mirror-image house next door owned by Americans who had stripped out all the moulding, doors and architraves and made theirs into a Manhattan-style dwelling. I seized their discarded fittings and reopened closed doors and fireplaces at number 10, to return it to its former glory.

Mrs Hartley had told me that during the war the house had been made into a billet for officers and divided into many rooms, and was pretty run down when she moved in. She also told me that Lloyd George had lived there for a short time. She had tried to have a plaque put up but the council said he had lived in too many places – he got around, Lloyd George, if you remember.

When I bought it some of Mrs Hartley's lodgers were still there, living at the very top of the house. I said they could stay as long as they wanted at the same rent until they were ready to leave. In particular I recall a lady called Penny, as she later became the second wife of barrister and author John Mortimer, but was then a girlfriend of one of the lodgers. After they left I let their flat to an American writer to help pay the mortgage. He wrote me notes occasionally which always ended with 'Oh – and that other curtain . . . ' When he first moved in he'd pointed out that his window was only covered by one curtain. The other was missing. I promised to supply it, but somehow never did. After he left, Mr and Mrs Hulbert arrived. Mrs Hulbert also used to write me notes, on expensive headed paper: 'From the desk of Louise Hulbert'. They left rather abruptly and she wrote me a final note from her desk explaining that 'the stairs finally got to me'. There were 110 steps in the house from basement to attic. It kept me spry over the years. It's the only fitness regime I've managed to maintain apart from walking to my car.

My last tenant was 'The Brigadier'. Once he'd 'got his kit in' he was very quiet, came and went silently. Occasionally he was visited by 'The Horse', as my brother and I called her.

I called another visitor 'The Thespian'; he came soon after Mrs Hartley had left. He wore a black homburg and a long black overcoat and walked with a silver-topped cane. A dodgy-looking character who had not been on the boards but had apparently, I discovered later, been 'inside'. Brixton, in fact. He would arrive with a crop-headed youth who looked as though he had also been housed at Her Majesty's pleasure. 'Ah, dear boy,' he would say to me, 'I've come to pick up Mrs Hartley's silver cutlery set.' I didn't give it to him. I didn't have it anyway – Mrs Hartley had wisely taken it with her.

I had a friend at that time who said it was the only house he knew where the wind blew out when he came to call and looked through the letterbox. The wind did blow out – it was warmer in the street than in the house. It was very, very cold in the winter. I had a few sticks of furniture that Mrs Hartley had left me, but very little else in those first few months.

Originally my studio at Cheyne Walk was at the back of the house on the ground floor, but later I had a studio purpose-built at the top of the house. I would often go there at four a.m. to relax with a cup of tea and a newspaper. I sleep less as I get older. An artist's life is a lonely one and my radio is a real friend. I'm an avid Radio 4 listener. If I didn't have my paint-splattered radio for company I think I'd succumb to cabin fever. I listen to Radio 4 from the *Today* programme right through *Women's Hour*, the news and the afternoon play to *The Archers* and *Front Row*. Then – finally – back down for that glass of wine with Jane and a meal with the family.

My secret domain was my library of art books, a room where it was comforting to be able to take down a book and open up my own private gallery. A room where I could mix with Picasso, Daumier, Goya, Rembrandt. I have many large weighty glossy coffee-table tomes of Gillray, Bacon, Van Gogh, Delacroix. It is always comforting to see that others have spent a lifetime in this strange pursuit of sketching, painting and sculpting and have apparently been thanked for giving pleasure to others.

Many artists and writers have lived near the river. On one side of my house lived George Eliot, on the other Dante Gabriel Rossetti. Nearby, in Tite Street, Oscar Wilde. I think the river attracts artists. Turner lived in Cheyne Walk, and we know that he was drawn to depictions of water. Whenever I drank my morning tea seated in my armchair with a view of the river I could see how the mood of the Thames was continually changing. It could turn from a glittering silver to a bright sky blue and then, in the evening, to a red-tinged ribbon of gold.

The house is ten minutes from the Chelsea Arts Club — too convenient in a way because in the 1970s I would finish a drawing and think, I'll just pop round to the club for a quick half. That quick half very often turned into a pint, and that pint turned into another pint. And so on. In addition I had become obsessed by the game of snooker and I thought (wrongly) I was rather good at it. In the seventies the club had two snooker tables and I could be fairly sure that some other ne'er-do-wells would be there looking for a game. So I'd think, OK, I'll just have one game and then go back to the drawing board. But that game inevitably led to another one, and then a decider, then maybe another one, and possibly another pint too. And the day would wear on into the evening.

Another reason for this misspent youth was my actor friend David Hemmings — a competitive snooker player if ever I saw one. And always up for a game. David and I would often be there until two or three in the morning thrashing it out. With David, every game would have to be for cash — maybe a pound, maybe a fiver. Just something to give the game an edge. I'm not sure whether betting broke club rules or not. Anyway, that's what we did.

After walking unsteadily home I would sometimes feel inspired to draw some of the characters I'd seen at the club. One evening an amorous middle-aged couple, fired by an afternoon's drinking, were seated at the bar and getting on splendidly. After a while the inevitable happened — she slid slowly off her seat and with a resounding thump landed on the beer-stained floor. Without stirring from his seat her gallant gazed down at her slumped figure and said, 'Oh, pussy, you've fallen off your stool.' I made a drawing of that moment.

Early in the seventies the committee asked me to design a poster for the Chelsea Arts Club Ball. The chairman, Dudley Winterbottom, thought it should be of the Lord of Misrule. I submitted my drawing, a Pulcinella-like figure with a penis for a nose (years ahead of the Chapman Brothers), but the committee thought it was far too rude. 'Why,' I complained to David, 'did they ask me when they know what type of work I do?' He was on the committee and got the ban reversed. That was the year I helped design the ball with David. I went in a blond wig as David Hockney.

At a charity dinner for the Royal Hospital in Chelsea, Lady Cadogan, wife of Lord Cadogan, who owned the freehold on my house, bid £5,000 for me to make a portrait of her husband, and asked me to be kind to him. I felt that I was not known for or in the business of flattery, and caricature can be a cruel art form, but I said I would try. I didn't want to upset my landlord.

I had several very pleasant and chatty sittings with Charles Cadogan and I think we got on well. He had a bad leg. As always I took my sketches back to the studio and made the finished work there. I tried to be gentle. The chauffeur who came to pick it up said it was just like him, a good likeness, and I heard no more. Later, at one of Lord Cadogan's birthday parties, he let drop that Lady Cadogan was not over-fond of the portrait and I feared it might have gone the way of Sutherland's portrait of Churchill. But at another party he showed me that it had survived and was hanging in a back passage of the Cadogan offices.

I felt perhaps I was making myself a hostage to fortune in caricaturing my freeholder, but I'm sure it had nothing to do with Cadogan Estates refusing my appeal for another short lease.

7

From The Suez Canal to The Mekong Delta.

Reportage illustration has a long history – going back to stone friezes depicting wars in ancient civilisations, the Bayeux Tapestry, and in the seventeenth century woodcuts were used to illustrate cheap publications, focusing on murders, robberies and executions. It became a widely used form in the nineteenth century as demand for newspapers and publications grew. Artists would be sent on location to areas of disaster or conflict, such as during the Boer War. They would make sketches and notes on the spot and then the sketch books would be sent back to the publisher of the magazine or newspaper to be redrawn, organised and arranged into composite etchings showing the whole battle in one picture. This was all done by specialist engravers who had never been anywhere near a battle in their lives. When I worked for *Time*, writers on the spot would complain bitterly that the pieces they sent back from countries like Vietnam were rewritten in New York by people who had never travelled, whose job it was to translate it into '*Time*-speak', thereby losing all the local colour and feeling of authenticity. Eventually photography became the main source for newspapers but illustrated reportage has continued to have its place.

In 1956 President Nasser of Egypt nationalised the Suez Canal. He scuttled large ships at the mouth of the canal making it unnavigable and forced shipping to go the long way round Africa, past the Cape of Good Hope. This initiated what became known as the Suez Crisis. The scuttled ships were removed and the canal reopened when this was resolved in March 1957. During his presidency Nasser began a series of major socialist measures and modernisation reforms in Egypt, but by the mid-sixties the country's economic problems had grown substantially. To uphold his authority he held an unopposed election.

In 1965 the *Sunday Times* colour magazine sent the writer Martin Page and me to report on how well the canal was running during the economic difficulties Nasser was facing. The simple premise was – can the Egyptians run the canal? Well, the short answer was yes. But that was our brief.

The statue of Ferdinand de Lesseps, who built the Suez Canal, originally stood at the mouth of the canal but had been blown from its plinth by explosives in the wake of the Suez Crisis. When we were in Port Said only the plinth remained. We stayed first at the old Casino Palace Hotel, which was on the sea-front at the mouth of the canal. While taking afternoon tea I made a drawing showing the famous veranda – it was fashionable to take afternoon tea or drinks there, with its spectacular views. In the drawing the hotel manager lounges in a wicker chair, while behind him stands the head waiter in a white jacket and black tie. Two other waiters stand in the background. Alongside the ornate veranda with its art nouveau lamps a giant ocean-going ship can be seen through the tall wooden columns that hold up the veranda's broad canopy. The hotel, sadly, is no longer there. It was used as a barracks by the invading British soldiers and survived that, but was torn down by developers in the seventies.

By the Mena House, the most luxurious hotel in Egypt, located at the foot of the Pyramids, camel drivers plied their trade. With sticks they urged the weary, grumpy beasts to sink to their knees in order that camera-laden tourists could board them, and then set off on a slow, leisurely, unenthusiastic, lolloping walk, tassels swinging, through the sands to allow their passengers to view the amazing Pyramids. Day after day I returned to draw those camel drivers at the Mena House. I became quite friendly with some of them. While waiting for business they came to watch me draw, laughing and pointing at my sketches. In general people are fascinated by artists at their work. It is readily apparent what an artist is doing. She or he is not scribbling unseen notes in a notebook. It's all on view, and one can watch and share the drawing with them as it evolves. Nothing is secret. Pictures are the most immediate form of communication.

Sitting in the baking sun among the bulrushes on the banks of the Nile, I sketched the scene before me – the sluggishly flowing dark-green river – occasionally dipping my brush into the edges of the muddy water to apply my watercolour, using the sandy texture to make my picture. Painting with Nile water. The only problem I had was being bothered by the huge flies, swarms of them that pestered and tickled my face and hands. They seemed to be attracted by the whiteness of my cartridge paper and covered my sketch book as though watching me draw. On one of my paintings I drew an ominous life-size *trompe l'oeil* fly.

After the Suez Crisis the British were not popular. I was in the desert outside Cairo sketching the canal and the giant tankers that appeared to glide surreally through the desert sand when I was arrested by two police officers and accused of spying. The police took me to a small wooden hut on the banks of the canal and sat me on a chair in front of a simple desk. They took my passport and disappeared outside. Feeling naked without my passport I sat there for a while until a very large and menacing Egyptian police inspector came in and parked his enormous backside on the chair opposite me. Holding my passport, he asked what I was doing and why. Endlessly he looked through the document, page after page, occasionally glancing up at me. It seemed like an age. Martin, who had been checking out something in the neighbourhood, returned and managed with various papers to prove that we were journalists, and I was free. Back in the hotel I made a sketch of the inspector from memory.

Martin and I had some enjoyable days. Late one afternoon when the dusty yellow and orange sky had turned the towering Pyramids into grey silhouettes, we hired two white Arabian horses from a camel driver at the Mena House and set off into the desert. Soon we were taking the horses at full gallop down the sloping sand dunes, without wearing helmets. It was incredibly dangerous, but totally exhilarating. Whooping with excitement we urged our steeds to go faster and faster. Eventually, as the horses tired, we brought them to a steady walk and enjoyed the still loneliness of the desert. The light was now dropping fast and it was becoming cold, as it does in the desert when the sun goes down. Martin told me apologetically that he suffered from night blindness and couldn't see a thing. I took his bridle and led him back to the hotel.

The next day Martin was absolutely adamant that he had to buy some 'dirty' postcards. He insisted it was essential for his written piece on Egypt. How could you go to Cairo and not buy dirty postcards? It was very much the cliché, uninformed cartoon view of Arabs in those days, that they were likely to sidle up to

you and produce an envelope from beneath their robes. 'You
want filthy postcard? Man with woman, man with man, woman
with donkey?' So we set off one afternoon to the hot and dusty
kasbah. Martin approached various wary-looking shopkeepers
in what he thought were likely places and asked, in a lowered
voice, 'Do you have any dirty postcards?' Many of them looked
startled, even frightened; none of them had what Martin wanted.
They offered him various postcards with moody views of the
Pyramids and picturesque views of the Nile, but nothing filthy.
We trekked on in the afternoon heat. Eventually, in a shop selling
tourist tat – copper bowls and rugs – one shopkeeper thought he
might have something helpful. He disappeared into the back of
his grubby shop and returned with a brown tattered envelope.
Martin opened it with excitement. Was this it? The Holy Grail?
I looked over his shoulder as he sorted through the dozen black
and white cards. They were what he wanted. Sort of. A Japanese
couple entwined in various positions, and for the connoisseur
enlarged photos of the 'important' areas in a separate circle set
into the main photograph. They were disappointingly anodyne,
rather blurred, but Martin seemed happy and (unaroused in my
case) we returned to the hotel.

I didn't see these cards again until the day Martin left. I was
staying on for a few more days to finish a couple of drawings.
Martin came to my room in the Shepheard Hotel to say goodbye
and as he went out of the door he said, 'Can you take care of these?
I don't want to take them through customs.' He threw the cards
on my bed and he was gone. This was awkward – I also didn't
want to take them through customs. There had been stories of
people being arrested for carrying pornography. I think Hockney
was held just for having adult magazines. I thought I would dump
them in the Nile. I tore them into very small bits in the hotel and
walked to the Qasr El Nil Bridge. There weren't many people
about but a couple of policemen with guns were crossing to the

other side so I waited for my moment and then threw the Japanese porn stars over the parapet and into the water. That was the plan, anyway, but an updraught caught the tiny pieces and blew them like confetti back on to the bridge. Amid a shower of porn I hurriedly walked away. Nothing to do with me, guv'nor.

During my time at the *Daily Mail* it was clear the newspaper deemed me a brutal artist, so they sent me to a brutal situation – the war in Vietnam. They failed to understand that the brutality in my drawings comes from things that I fear, not things that I advocate: I abhor violence.

The journalist Richard West asked if he could come with me and my editor agreed, so the two of us flew to Saigon. Within a day or two we were deep in the countryside staying at an American army base and living under canvas in the sticky humid heat of the Mekong Delta, eating slop from compartmentalised tin trays. My first night in my bunk I slept like a top. Dick West said he didn't sleep a wink as the guns were blazing and booming all night. He said the noise was insufferable – but somehow I was so exhausted I didn't hear a thing.

Up until my visit, Vietnam was just a name on a map to me, or a film of gung-ho marines jumping out of helicopters on the television news. I felt sympathy but only saw it symbolically, and made symbolic drawings. The reality was far different. Vietnam is a beautiful country with gentle people who, like most civilians in wartime, were confused and frightened. They did not want to die. They had the misfortune to have the war between communism and capitalism being fought out in their country. They did not want a war and I realised, for the first time, that apart from the tough professionals, most of the soldiers did not want one either. The majority of the soldiers seemed to be young college kids, hoicked out of their studies, flown to some strange jungle and told to go out and kill 'gooks', as they contemptuously called the Vietnamese.

The only way to travel in Vietnam was to hitch a lift from an American military aircraft going towards your destination. Wherever it landed, you hoped that another one would turn up in which you could continue your journey, leapfrogging across the country. We spent many hours in jungle clearings desperately hoping that something would turn up, and many more bouncing about in the sky in strange aircraft. The helicopters were the worst. Occasionally brought down by a lucky shot from a Viet Cong rifle, they were most at risk on take-off and landing. I hated travelling in them. The passenger seats faced the side of the heli-copter, the huge sliding doors were open on both sides, and the pilot continually banked left and right so that the two machine-gunmen could fire at the puffs of smoke from the countryside below – tell-tale signs that the Viet Cong were shooting at us. I continually found myself staring at the sky and then suddenly at the jungle below, over which I was suspended like a sitting duck held in by a simple belt around my waist. Almost as bad were the transport planes, huge beasts used for moving very large vehicles about – tanks, lorries. Rattling ponderously through the sky, it was like flying in the Albert Hall. Then there were the large troop-carrying planes full of anxious, silent young soldiers with their parachute packs, the backs of the planes open ready for them to leap out and drift down to the unfriendly jungle floor below.

I arrived at a camp in the jungle. Everything was in disarray. I was told by a tough sergeant that the previous day a platoon far from camp had been surrounded by the Viet Cong. They had radioed for help and were told that a napalm air strike would be carried out if they gave the precise position of the Viet Cong. The surrounded soldiers radioed that they were pinned down in a circle about a quarter of a mile wide, gave their position, and asked that the air force strike should be outside that circle. The pilot had misheard the instruction and dropped napalm inside the circle, killing and maiming his own men. As the sergeant told me this story, a few wounded, dazed and bewildered survivors of the disaster were still wandering back. Others had deserted. I drew one confused and lost nineteen-year-old American boy sitting on his bed, next to the empty bunk of his dead buddy, a guy he had become very close to, although they had only met a month earlier. He had been killed in the so-called 'friendly-fire' incident.

In those days I prided myself that I could draw anything, and I applied to sketch inside the American morgue in a hangar at the Tan Son Nhut airbase in Saigon, in order to get a fuller picture of life and death in Vietnam.

The sergeant who met me outside said, 'You sure you wanna do this?'

'Sure,' I said – unsurely.

And when he opened the door, I nearly fainted. On slabs in front of me lay the remains of a platoon: mutilated bodies, bits of bodies – no heads, no limbs – disembowelled half figures. Lumps of meat. They were being cleaned up before their return to the States by a group of cheerful young orderlies in bloodied white coats. I noticed several were whistling. What a job. The floor was awash with blood and flesh: it was hell.

'I'm sorry,' I mumbled. 'I can't draw this.' I found myself clutching my armpits and sweating.

'Thought not,' said the sergeant, and he took me back into the fresh air.

Even as I walked across the yard outside I found myself dodging slivers of flesh and entrails on the hosed-down concrete yard. I reasoned the only way the medics and orderlies could handle this hell was, as far as possible, to treat it as a normal job. Hence the whistling and everyday behaviour. Living a dual life.

We took a plane to the highlands of Dalat, about 150 miles from Saigon. Unlike the wet, humid air of Saigon, Dalat's air was cool and fresh at 4,500 feet. I felt a million miles away from the war and yet Viet Cong strongholds were only fifty miles away.

Pine trees and oaks grew alongside lush tropical plants and banana trees. Giant grasshoppers and other large insects hid among the exotic flowers that covered the hills and grew along the lakes, and I included them in my drawings. Like the medics, I wanted to pretend all was normal. Amid the terrible bloody violence and carnage that was Vietnam I had the urge to capture the beauty of its gentle people and the flora and fauna as an antidote to the horror that was everywhere. In the countryside I sketched butterflies, bees, grasshoppers, banana trees, pine trees and exotic blooms. I put my drawing board down on the dusty dirt road and, crouching uncomfortably, attempted to capture the scene in pen and ink, Dick West hovering uneasily in the background. It was certainly not a good idea to stay too long in one spot in case word got around in the wrong quarters. The Viet Cong were not far away, but I didn't have the advantage of a photographer who could snap and run. Mine was an outmoded method of reportage. 'Are you going to be much longer?' Dick would ask anxiously.

We stayed in a baronial hotel that had an almost Scottish feeling, with stuffed animal heads on the oak panelling and a duck press on the sideboard. I slept in a cool room covered in a white mosquito net, and when I woke to birdsong in the morning it was raining. During breakfast the rain cleared to a fine drizzle, and in the mist several Vietnamese left the hotel for a round of golf. It is extraordinary how in times of stress we all try to revert to the normal. Everyday life carries on. Incidentally, Dick's breakfast was two boiled eggs and several bottles of Vietnamese beer. Normal or what?

On our return to Saigon we stayed at the Hotel Royal. It wasn't the best hotel in town by any means, but it didn't invite the unwelcome attention of the Viet Cong who attacked the Americanised Continental across the square. Monsieur Octavj, a world-weary French colonial with a lugubrious, heavily lined face, was the owner and could occasionally be seen in the bar. The bar was run by his Vietnamese staff, one of whom would frequently slip photographs of war atrocities to you as you sipped your beer. The beer was Bamibah 33 – thirty-three being a lucky number in Vietnam. It was not unusual to have to return the beer as some bottles were off – not so lucky. As I sat there, cockroaches with enquiring feelers would wander around the metal top. One huge lone cockroach lived in my room on the first floor. I didn't like him much because he kept surprising me. I bought a spray can of insecticide, but I couldn't bring myself to kill him. When I returned each evening from my day's travels, I would lay the sketches I'd made across the floor like a carpet so that I could look at them all from the bed – and there they stayed. At night when I put out the light, I could hear the progress of my room-mate as he scuttled across the dry surface of my sketches with his scratchy legs.

One evening, Monsieur Octavj took me to an opium den, a small room in a back street in Saigon. Several figures sat or lay blissfully around the bare room while the pipe was lit by an emaciated man with greying hair. He handed me the pipe. The smokers lay peacefully on the floor in their underpants, elbows down with hands suspended over their chests. Others lay on their sides, their heads resting on small wooden blocks. This looked very uncomfortable but seemed to do the trick. I lay on a large shelf. I am not a smoker and inhaled tentatively. I don't know how long I was there but that night, when I returned to the Hotel Royal, I made a very careful drawing of the opium den from memory. I was hours on it, working all through the night, drawing each line very, very slowly – it seemed wonderful at the time, possibly the finest drawing I had ever done. It was only when I looked at it the following day that I could see it was average, just another drawing. I had been looking at it through opium-tinted eyes.

Several days later I had a fever. I don't think it was the opium. More probably something I had picked up on my travels. I felt slightly delirious. Monsieur Octavj invited me to a 'special' dinner in the dark shuttered dining room of the Royal. A long table with twelve chairs either side was set with a white cloth. Only half the guests seemed to have arrived and I sat with them on one side of the table but, although places were set, the other side remained empty. The first course arrived, a watery soup, and twelve bowls were set at the empty places. Octavj explained that this was the 'Feast of the Dead' and that opposite us sat the souls of twelve deceased relatives. In my heightened delirious state, and under the nervous strain of all that I had seen, I believed that the dead were there. I could barely face the rest of the meal. Course after course arrived and I struggled to eat under their invisible scrutiny. As soon as I could, I excused myself.

I went up to my room and lay on the bed, staring at the large fan turning slowly on the ceiling. I turned on to my side and almost crushed the giant cockroach with my head as it sat alongside me on my pillow. I leapt out of bed, seized the can of insecticide and sprayed it all over. The force of it blew him off the bed. I gave him several more squirts, blowing him around the room, but suddenly he was up and running. He looked bigger than ever. I leapt back on to the bed and watched his mad agonising progress as he tore around the room. It seemed as though he took an hour to die, scuttling blindly and noisily around the room. Eventually he went quiet and I fell into a disturbed sleep. The next morning I felt better and carefully set about picking up my sketches, expecting to see his huge corpse at any moment. But I never did find him.

As part of my self-imposed duties I felt it right that I should draw some of the Vietnam wounded. I was given permission by a French surgeon to be present at a minor operation on a wounded man. His hand and arm had been lacerated when a mine exploded and he was going to have several dangling fingers amputated. I steeled myself for the scene and entered a rudimentary operating theatre – an operating table with a patient lying on his side, a trolley of instruments, a nurse, and very little else. The breeze-block window on to the courtyard was open and a crowd of curious onlookers gazed in, impressed by the fact that there was an artist present – more interesting than the sight of an injured man, which was much more common. They found me a chair to sit on while the patient squirmed in agony. I was upset that they should pay me any attention while there were far more important matters in hand and set about making myself as inconspicuous as possible.

'Ah, yes,' said the French surgeon, as he picked up the surgical scissors, 'I studied art in Paris.'

He took up the patient's hand and cut off one of the damaged fingers that was hanging by shreds. 'But I was no good as an artist.' Snip, snip, off came another finger. The patient writhed in pain but still, apparently unconcerned, the doctor chatted to me. I wondered how good he was as a surgeon.

'Keep still!' shouted someone in the crowd of onlookers outside the window. 'There is an artist here trying to draw you.'

'Oh no!' I said. 'Please, please!'

But the patient stiffened into a pose.

Dick and I decided to go to a recommended fish restaurant in the region of Dalat. We were shown into a very simple hut with rudimentary tables and chairs. Outside the window we could see the countryside and part of the lake from which the fish were taken. Altogether very idyllic. The various fish dishes were put before us one after another and were stunningly delicious, and a welcome change from the mush of chow we had been served at American bases. Together with a few beers it was one of the best meals we were to have in Vietnam.

After a couple of hours or so of chat, as we left the restaurant, outside the building I noticed a wooden walkway of planks about eighteen inches wide stretching out across the fish pond. They led to a small thatched hut about six foot square on a raised platform in the middle of the lake. Inside the hut was a crouched figure of a man. What was he doing? The distant plopping sound gave me the answer – I later learned that the Vietnamese build their latrines over fish ponds in the belief that nothing should go to waste. I was so glad I hadn't noticed him on the way in. Waste not, want not.

It's an ill wind that blows nobody any good. For most, war is a horrific, apocalyptic experience. But for others it means big opportunities – money. Like camp followers, the construction industry follows the destruction industry. Where war has cut a devastating swathe of chaos destroying cities, roads, railways and homes, along comes the construction business with its civilian engineers to rebuild the infrastructure. Many of the construction engineers I encountered were foul-mouthed drunken slobs. In the bars and brothels they were the most unpleasant. By contrast, the petite Vietnamese bar girls in their áo dài (traditional long-sleeved tunics) were beautiful visions. I saw one huge, lumbering, drunken redneck engineer lurch unsteadily across a bar, his arm around a beautiful Vietnamese hostess, shouting to all and sundry, 'Let me tell you, the Vietnamese are shit! They are all shit!'

The hostess turned on him. She was transformed into a tiny bundle of spitting fury. Incensed, she flew at him, small fists flailing and hammering on his great barrel of a chest. 'You no shit Vietnamese!' she blazed. 'You shit Americans!' With flying fists, this small girl drove the drunken hulk back against the wall.

'OK! OK!' he said, hands raised in surrender.

'You shit!' she told him again. 'You shit American!'

Soon after that incident I returned from Vietnam and went to dinner with Peter Cook and his wife Wendy at their house in Church Row. One of the other guests was David Niven, the film star and raconteur. And raconte he did, on and on. He dominated the evening with undoubtedly hilarious stories of showbiz, but no one – not even Peter – could get a word in. It was really like an endless version of the *Parkinson* show. Eventually Peter asked me to talk about Vietnam but I was too intimidated to do so. I felt I could not follow David Niven — he was the main act — so I made my excuses and left.

Several years ago I visited Vietnam again, this time with Jane, on the huge *Queen Elizabeth 2* cruise ship where I was lecturing. After days on the South China Sea I had become accustomed to the sound of the wind and the crashing sea. I awoke just before daylight that morning to feel that the ship was moving slowly but with no sound of slapping waves. Instead there was the sullen silent swell of the Mekong, fisherman's boats bobbing and rising on the ship's wake like little corks on the silky surface as the lush dark-green foliage slipped by. The city of Saigon (now Ho Chi Minh City) is on the Mekong Delta about thirty miles inland; but the river is still deep enough to accommodate these huge ocean-going liners, so after many years I was back in Saigon.

What had been war-torn Saigon, and Vietnam itself, is now a major tourist destination. The beaches at Da Nang, where the American soldiers had waded to shore, rifles held high, are now covered with luxury hotels with waiters serving cocktails to tourists on loungers around the pool. When I was there during the war half a century earlier I'd thought beautiful Vietnam would make a wonderful holiday destination, and it does. I could find no sign of the Royal Hotel in Saigon. All I would rediscover was the Catholic cathedral in the centre of the city. Very little of the world of Graham Greene's *The Quiet American*.

On my original visit during the war I made drawings of the girls in their beautiful flowing white áo dài, riding bicycles through the streets. Now dressed in T-shirts and jeans they rode motorcycles, hundreds of them, through the crowded streets. The same tangle of electric cables hung from the corners of buildings and telegraph poles. The Vietnamese seem never to remove a cable when it goes wrong — they simply add another on top.

While on a little island I visited, there in a clearing outside a ramshackle hut I saw a local crouched on his haunches whittling a piece of wood into a tourist souvenir. He wore a pair of tattered jeans and a T-shirt bearing the logo Hard Rock Café. America may have lost the military war in Vietnam but they most certainly won the sartorial war.

Memories of the war are now part of the tourist industry. There is a museum showing the ingenuity and cruelty of man with his numerous ways of killing his own kind. It shows pits like elephant traps but intended for humans, with sharpened bamboo spears pointing upwards, waiting for a heavy falling body to impale itself and die in lingering agony. Against my better judgement I thought I should see the conditions under which the Viet Cong had lived during the war. I steeled myself to descend the muddy steps cut to bring visitors to the entrance of the Cù Chi tunnels about six feet below ground level. This labyrinthine system was where the Viet Cong lived underground, with hospitals and even schools. It was from here that the VC attacked the lumbering tanks and heavy US machinery that became bogged down and stuck in thick mud. Sliding from their tunnels like snakes, they struck lethally and were gone, disappearing back into the ground unseen. Historians say that the Americans were over-equipped and laden down with heavy armaments, while the VC nipped and sniped with much more mobility. They should have learned the lesson from the French. Jane and I joined a line of waiting tourists and dropped on to our hands and knees to enter the tunnel. It was frighteningly small, at most three feet high. I had only crawled a few yards when I felt an urgent need to get out, but by that time I had three other crawling tourists behind me. I suppressed my claustrophobic panic and crawled on. What if the roof caved in? I had seen *The Great Escape*. What if the tourist whose fat arse I was following had a heart attack? How would we get out? Thoughtfully, there are three escape exits spaced along the tunnel at regular intervals. I wimpishly took the first. Jane, more intrepid than I was, crawled the whole length.

8

PINKO ARTIST AT THE SUNDAY TIMES

'You are a radical and I am a radical' were Harry Evans's words to me when he asked me to join the *Sunday Times* as political cartoonist in 1967. After being given the E-Type and free petrol when I joined the *Daily Mail* I thought I'd give it a go with Harry. Would there be a car? He laughed and responded with a polite version of 'fuck off'. I persevered – how about petrol? 'Well, I don't know about you,' said Harry, 'but I get mine at a petrol station down the Gray's Inn Road.' I think that was a no.

Things were pretty good at the *Sunday Times* in those early days. Every Saturday I drove to the Gray's Inn Road in my Ferrari Dino to deliver my drawings, which would be laid flat on the seat beside me in the car, often still wet, sticky black Indian ink lines glistening and bearing my message – hot off the press. Sometimes, in the early days of our 'courtship', Jane would come with me and patiently wait in the Ferrari for me to make my delivery.

I always seem to have been unable to draw small. Even if I began small the drawing would grow and grow as I added more and more lines. Occasionally I would come to the edge of the paper and feel I should add a little more length to Nixon's nose, for instance. No option but to Sellotape an additional piece of paper alongside and continue the nose on that. Some of my drawings were enormous – sometimes six feet in length. The production department had to add a length of track to their large camera in order that it could pull back far enough to get my drawings in focus. I would unroll and present these beasts to a sometimes bewildered Harry. But he was always supportive. 'I don't really understand all of your drawings, but I think you're some kind of genius,' he told me.

Harry Evans was here, there and everywhere on the paper; he would be with the Insight team in their office or in the art department with Edwin Taylor, then down on the stone with the compositors. I liked him – pretty well everybody liked Harry. Unlike the previous editor, C. D. Hamilton, who was aloof (I was told) and spent most of his time in his office, Harry was level with everyone. He was easy to talk to, did not pull rank and had his fingers in every corner of the paper. His catchy enthusiasm was hard to resist. He gave me full rein and encouraged and printed everything I produced. Harry had a strong reputation for understanding what power and importance visuals and pho-tographs held in journalism. I always dealt directly with Harry and presented my drawings personally to him.

An editor, Harry told me, is like the conductor of an orchestra. He only has to direct. If he has a good team they will be brilliant at their particular skills and will do their best for themselves, the editor and the paper.

The columnist Hugo Young told me that he was in Harry's office once when Rupert Murdoch strode in. A copy of the previous week's *Sunday Times* was lying on Harry's desk, open at the editorial page. There he could see my cartoon which showed Ronald Reagan stepping out of Vietnam into San Salvador and implying America was making the same dreadful mistake they had made in Vietnam. Murdoch pushed the paper away. 'We've got to get rid of that pinko artist,' he muttered. Harry didn't get rid of me, and I lasted a further thirty-five years.

Harry moved from the *Sunday Times* to *The Times*, where Murdoch sacked him one shocking day in 1981. Many journalists' lives changed. Harry refused to go but had to capitulate, and after Frank Giles had held the *Sunday Times* tiller for a couple of years Andrew Neil was brought in as editor by Murdoch. He was a different kettle of fish. Just as hands on as Harry but a more distant, frightening figure – certainly for me. I was in the middle of negotiating a rise when it happened and had to deal with Andrew.

'I'm not so sure I will want you as cartoonist,' he said in his forthright manner. 'I haven't decided yet. Frankly, I was thinking of something more in the American style.' (He did explain what he meant but I can't recall what he said now.)

'Well, let me try,' I said. 'I'd rather adapt than die.'

He agreed, and I stayed. But looking back, I think that was a mistake. I was never at ease with Andrew. I didn't dislike him, I just couldn't connect with him, and I think he was equally uneasy with me. Perhaps it was his brusque Scottishness. I produced very few 'good' cartoons in that period. Many journalists left the *Sunday Times*. Both Hugo Young, who said he had always thought of himself as 'a lifer', and my friend the brilliant photographer Donald McCullin were let go by Andrew Neil. In retrospect I wish I had gone too but insecurity got me and I stayed – gradually, to my mind, slipping down the system financially, but I was lazy and it was easy doing one cartoon a week. As an uncle of mine once said, 'You're like a vicar, you only work one day a week. What's not to like?' Well, lots.

One day in 1986 Andrew called all the journalists together at a secret location and told us, unbelievably, that we and the *Sunday Times* were all moving, lock, stock and barrel, to Wapping. A new era. The unions, he said, had brought this about with their strikes. Unbeknown to me and many others, for over a year Murdoch had been building a new, fully computerised *Sunday Times* base in the East End.

It was Eddy Shah, owner of several newspapers including *Today*, who first computerised Fleet Street, a move which was eventually to revolutionise news printing. The print unions had been out of control, demanding more and more, and striking continually. I admired the composite printers, who composed the pages of news out of metal letters which they put together into words and sentences at a quite incredible speed, also upside down and back to front so that it appeared the right way round in the newspaper, but it was an unhappy time. I'd resented not being able to publish my drawings for almost a whole year in 1978–9 during Kenneth Thomson's generous ownership, when the *Sunday Times* was on strike. It felt like some sort of censorship by an outside force. It led to Thomson selling the paper to Rupert Murdoch and thereby subsequently bringing about the print union's eventual downfall. There were various workers who were claiming two or more false wage packets each week and getting away with it. One was said to have claimed false wages contemptuously under the name 'Goofy'. Literally overnight all the journalists left Gray's Inn Road and moved to Wapping with its gleaming new technology. A huge shock to most. The look of a newspaper office – the typewriters, stacks of papers and other detritus – disappeared instantly. Instead each desk featured a brand-new computer terminal.

Wapping brought about a new misery. The *Sunday Times* part of Murdoch's empire was housed in what had been a banana warehouse in the days when Wapping docks had been operational. Surrounded by barbed wire, like an internment camp, for the journalists' safety, the buildings were besieged every day by angry pickets. I suffered less than most as I rarely worked in the building but I still had to deliver my drawing personally every week. Perhaps unwisely – or arrogantly, certainly lazily – I drove my BMW through that checkpoint, past the waving placards, to meet what the art department called 'a visually illiterate' Andrew Neil.

My next *Sunday Times* editor was John Witherow, who took over from Andrew Neil in 1994. He had been at the paper since 1980 in several roles including Foreign Editor and Head of News. He was a tall, quiet, intellectual journalist, and I felt more at home with him than with Andrew. But apart from Harry Evans, I can't say I've had a great rapport with any of my editors. Perhaps because I've never sought their company or they mine, or perhaps because most of them seem more at home with the written word than the drawn image and don't really know how to have any input with a cartoon, whereas they know how to edit or improve a written article by taking out a word or rewriting a sentence.

Maybe it was a mistake that I never went to editorial meetings, dined or drank with my editors. I was always a loner, and the ideas and point of view I brought to the paper were always my own – unless I was illustrating a particular article.

In my early days at the *Sunday Times*, just as at the *Daily Mail*, Harry had had difficulty placing me. He certainly couldn't print the overt drawings I had been able to make at *Private Eye*. So he sent me on many reportage commissions. I felt exposed as I sketched away in troubled areas like the Middle East during the Six Day War and Northern Ireland during the Troubles. While photographers can click and run, I was left sharpening my pencils as the bullets flew. Other less intense assignments sent me to the London Docks during the dockers' strike; to Paris for an audience with 'God' (General de Gaulle) at the Élysée Palace; 'up north'

with Harold Wilson ('What's he bothered to come for?' he said);
to draw the deprived and poor in Paddington; to Washington for
a portrait of US Secretary of Defense Robert McNamara; and to
Cannes for the film festival.

I went to Plymouth, USA, looking for the boxer Sonny Liston
at his training camp in Buzzards Bay, Massachusetts. I was to
capture him at the table where he sat with his wife in the camp
restaurant. The great bear stared at me, chewing ponderously, a
fork suspended in one hand. He probably thought what a strange
creature I was with my long hair (it was not actually that long
by today's standards). Sitting several tables away a crop-headed
sparring partner also stared at me. After a while he bellowed
across the restaurant, 'Hey buddy, I know where you can find an
English barber.' He probably thought I was what they would call
an 'English faggot'.

Later I sketched him in the gym where he hit the punchball with
frightening force and sparred with his partner. Worryingly, his
manager told me he didn't like to be looked at while he was training and that he was likely to bawl me out. I kept at a safe distance.

I also drew Muhammad Ali – or Cassius Clay as he was still
called at the time – at his training camp in Boston. He struck a
pose for me and said to all and sundry, with a self-important swag-
ger, 'Lookee here, I got an English artist drawing me!' On seeing
his portrait, his expression darkened and he growled, 'Ahm pret-
tier than that!' Indeed he was – but I find it hard to flatter my
sitters, even if they are world champion heavyweight boxers. The
British boxer Henry Cooper, who famously knocked Ali down,
trained above the Thomas a'Becket pub on the Old Kent Road. I
made a drawing (which is now in the National Portrait Gallery)
of 'Enery' having a rub-down after his training in the ring. I left
out one part of his physique which was as large as the rest of him.

On another American trip I shouted, 'Two more mint juleps
over here, waitress.' It was late, and the writer and journalist

David Leitch and I were sitting in a bar in Tennessee (naturally —
that's what journalists do). The waitress asked what we were
doing. When we told her we were following the Poor People's
March to Washington, she sneered, 'What do you want to do
that for? They're no-good folk — you don't want to give them any
attention.' This was because most of the poor people were black
and we were in Tennessee. We had several more mint juleps and
retired for the night. The following morning we both woke late
and the march had already left so we hitched a ride in an old jalopy
taking several people to catch up with and join the march. 'Why
are you so uptight?' one guy asked me as we sat together in the
back of the station wagon. I explained to him I was English. He
seemed satisfied with that and we drove on.

Back in England, I crawled along two-foot-high tunnels miles
underground in Mosley Hill Colliery, once again stifling my claus-
trophobia, with water dripping down my neck; visited Aintree
Racecourse to draw sporty types; then, when the Greek colonels
carried out their coup and the seat of democracy was taken over
by the army, I was sent to Athens. I had great experiences in
those days, when the *Sunday Times* was owned by Roy Thomson,
the Canadian multi-millionaire. One reporter allegedly bought a
Mini Moke Jeep on expenses. Expense seemed to be no object.
That certainly changed later with Mr Murdoch.

Another assignment led me to walk with Danilo Dolci, a coura-
geous priest who marched against the Mafia in Sicily. His crusade
denouncing the stranglehold the Mafia held on the Sicilian people
took him right through the main towns where the movement had
been born. His brave uniform was a white polo neck, flaunting
his presence and making him a sitting duck for any sniper. By a
strange coincidence on the first day I found myself wearing a similar white jumper. The next day I changed my clothes and dropped
the polo neck. I didn't want to wake up with a horse's head on
my pillow. I walked with him to one town where he lectured the

locals in the town square on the evils of the Mafia. Engrossed in my sketching I didn't notice a mob of youths gathering behind me, until one came alongside and said something unpleasant in Italian. They clearly thought that I was a sympathiser. I ignored them and continued sketching uneasily. The ringleader taunted me again. I was surrounded by them and felt trapped. I didn't quite know how to defuse what was a worsening situation. So I explained I was working for a newspaper, and turned my sketch pad on to the ring-leader and began drawing him. The effect was magical. Flattered and embarrassed, he melted into a grinning booby. Luckily the drawing was a good likeness and his friends began to barrack him about the size of his nose. The crowd began to laugh, and when I showed him the drawing he nodded sheepishly. Collapse of stout party. It showed me that it was possible to use art as a weapon.

Other times I found it very difficult to draw at all. I was sent by the *Sunday Times* to report on a cholera epidemic that was raging in Calcutta. My friend, the photographer Peter Dunne, and I clung to our seats as the Land Rover slipped and slid through the milk-chocolate mud in torrential rain along an unmade track towards the hospital. We peered through a waterfall of rain as it cascaded down on to the windscreen to catch sight of the hospital.

The 'hospital', when it came in sight, was no more than a huge corrugated-iron barn. A temporary refuge set outside the city for cholera sufferers. In the stifling heat we stopped, got out and went in. As soon as I saw the scene before me, I knew I was going to have difficulty drawing it. There were only a dozen or so iron-railed hospital beds with filthy mattresses, and four or five cholera patients on each. Every inch of remaining floor space – even under the beds – was taken up by more people: men, women, children and babies, all extremely ill or dying. A terrible sight. I couldn't stand it, went back outside and stood under the dripping eaves as the rain bucketed down, trying to clear my mind. I felt

I couldn't possibly invade the privacy of those poor, ill or dying people, peering at them as thought they were some sort of curious other beings from another world. However, Peter, professionally, had got to work immediately, crouching with his Nikon, getting this and that angle. I knew he was right, of course. This was our work; this is what we had been flown five thousand miles to do. Our job was to report, and, in so doing, bring the plight of these people to our readers in the hope that they would send money or help in some way. Treading carefully, and stepping over limbs, I picked my way through the sprawled figures, clutching my sketch pad, and started work – nobody objected. Most were too ill or resigned and just couldn't care.

Then I entered another state and almost forgot where I was. This often happens when I am drawing: my whole concentration is on the tricky task of transferring the scene I see before me on to the paper. It becomes an intellectual exercise of getting proportions right; achieving the awkward foreshortening of an arm or the expression on a face. However, I don't suggest it is an entirely mechanical process: in Calcutta that day, I still felt an overriding pity for those people. But, to a certain extent I could take cover behind my pencils and sketch pad, as Peter could do behind his camera.

In June 1967 I was back in a war zone, having been sent to Israel to draw the Six Day War. I took a taxi from Jerusalem across the border to Jordan. I noticed the driver's automatic pistol hanging from the window-winder and uneasily questioned him about it. 'We may need it,' he replied. 'There is a war on.'

I was puzzled to see expensive Mercedes and BMWs parked at the roadside among the rubble with one side perfect and the other flattened like a tin can. Elated young Israeli tank drivers were driving over them for fun. One gung-ho Israeli tank drove straight at our taxi, causing us to swerve violently. 'Bastards!' shouted my driver.

It was said much of the reporting of the Six Day War was done from the bar of the King David Hotel in Jerusalem, but I still felt very much in the heat of the action as I crouched on the ground in the dust of the road with my drawing paper, sketching the sad sight of refugees flooding across the bombed Allenby bridge.

The 'Troubles' in Northern Ireland were in the papers and on TV news daily in the late sixties and early seventies – mainly shootings and car bombings. The *Sunday Times* asked me if I would be prepared to make some drawings for them in Londonderry, as it was more often called then. Jane said she would come with me and I promised her mother faithfully that I would not take her anywhere dangerous. We flew to Belfast, where I hired a Ford Cortina. It was slightly worrying that Avis would not give me fully comprehensive insurance, only 'third party', because it was a 'troubled area'. In Belfast we stayed overnight at the Europa Hotel, which was ominously covered in barbed wire.

On arrival in Derry I made contact with my friend, the *Sunday Times* journalist John Barry, who explained the layout of the 'Bogside'. I wasn't sure how dangerous it was. 'Well, we'll have a look if you like,' said John, and on foot all three of us entered the Catholic quarter. I was surprised that we could move around so easily. It was a seemingly quiet working-class street in the early evening. There were few people around. Those we met paid us very little attention. Everything seemed normal until we reached the first barricade. Ahead of us we saw a line of burned-out cars and vans stretching the width of the street, leaving only a gap at one side large enough for one car to pass through. Thirty yards further on was another barricade – this comprised concrete blocks as well as destroyed cars. After walking without incident for half an hour we returned to the hotel.

The following morning I assembled all my sketching materials in the Cortina and Jane and I drove into the Bogside, wending our way through the chicane of burned-out cars. I chose a spot overlooking the Bogside area spread out below. After about five minutes a kindly lady passing by said, in a matter of fact way, 'I wouldn't sit there if I was you, you'll get shot. They sometimes take shots from the houses below.' So we moved and I drove the car to a spot where I could draw the Ross Hill flats and the barricades. I parked, got out of the driver's seat and walked around to use the passenger seat so that I could hold my large sketch book in front of me without being encumbered by the steering wheel. Jane sat curled up in the back of the car reading her book.

After I had been drawing for about fifteen minutes a sharp rap on the window made me jump. A pleasant-looking young man in his early twenties indicated that I should wind the window down.

'What are you doing?' he said in a strong Northern Irish brogue.

'I'm making a drawing for the *Sunday Times*,' I told him. 'Why?'

'Well, we might need your car,' he said.

I was shocked. 'If you take my car I will have to pay for it,' I said, hopelessly. 'Avis wouldn't insure me.'

He seemed sympathetic, nodded and went away.

Jane and I discussed what we should do – stay there or run for it. We'd never make it through the complicated chicanes. Before we could decide a Ford Zephyr pulled across the front of our Cortina and three men leapt out. Without a word they got into our car, one either side of poor Jane and the third, a dangerous-looking unshaven guy with dark and dirty shoulder-length hair, behind the steering wheel. He started the engine and began to drive away.

'What's happening?' I said. We were both very frightened.

'This is official,' said the young man behind me in the back seat and he pushed an automatic pistol through the gap between the two front seats and into my ribs.

'Where are we going?' I said. 'Look, if you want the car, take it – take it. We don't want trouble.'

Nobody answered. It's extraordinary, but at moments like this time expands – milliseconds seem like hours. If these desperate men could go this far, how much more were they capable of? After what felt like an age we stopped in the shadow of some flats and they began to discuss our situation. The *Sunday Times* was mentioned. Apparently Murray Sayle, an Australian journalist who worked for the paper, 'had done them down' by naming some individual IRA members who had been passing gelignite in the Bogside Inn. They seemed to be talking reprisals. Whether this was done to frighten us or not we'll never know. It was certainly very scary.

The break point came when the young man suddenly caught sight of my drawing of the barricades. 'Ah!' he said. 'You're a brave drawer.' They all agreed, except for the sullen, dangerous driver. 'Well, you can get out here,' the young man told us.

A fantastic wave of relief spread through us. Still alive.

'Do you have anything you want in the boot?' he added, thoughtfully.

We did, and while we retrieved it I still had that lingering feeling – 'is this a trick?' The wave of relief tightened into apprehension again. Once the rules of civilisation have been broken, anything is possible. We walked away as if in a dream, the back of our necks prickling with expectation.

They took our Cortina. Later we learned that Cortinas have very large boots – excellent for accommodating large amounts of gelignite and turning the car into a horrendous bomb. The next day they blew up the post office.

Alongside me on the driver's seat I'd left an open razor blade that I used to sharpen my pencils while I was sketching. Mr Dangerous had leapt in and plonked himself down on the naked blade when he hijacked us. If it had cut his balls off the story might have had a different ending.

9

Hung by Scarfe

The teacher of our six-year-old son Rory thought we should see an essay he had penned on the subject of 'My House'. He'd written: 'At home we have a dog, three cats, a goldfish and two naked Mrs Thatchers.' Indeed we did. I had made two seven-foot-high sculptures of Mrs Thatcher, one as the unadorned Venus arising from the waves and the other as Michelangelo's *David*, both of which stood for many weeks in our hallway awaiting collection for a TV show. All of our children grew up in this type of environment. This was part of a normal household for Rory.

Being an artist is, on the whole, a lonely job. So I do like putting my work on display in exhibitions and seeing the public reactions to it. I sometimes can feel embarrassed standing in front of my own pictures knowing that people will see them and know they belong to me, come from my mind – warped mind, they may think. Often a gallery will have a 'comments book' which I see at the end of the exhibition, and they are always fascinating.

Like many artists, I have an urge to bring my two-dimensional drawings to life. The ancient Greek myth tells us that Pygmalion sculpted a beautiful young woman and wished his creation could come to life. The three ways I can bring my creations to life are to animate them, to dress actors for the stage or to film them.

I have always enjoyed the challenge of sculpture because, unlike my drawings which are organised and presented to confine the viewer to one point of view, sculpture can be seen from all angles. One must retain a likeness and still convince the viewer from all points of the compass. This challenge fascinates and inspires me.

In my 1969 exhibition *Hung by Scarfe*, at the Grosvenor Gallery in London, I was no longer restrained by the edges of the paper and my contorted, cramped fingers began to grow, bulge and spill from their paper boxes, crooked limbs to unfurl and spew and sprawl across the gallery floor. The art critic David Sylvester said to me at the time, 'Now – let yourself go!' I did. I made a pregnant Pope with bulging belly resplendent in his Papal gown holding aloft the contraceptive pill bearing the message, 'Thou Shall Not Pill'. Nixon's jowls were no longer restricted by the edges of the paper, they were free, uncontrolled; they flowed across the room and tripped up the gallery director, Mr Estorick. 'What the hell's that?' he growled, irritably. 'The kid's trying to kill me.'

It was a great release for me. I seemed to be at the beginning of something new again. It was also wonderful to see the public among my creations. They mingled with them and became part of the show. I saw them laughing out loud and realised I was really in the business of entertainment. Now that my figures could unleash their limbs it also meant that I could achieve simpler, bolder shapes. I began to aim for simplicity, leaving behind the nooks and crannies I had explored so often in my *Private Eye* drawings.

My first exhibition in America had been at the Waddell Gallery in New York in 1968. Because of its success I was given another in 1970, again at the Waddell Gallery. It was sculpture as political comment, three dimensional political comment – my way of protesting: Governor Wallace hung from the ceiling like an ape in the costume of a Confederate soldier; a larger than life size Mayor Daley of Chicago beat the living daylights out of a young student. The rejected papier-mâché model of Richard Nixon stood forlornly in the corner. Nelson Rockefeller bought the sculpture of himself. Apparently it sat at the top of the stairs in the Gracie Mansion, the mayor's residence in New York. The director William Friedkin bought my sculpture of Francis Bacon.

Gallery openings can be depressing affairs for the artist. The same fashionable New York crowd came to every one, jam-packed in so tight that the drawings and sculptures not only weren't looked at but were in danger of being damaged. 'Mr Scarfe, I got to tell you, you're a genius' they trotted out, as I'm sure they did to every artist, while upsetting white wine over the pictures.

I took my sculptures on Johnny Carson's television show. During the interview I explained to Johnny that drawings bottled themselves up inside me and I didn't feel right until I'd got them out on to the paper – 'A bit like being constipated,' I remarked.

'Uh-huh,' said Johnny, 'that's a no-no.'

Robert LaPalme, the Canadian caricaturist, was a great fan of my work, and every sculpture I completed he wanted to put on show in Montreal in his Pavilion D'Humour. So every time a sculpture had finished its round of the galleries I sent it to Robert in Canada. After some years I decided to ask Robert to return to England what amounted to most of my sculpted work, only to find on its arrival, to my devastation, that most of it was either badly damaged or destroyed. Robert was apologetic. They had been badly handled by the shippers. I had to fly to Montreal, hire a lawyer and sue the City of Montreal for damage to my artwork.

The lawyer thought I was crazy but took my money anyway. He didn't think I would get in to see the mayor, let alone win a settlement. But eventually we sat before Mayor Drapeau and did arrive at a settlement. Alas, little work from this period has survived.

Monsieur LaPalme was a tiny, wiry little man with a small grey moustache and wandering hands – so my American girlfriend at the time told me after she had travelled in the back of my Mini with him. He was Artistic Director of Expo '67 and wanted to exhibit my work in the show. He was obsessed with sex but it seemed only as a voyeur. Indeed, when he came to London he wanted to buy two prostitutes for my brother and me on the understanding he could watch. We declined. He then wanted to go to Soho to 'see something dirty'. We took him for an educational stroll around Old Compton Street and Greek Street. Outside one of the clubs advertising its wares a heavily built bouncer asked if we were interested and if we'd like to step inside. I explained that it wasn't really for us, but that our visitor from Canada was looking for something dirty. 'Tell him to come here,' he said. 'I'll piss on him.' Always ready to please.

My show, *Hung by Scarfe,* travelled on to the Sears Vincent Price Gallery in America. Vincent Price, a famous actor in the sixties and seventies, invested much of his earnings wisely in art. In the 1960s he had partnered with Sears Gallery in Chicago and developed the Vincent Price Collection of Fine Art, which would make original works of art available for purchase to Sears customers. There were pieces by Rembrandt, Chagall, Picasso, Whistler and many contemporary artists of the day. When the time came for me to publicise my exhibition at the Sears Vincent Price Gallery I found myself on the main TV chat show in Chicago – *Krupps Show.* One of the other guests, a strident New Yorker, went ape when I explained that my drawing of Jackie Onassis kicking the American eagle up the backside was a symbol of the way Jackie had disdained the American public by marrying Aristotle Onassis, after her husband, the hero Jack Kennedy, was assassinated. She flew at me, eyes blazing, screaming, 'She did not! She did not disdain the American public!'

In 1970 I was commissioned by the Central Office of Information to provide a series of sculpures for the British pavilion in Expo '70 which was to be held in Osaka, Japan.

The theme for the exhibition – my first in Asia – was British literature. I made sculptures of Mr Pickwick, Sherlock Holmes, Alice through the Looking Glass, and Gulliver. Gulliver was the biggest task. I constructed a thirty-foot-high sculpture of him in my back garden, made entirely of welded scrap metal. I toured scrap metal yards looking for suitable pieces to have delivered to Cheyne Walk and into my small back garden. Talk about lowering the tone of the neighbourhood. Many of the armatures were made of gas piping which we took to the front of the house to bend in the railings. I found a lad called John who said he could oxyacetylene-weld with a blowtorch. To the neighbours' further dismay oxyacetylene cylinders were delivered. I'm not sure John really could weld or whether he had simply mugged up on it the night before, but it was all highly dangerous. 'Careful, I nearly had your eyes out then!' he'd say as he wielded the torch. The whole house was crammed with scrap metal and welding equipment. It was a disgrace. Strangely, my neighbour who had complained about the previous owner of my house playing the piano didn't say a word about my garden being a junk yard.

In order to clothe some of the other figures in my exhibition I bought the entire wardrobe of a defunct theatrical company. It was bitterly cold working outside on Gulliver, so my brother Gordon, who was helping me, took to wearing some of the costumes to keep warm. One day the gas man came to read the meter while we were working. Gordon opened the door wearing three frock coats, one on top of the other, and a Thomas Wolsey four-cornered skull cap. The gas man didn't say a word – probably thought it was the thing down in Chelsea.

When I had finished, eight or nine soberly suited men from the COI filed apprehensively into the alien territory of my studio. They had come to look at Gulliver. As he was two storeys high he had been made in two halves, the head and torso separate from the legs. Unfortunately only the head and torso was on view. Silence and shuffling from the COI gents. 'I think he's absolutely wonderful,' said one of them, 'but isn't he a little short for Gulliver?'

An enormous crane was hired to lift Gulliver over the garden wall into the side street, Chelsea Manor Street, where he was carted away on a very long lorry. Off he went to Osaka to confuse the Japanese. I followed a week or so later to put the whole exhibition together.

I have always been fascinated by Japanese prints, and I still draw feet like the feet I've seen in Hokusai's notebooks – he's another of my artist heroes. Japan is fascinating. I sketched sumo wrestlers: gigantic men of blubber and muscle raising one leg and then the other with much ceremony. Suddenly they rush one another, their two bodies colliding like express trains with frightening velocity. The first to be thrown out of the ring loses. It takes enormous strength for one to topple the other. Sometimes they teeter there for seconds before they thud to the sand.

From Japan I travelled on to India – Udaipur, Jaipur, Agra. I have no idea what ultimately became of Gulliver. Back to the scrap metal yard whence he came, I imagine. Ashes to ashes.

In 1971 I was extremely flattered to be asked to exhibit at the National Portrait Gallery in London in a show called *Snap!* with two other portraitists: the painter David Hockney and the photographer David Bailey, both of whom I admired enormously. Although I have drawn Hockney several times, I've never been drawn by him. I have had my portrait taken by Bailey several times, most recently five years ago. David's approach is to put his sitter at ease. Arm around the shoulder, 'me old mate' sort of approach. It has the reverse effect on me. I become as tight as a drum. I feel patronised. I don't take easily to being directed at any time – I prefer to direct. On this occasion Jane and I were being photographed for *Vogue*. He kept urging me to get closer to Jane. Not a difficult thing to do, but I asked why. 'I want her hair to hide all this,' he said, slapping his jowls. 'Anyway, darling,' he added to Jane, 'I'm going to have to get it all from you – I'm getting nothing from him.'

Since he'd first arrived in 1967, Roy Strong, the trendy director of the National Portrait Gallery, had been sweeping away the dusty old fuddy-duddy image of the NPG and bring in exhibitions that were relevant to today. The exhibition contained many of my drawings and paintings. I set about making new sculptures but this time, remembering that my Beatles had been eaten by beetles, I used more durable materials. A fibreglass Edward Heath oozed across the floor as a spilled egg leaking from a cracked polystyrene shell. A collapsed old armchair from the basement, reupholstered in red leather in the shape of the Chinese leader Mao Tse-tung, became an expensive pun: *Chair Man Mao*. Richard Nixon was an example of pushing caricature to the extreme. I wanted to encapsulate him in the simplest shape I could achieve. He was made of wood, and this time his jowls were separated from his face and hung independently beneath his ski-jump nose

I also made a sculpture of the controversial racist politician Enoch Powell which consisted of four figures made of cloth, wire, leather and metal, all linked to one another. It showed the progression of Enoch from a seated figure to an abstract pair of steel jaws in which was clutched a 'golly'. The BBC featured my Enoch when I was interviewed at their studios for an arts programme and he was stored there overnight. The next day he was discovered badly beaten up and partially destroyed, and that was the end of Enoch. I have always wondered whether the vandals were anti-Scarfe or anti-Powell.

*

I arrived in Newport by train and, pausing only to buy a screwdriver from Woolworth's, I made my way to Newport Art Gallery and started unscrewing pictures from the wall. The director of the gallery was appalled. He ran around flapping his arms. He told me to stop or he would call the police. I told him to go ahead. After I had taken down about ten pictures the police arrived and the director pointed me out in excited fury. I thought he would explode.

'Now, sir,' said the sergeant, 'what's this all about then?'

I explained that my exhibition from the National Portrait Gallery was to be shown in its entirety at Newport but a councillor and the committee had objected to three of my drawings, calling them 'lavatory wall artistry', and wanted to take them out of the exhibition. On hearing this, I had told the Arts Council, who ran the exhibition, that it was understandable if they didn't want to show them, but they must remove all of my work or none of it. I had taken great trouble to pick a balanced, representative selection. The drawings they wanted to remove were sexual in content but as an artist I felt that there was no part of human activity that I should not show in my work, and indeed I was known for using human sexual activity as a vehicle in my drawing. Therefore it would be an incomplete collection if they were not included. What had spurred me on to take this action was that the committee had gone ahead with the exhibition without the three controversial drawings, against my will.

'Well, Mr Scarfe,' said the sergeant, 'you are completely within your rights to remove your property.'

So I did. The exhibition closed and the gallery director exploded.

My drawing of the Victorian artist Aubrey Beardsley, which was banned from that exhibition in Newport in 1971, was chosen to appear in a 2010 exhibition at Tate Britain, *Rude Britannia*, and will be included again in a forthcoming Tate exhibition about Beardsley in 2020.

My first large solo exhibition in England was at the Festival Hall in 1983. I feared that no one would come, so to people the exhibit I produced some realistic life-size figures in everyday clothes to face the paintings as though they were examining them. Several people bumped into them and apologised. I was relieved when the exhibition opened and there were long queues. Tony Banks, the right-hand man of the leader of the Greater London Council Ken Livingstone, thought it disgraceful that I had not been given a full-size exhibition before. He also wished to popularise the Festival Hall. It was felt by the left wing that it was a place for the privileged rich who went to classical music concerts. There was even a champagne bar. Tony soon closed that down. He chose me to bring the place downmarket, make it more of a people's palace, as it is today. As well as dozens of my drawings I sculpted a huge twelve-foot-high figure of Mrs Thatcher as Britannia with her shield and trident, wearing a breastplate bristling with razor-sharp, spear-like breasts, standing on the Tomb of the Unemployed. I also included a ten-foot-high sculpture of Ronald Reagan as a gun-toting Mickey Mouse cowboy (I often depicted him as Mickey because he had been a film star – as had Mickey).

Around that time I was approached by a professional portrait painter who wanted to paint me. I agreed, and she came up with a portrait that made me look rather good. I was very pleased with this benign, smiling representation, like many you see in drawing rooms and boardrooms today. But the painting was too flattering. The problem with this kind of portraiture is that the viewer gets little idea of what the person is really like.

The history of commissioned portraiture has mainly been one of flattery and sycophancy, which isn't surprising because the sitter is usually footing the bill. It's a bit like being an interior decorator. If the client wants a yellow wall, he gets a yellow wall. On a visit to the National Portrait Gallery I can spend hours looking at the portraits of people such as Henry VIII and Elizabeth

I – mostly painted by sycophants. Wouldn't it be better to know what these people really looked like? It is no doubt entirely possible that had I been asked to paint Henry VIII I would not have been brave enough to portray him as he really was. Nonetheless, flattery isn't a very good idea. Had the painter Hans Holbein been more honest, the whole course of history could have been very different. When Henry VIII commissioned him to paint Anne of Cleves, the resulting portrait was the basis on which Henry decided to marry her. He was appalled when the real woman turned up and he saw her in the flesh. He called her 'the Flanders Mare'.

In 2005 the director of the National Portrait Gallery, Sandy Nairne, approached me with the idea of drawing caricatured versions of some of the famous people currently hanging in portrait form at the gallery. My work would then form an exhibition, which became *Heroes & Villains*. I showed a drawing of Princess Diana dressed in white and surrounded by pigs in shit. The pigs are the press and their shit is smudging her white gown. I called it 'Live by the Sword, Di by the Sword'. I took this idea one stage further and drew Diana naked on her hands and knees, being taken by a pig from behind. She looked like she was being assaulted, but the question was, was she going along with it? I was trying to show what I believe was Diana's ambivalence towards the press and how she used them but also got screwed by them. Sandy thought it was 'horrid' and banned it from the exhibition.

Extraordinarily the BBC showed the very same drawing in a film made about me at that time called *Drawing Blood*. They filmed a lawyer looking at my drawing while saying something to the effect of 'I see nothing wrong with it – it is simply Diana being covered by a pig'.

The drawing caused a huge furore. When I revealed it during a subsequent talk at the Hay Festival, a very angry and offended woman on the top bleacher rose from her seat, noisily clattered down the metal stairs across the front of the stage and swept out of the exit. I managed to keep talking during her protest but it was difficult. Luckily the rest of the audience remained seated.

Even the artist Tracey Emin was appalled by my drawing of her. She spends much of her time in public galleries painting her private life in intimate detail. I drew her sitting naked on the loo, and around the bottom of the loo I had written, imitating her lettering, 'Me in the fucking shit house'. But Tracey was shocked. 'Not me on the loo!' she cried when she saw it. I was quite pleased to have shocked her, but it made me realise how much well-known figures expect to be flattered.

'But Tracey,' I said, 'you depict your private life through your work all the time – your bed, your tent!'

'Yes, I know,' she said, 'but on the loo – that is so very private. I wouldn't have minded if I had been throwing up . . . but that!'

The National Portrait Gallery was not happy with another of my drawings. My idea for it came from the phone call in which Prince Charles told Camilla he wanted to be her tampon. Camilla sits, looking large and solid, with her legs wide apart, while Charles, weedy and slightly cross-eyed, is peeping out from where a tampon would be. The Queen looks on, saying 'Anus horribilis'.

Censorship has always been a big issue and a sore point. Once, Harry Evans phoned me, and he was furious. I had deliberately tried to slip a penis into the *Sunday Times*, he stormed. I had no idea what he was talking about. He said, 'You know very well – Reggie Maudling's chin looks like a penis.'

I looked at that week's drawing. He was right, it did look like one.

'I'm sorry,' I said, 'I didn't intend it.'

I had done it unconsciously but he didn't believe me. He was convinced I did it on purpose. I told him penises are in the eye of the beholder, but he wasn't amused. I changed it for the second edition. I sent him a little drawing of Maudling with underpants on his chin. He was always worried when I drew phallic rockets. It's not easy being a cartoonist.

Frank Giles, during the short period when he was editor of the *Sunday Times* in the early eighties, once summoned me to his office asking if I could alter a cartoon of Nigel Lawson as it was a bit ferocious. I told Frank no, I couldn't do that. I was not in the business of flattering politicians. Frank looked taken aback. There was an awkward silence, broken eventually by a fellow journalist who said, 'Actually I believe the correct answer is "Up to a point, Lord Copper".'

As a cartoonist it is my job to dig beneath the veneer. The great and good, the powerful and the monied have always been flattered. Think of Mario Testino's photograph of Prince Charles and his sons for the royal Christmas card. It looked contrived and unreal, as though they were in a glossy magazine advert. There are few photographers or professional portraitists who dare to paint their subjects in a bad light. Lucian Freud is a notable exception. He painted people honestly. His painting of the Queen, with a distinct five o'clock shadow and a huge jaw, struck me as being nearer the truth, unlike Pietro Annigoni's effort in 1955, which made her look anodyne and unrecognisable – enough to ensure another commission a decade and a bit later.

'Ooh! Don't draw me, will you!' people say to me. 'Goodness knows how you must see me. Please don't put my big nose in.' Well, the truth is I don't see people with elongated noses and floppy ears. They look normal to me. Well, normal-ish. When I start to caricature someone I exaggerate their features or I may imagine them as something else entirely – a lug worm, a toad, a bat or a pop-up toaster. What I'm trying to do is bring out their essential characteristics, to bring their overall character on to paper. I find a particular delight in taking the caricature as far as I can. It pleases me to stretch the human face and figure and yet keep a likeness. There comes a point in that stretching process where, like a piece of chewing gum, it breaks and the likeness is lost.

It's part of my job to have frightful thoughts. I once drew John Major tiptoeing into bed with Edwina Currie, depicting her as a gargantuan, lip-sticked, bare-breasted harridan, with a tiny, naked, grey-looking Major. To encourage him she's tickling his private parts with her forefinger. We all know this was true because Edwina told us so. I called it 'A Ghastly Thought'.

Cromwell told the artist Peter Lely, 'Paint me, warts and all.' I'm sure Lely thought: Not bloody likely, my lord! People are frightened of power, and portrait artists are trying to make a living. A caricature of a politician can represent more than simply his views and character, and I tend to hit as hard as I can. But today the culture of flattery is insidiously pervasive. Celebrity magazines actually pay people to be interviewed and photographed. Some celebrities sell their most intimate moments – their weddings and family holidays. Perhaps the consumers of these publications don't want to read nitty-gritty stories; they want to believe there's a glossy world out there and they aspire to be a part of it. Through admiration and envy, the world is represented in a way that people would like to see it. The truth, even in art, can hurt.

There should be no taboos in my line of work, but I notice that when I experience difficulties getting work published it's often to do with sex. I think that sex is a big part of life and it's my duty as an artist to represent that. If we falsify the world around us, we are dishonest both to ourselves and to posterity.

Censorship is recommended by busybody individuals like Mrs Mary Whitehouse, and also practised by the nanny state who feel it is not good for us or for them to hear, see or do certain things. Controlling the world in which we live is their main concern. In general, I would think most of us object to that. I have been censored many times but not, as far as I can tell, for my political views. Certainly, many of my sexual drawings have been refused by editors – but offence comes from all quarters. Mary Whitehouse styled herself an ordinary housewife, but also a keeper of public morals. She often complained about what she had seen on television or read in the press, and she started a Clean-Up TV campaign, which later became the National Viewers' and Listeners' Association. Her complaints were usually about sex. At one point she went to Rome to see the Pope about the lax state of morals in Britain. At the time Rupert Bear was the symbol of the underground movement owing to the *Oz* magazine obscenity trial, and I made a drawing for the cover of *Ink* magazine in 1971 of Rupert and Mrs Whitehouse in the Vatican with the caption 'Mary Whitehouse explains her position to the Pope' (you can imagine what position she and Rupert were in). She wasn't pleased – she sued me. I received a hilarious letter from Mrs Whitehouse's lawyer in which he set out in legal language a description of my drawing, saying that I had suggested that his client was prepared to disport herself *in flagrante* in front of the Pope. *Ink* magazine settled out of court, donating several hundred pounds to charity, and it all died down. In the years since, it has been exhibited in the V&A and the Tate, which shows how tastes change.

'They will sue if these are printed!' exploded a French maître d' one day when I was sketching the punters gambling at Crockfords Casino for the *Sunday Times*. 'That is Monsieur X and that's Madame Y. They are so recognisable!' He took an eraser from his desk and began to rub them out.

Angry, I seized the drawing back. 'Listen,' I told him, 'you do not have the right to destroy them.' And I tore the drawing into tiny pieces. 'I do!'

The Frenchman was abashed. *'Ce n'est pas necessaire!'*

I didn't worry because I had taken the precaution of secreting my best drawing in between the pages of *Queen* magazine, which I was using as a rest for my sketch pad. I had anticipated trouble.

As I said, offence comes from all quarters. The *Sunday Times* editor John Witherow once objected to my cartoon showing Education Secretary Michael Gove being caned by a headteacher representing the teachers' union the NUT. Gove was answering through a puff of air from his bare bottom. I was puzzled as to whether it was the bare buttocks or the escape of air therefrom that was offensive. John said that the buttocks were acceptable but that the gush of wind was not. Having established our parameters we both agreed the *Sunday Times* was a 'fart free zone'.

I think Phillip Whitehead, the Labour MP for Derby North, explained the conundrum well when he made this statement to the House in November 1973, from *Hansard*:

> the difficulty is that even when we look at what comes through the mails, there can be differences of opinion as to what is indecent and what is not. Something which I received through the mails only the other day is a scatological cartoon of the reigning monarch seated upon the lavatory with the consort. It is a cartoon by Gillray and the reigning monarch is George III. Most of us would not now consider that material to be grossly offensive.
>
> But there may well be people who feel that it is extremely indecent, and there are certainly people who feel that the work of the modern equivalents of Gillray – cartoonists such as Gerald Scarfe – is extremely indecent and should be prohibited; and that some of the covers of magazines such as *Private Eye* come into the area of indecent display

There's one area where so far I've had no trouble: the F-word. One drawing I show in my talks is of President Bush flying like Superman over the burning oilfields of Iraq, which has the title 'Is It a Bird? Is It a Plane? No, It's a Fucking Disaster!' I never know whether to say 'fucking' or 'effing'. Jane always tells me, 'Don't be silly, say "fucking". Everybody knows that word.' So I do. And there is no doubt that 'fucking' has more impact than 'effing'. The first time Ken Tynan said the word on late-night television, in 1965, you would have thought the sky had fallen. But now Gordon Ramsay says it every other sentence. Times and language change, but I still couldn't write it in a newspaper.

'What's it like to have a genius in the family?' said my editor, Harold Evans, to my mother at the opening of *Snap!* at the National Portrait Gallery.

'It's all very well,' answered my mother, 'but I wish he'd draw something nice.'

For some time thereafter I always put a small watercolour of poppies at the end of an exhibition. Something nice.

10

This Business of Art

As the caves of Lascaux and Altamira prove, human beings have an urge to depict their experiences, whether on the walls of caves or on the walls of art galleries. This recording in pictorial form is an effort to explain the mysteries of our existence, whether done with a pencil, a sable brush or a burnt stick. The important element is the mind that drives the implement and its control of the hand that wields it. I feel a tremendous sense of satisfaction when I do this successfully. The graphic aspect of my work is important to me. I want my drawings to be precise and a steel nib used like a scalpel is my usual favourite. A steel nib can cut into the paper like a knife into flesh. My drawing pen is the simplest of tools. It is a wooden shaft with a metal ferrule on the end, into which I push a nib. I dip that nib into a small pot of shiny black Indian ink.

I have an image in my mind and need to get that on to the paper as quickly as possible. It is important that the ink flows steadily and freely. The pen's job is to transfer my imagination on to the paper. If it doesn't flow it interrupts my flow of thought. Damn it.

The transference of ideas in the mind on to paper or canvas is mysterious and difficult to understand. The hand has to move in tandem with the brain and channel the amorphous imaginings of the mind correctly on to two- or three-dimensional surfaces. Line drawing must be so precise, and once that line has been committed to paper in ink it's impossible to change or get rid of it without using white paint, which I hate doing. With oil paint one can cover the mistakes, even wrestle with the painting until you make it do what you wish. With oil paint you can even scrape it all off and still leave a ghostly echo of the image underneath, then work back on top of it and into it.

With a certain amount of application one can achieve a high standard in drawing. The old cliché that says genius is 5 per cent talent and 95 per cent hard work isn't far off the mark. The crunch comes when you have achieved that high standard of drawing and don't know what to do with it. That is why so many artists abandon the academic representational drawings of their student days for the abstract. Having achieved basic drawing skills they are searching for their particular contribution, something that will make them unique. The rules of art are there to be broken. In fact I'm not sure there are any rules, only personal ones.

If you visit the Musée Picasso in Paris you will see how Picasso could draw perfectly by the age of fourteen. It seems that bored him. He grew tired of his representational drawings and pushed on to discover cubism.

Although I appreciate Pollock and Rothko, I find I respect an artist who has been taught the basics of drawing because I can feel it as a solid basis to his work. That is why I appreciate the work of Picasso or Matisse. Whenever I need inspiration I turn to them or to Michelangelo, da Vinci, Rembrandt, Goya, Daumier. But I think art is ultimately just a wonderful way of expressing yourself. If you're happy with it, it's successful. Many Sunday painters get more joy from their work than Van Gogh or Toulouse-Lautrec ever did.

Artists should always be striving to move on. Within my limited field of caricature I do try to push the limits but it is more difficult to do so as a cartoonist working in the popular press. One cannot become abstract, for one of the requirements is that one stays within recognisable boundaries. However, I feel I have pushed boundaries outside my newspaper work. My work with Pink Floyd on *The Wall*, for instance – which I talk about in a later chapter – was much freer and more expressive. I could let fly because that audience would expect something different, more challenging and 'outside the box'. I've always thought that animation is to some extent an unexplored medium: moving art. The sheer magic of taking still single drawings and running them one after the other to give the illusion of movement.

In the early twentieth century the work of 'R. Mutt' (Marcel Duchamp) opened a whole new box of tricks, exhibiting a urinal as art. The floodgates to 'conceptual art' were flung wide open and many artists felt free to experiment. Undoubtedly many charlatans and lazy flavours of the month sneaked through those same floodgates. Really it's up to you to decide what you will or won't accept personally. Confused and puzzled? I'm not surprised – much cobblers is talked about 'Art'. You may feel there is some secret art club or language recognised only by artists. Van Gogh was a struggling, not popular, artist in his day. Fashions change. Now his work is ubiquitous, decorating calendars, tea towels, waste paper baskets. Was he ahead of his time? Why was he difficult to understand then and not now? Will we feel the same about some of the 'difficult' artists practising today?

Many people are puzzled by art. They think they ought to enjoy it but on entering a gallery feel insecure and don't know what to think or what they ought to think. They may think 'What a load of old tat – my five-year-old could do better than that' but dare not say it for fear of being thought uneducated or stupid. Some conceptual art is difficult to appreciate. Martin Creed's Turner Prize-winning *Work No. 227: The lights going on and off* puzzled me.

I struggled with my artwork. Not coming from an artistic background and not having had any artistic training I was continually puzzled as to what 'good' art was. During my teens there was an artist named Rowland Hilder who painted watercolours of the English countryside. Frozen fields of snow sparkling in the thin winter sun, the black lacework of bare trees lining the horizon, black crows circling in a cloud-blown grey sky. That sort of thing. I thought he was very good but I knew he was derided by those who regarded themselves as 'true artists'. 'Too commercial,' they said. 'Slight, flippant.' But why? Was there a common rule that decided what was and what wasn't good art? I knew there was more to learn but I didn't know how to get there.

It is a strange newspaper tradition that you should turn a page and be confronted by a cartoon. It's probably the only daily dose some people get of 'art'. But I'm convinced that many people do not see the cartoon. Their eyes, untrained, seek out the written punchline, or skid over it to headlines and text. I often find the explanation by the artist helps to point one in the right direction or give one help with their thoughts and aim. But should a work of art stand on its own without needing a verbal account? I feel it should.

Imagine yourself as an editor sitting at your desk. The door opens and an artist comes in and thrusts under your nose a piece of paper with a 'joke' drawn on it. 'Go on, laugh, damn you!' What do you do? That is probably what it's like for the editor when the cartoonist confronts him. God, what's this one about? Who's that? Trump? Putin? What are they doing? Why do they look like sponge cakes? Who's the man upside down in the background?

I learned in my early years to go in firing from the hip. Explain the idea verbally. 'This is Trump and this is Putin and they are symbolising world disunity.' Relief on editor's face. Pass. Then it's over to the readers to sort it out. Today there are no such embarrassing confrontations. All of my drawings are sent electronically and I very rarely meet my editor. Some cartoonists will go to the daily conference to pick up ideas. I have only done this once or twice, in the far distant past. I prefer to be completely independent with an outside view.

Cartoonists are mavericks in the art world. They fit in uncomfortably, if at all. They are part artist, part journalist, making weekly comments and judgements on their environment. They are not regarded as real artists: one only has to go to a Chelsea house to see that the real art is hung in the drawing room and the cartoons are hung in the lavatory. 'Really frightfully amusing. You must have a look next time you're in the loo. They are a real hoot!'

The word 'cartoon' itself is very confusing. In its original meaning a cartoon (from the Italian word *cartone*, meaning 'big paper') is a full-size drawing made on paper as a study for a more developed artwork. Cartoons by painters such as Raphael and da Vinci can still be seen in museums around the world. A cartoon, then, can refer to one of a vast range of styles and subjects, from that ridiculous man with a big nose and stubble sitting on a desert island putting a message into a bottle to the sublime drawings of Honoré Daumier. He illustrates some of the eternal questions: a couple gazing at the moon trying to understand what it's all about, for instance; beautiful, poignant drawings revealing the hopelessness of mankind through brilliant observations of the bourgeoisie and ordinary citizens grappling with the impossibilities of life. Incidentally, Daumier was spurned in his lifetime as a mere cartoonist but his drawings and paintings now hang in museums all over the world.

A cartoonist is a much rarer beast than a journalist, or even an editor – we're much thinner on the ground. A cartoonist must possess not only a journalistic sense but also a sense of humour or wit, and then the ability to draw it. Cartoons must fight for attention among screaming headlines, dramatic photographs, and advertisements designed for impact. I have either to shout louder to survive or make a drawing that is simple, direct and immediate – and hopefully punches you in the eye.

It's difficult to translate ideas to paper: like butterflies they seem exquisite when they are free and fluttering in the air, but once nailed into position they lose their magical possibilities. Visions dissolve and disappear like dreams in the telling when made concrete.

I read newspapers, watch the news on TV and keep abreast of the political scene. I don't sketch out my drawing in pencil first, but bash straight in with pen and ink hoping to get every line in the right place first time. Unlike oil painting, where each succeeding layer hides the last, there is very little room for error. The simplicity of shape, the volume of the figure, the likeness (if it is a caricature), all have to be achieved in the initial drawing. It's tricky. It's like running across a tightrope. A high-wire act.

Sometimes the image is already formed in my mind, or I may make the briefest sketch or a few lines to get the composition to my liking. Then all I am trying to do is get that preconceived idea on to paper. Other images may unravel of their own accord in front of me, taking a direction I wasn't expecting. They appear to lead me, dictate the way I should go.

I have ways of making myself work. Don't just sit staring at the daunting, expectant paper. Just put something down – hopefully it will lead on to another thing, and before you know it the drawing may be underway like a slow locomotive pulling out of the station before it speeds down the track. The first mark the pen or brush makes is like laying the foundation stone of a building. It can decide what happens thereafter.

Standing at the drawing board in my studio, about to pin my butterfly to paper, I dip the steel pen nib into a tiny bottle welded to a plate by years of congealed black ink. Now comes the moment of capture, the moment of commitment: half looking at the paper, and half hanging on to my vision, I place the point of the loaded nib on to the paper and make that first mark. It commits to the shape of the final creation, and within a split second I can tell whether the drawing will work or not. The floor of my studio is often littered with many false starts.

I may abandon a drawing with only one line completed, because I feel it is in the wrong place and I can see what, now that it is committed, the line will lead on to. Each successive line bears the same danger – it may wreck the drawing, just as each added card can weaken a house of cards. If I'm trying to find something, I may get thirty lines right and the thirty-first will wreck the image. Sometimes it's evasive and just out of reach. It seems right, then evaporates before my eyes. A trance-like state of mind is what I'm trying to work from but I so seldom achieve that. Every time I restart, my vision becomes fainter until, after many false beginnings, it has disappeared, and I am merely repeating the previous mistakes. Then I must begin again with a new idea, or rethink and draw the same picture from a different angle. Occasionally, even if the line is in the wrong place I feel I can go on to fight and wrestle the picture into place. Lost in a wilderness, a deep forest of sticky black lines, I can sometimes emerge triumphant.

I would like to think that artists have the heightened powers of observation that some professions require. While I was feeding a parking meter one morning I became aware of two approaching policemen. When they drew level one eyed me suspiciously, but they passed on by. What's all that about? I thought. I checked the meter to make sure I wasn't doing anything wrong. At that point they turned and strolled back, and, in that leisurely arms-behind-the-back way they have, one said, 'Excuse me, sir, would you mind telling me why you are wearing one black shoe and one brown?' I looked down. It was true – I was wearing odd shoes. Eccentricity? Artyness? No. That morning, in order not to wake Jane I had dressed in the dark without putting the light on. The policemen had noticed my odd shoes. Patrolling the streets they have every opportunity to notice anything that does not seem quite right, anything out of the ordinary or suspicious. Something out of place. Anyway, odd shoes are thankfully not a criminal offence and they let me go.

I know I often see things that others don't seem to have noticed. Someone in a restaurant may remind me of or may look to me like a crocodile or an aardvark. Is it just me? There are quite a few hippopotamuses around in these fast-food days I can tell you. You must have seen them?

To a certain extent I have a photographic memory. As an exercise I shut my eyes, take a 'snapshot' in my mind's eye, freeze the scene, then see how much I can recall and draw from that image. I may practise with the flickering flames of a fire or the billowing smoke from a bonfire. Perhaps swirling eddies of water as they rush around rocks. Leonardo da Vinci became obsessed with drawing the movement of water.

It's all too easy to slip into an unthinking, automatic way of drawing, resting on lazy, preconceived, well-tried methods. My friend Ronald Searle used to bind his fingers to make it more difficult for him to draw, to make him rethink, to struggle, to consider what he was trying to depict. It was the same principle Sophocles used when he put pebbles in his mouth to correct his stutter. His theory was that when the pebbles were removed his speech would improve.

I have always been interested in doing the best drawing I can. There are other cartoonists who are happy with their idea, a funny idea, and they don't necessarily care about the drawing itself. I have always cared tremendously what the drawing looks like, and I always do my best to organise it graphically and make it aesthetically pleasing even though it may be grotesque, even though it may be horrific.

Ideally I have to feel the flesh and bone when I'm getting a likeness. I can't even add the eyebrows without feeling them. It's like being a method actor or impressionist: I have to get into the mood and the feeling of that person. Often when drawing a character I can hear his or her voice in my head as I transfer that image to paper. The image I see in my mind's eye is not fixed and can evaporate before it reaches the paper. To a certain extent there is a lack of control in getting to the end result. I try to free myself and fly away from the obvious, the mundane image, separate myself from the lazy photographic snapshot and achieve a boiled-down, distilled image that captures the very essence of that person. I have to uncouple myself from reality yet remain tethered to that person.

My drawings are very personal acts made in the privacy of the studio in my home, but when they leave my hands they escape into hundreds of thousands of copies and may be seen by millions of people. I don't think about that when I make the drawing – it's just between my imagination and that piece of paper – but if a drawing is particularly ferocious or overtly sexual and someone looks at it in my presence I have to admit sometimes to feeling shy. I feel so personally about it, it's almost like undressing in public. My drawings are often a cry against that which I detest, and in showing my dislike I have to draw the dislikeable. To horrify people with a drawing about the waste of war I must make a horrific drawing of war, and when I come to draw people, their bodies become vehicles for emotions – greed, lust, cruelty. It's not that I have a dislike of human flesh: it is that I have a dislike of human frailties and the flesh becomes a medium for depicting them. However, as there is a percentage of prudery in my make-up I am embarrassed if, for instance, the drawing is highly sexual and the onlooker is shocked, even when that is what I set out to do.

Politicians have been my bed and board, my food and drink, my way of life. In a way I have lived off them, but in general I'm not particularly fond of them as a species. Many of them are blatantly ambitious, self-seeking, arrogant individuals who see themselves (incorrectly) as leaders. They love the power it can bring them and the flock of fawning sycophants who see them as their bread and butter and who follow them, picking up scraps. How extraordinary that they feel they have the answers to so many things and seek to persuade others to follow their lead. Does it never strike them they could be wrong? Having said all that, by the law of averages I must admit some politicians have the best intentions. They genuinely feel they want to and can change our world for the better. The rest – the majority – are a necessary evil.

I often went to the party conferences. In the days before the internet changed the world and gave us the ability to research people at the click of a mouse, and long before the days of twenty-four-hour news, I needed to go and seek them out. Blackpool or Brighton at conference time is the natural habitat of the politician. I was able to draw them unobserved – braying at breakfast, basking on the prom, lolling at their watering holes, snorting at the best troughs in town, slumbering in the afternoon boredom of unmemorable speeches. The *Times* foreign correspondent Louis Heren once said we should approach all politicians by asking 'Why is this lying bastard lying to me?' Politicians say, 'Let me be perfectly clear about this' – meaning 'I'll fog this up and hope to get away with it'. They say 'To be honest', which means 'I'm going to lie through my teeth'. Many politicians have the astounding arrogance to think themselves superior beings who have a duty to tell other citizens what to do, where to go and how to behave. They are not quite as bad as religious bigots but they are getting close. Somewhere I acquired or inherited a strong dislike of authority, of people throwing their weight around. I cannot bear bumptiousness, superiority, those who think themselves a cut above others because of birth or money. Those who misuse their power drive many of my drawings. What arrogance and stupidity makes a mere mortal think he is the one chosen to lead others?

I find that when a new politician is elected to high office and it becomes necessary to caricature him or her, at first it may be difficult to understand how they should be depicted. They could be drawn in an almost realistic likeness with only slight exaggerations – a marginally bigger nose for instance. Then drawing by drawing, week by week, the exaggerations become more extreme and distorted as I come to understand the face more. The advantage of working on a daily or weekly newspaper is that the readers can be slowly led over time to accept the extremes of caricature.

Drawing politicians over and over again is a tedious business and I've always looked for new ways to depict them to relieve the boredom. A public figure can become a symbol. I get a particular satisfaction from drawing politicians as animals. I saw Harold Wilson as a crafty old warty toad, puffing and swelling with self-congratulatory pride. James Callaghan was a sly old pig, snuffling and snouting for truffles in the political sty. Enoch Powell was the Hound of the Baskervilles, baying for immigrants' blood. Edward Heath became a beached whale. Richard Nixon was the old rogue Republican elephant, a sad, sagging leather sack hung on whitened bones, bleached in the heat of the Watergate sun. I drew George Bush (Dubya) as a bewildered ape, his close-set eyes beneath a wrinkled and puzzled brow, his knuckles scraping the ground as he wandered aimlessly, his arse stuck out behind with 'Iraq' branded on his buttocks. All in the name of God. Permanently licking Bush's backside was his sidekick, the poodle Blair. Also, more recently, Putin – the unpredictable Russian bear, code name 'Novichok'. And now there's one of the worst of them all, the vain, pussy-grabbing Trump: a pile of horseshit. A 'shithole' president for sure, to use the word he used about African countries.

Yes, it all went very, very wrong in 2017. A rogue president moved into the White House. An immature bully, a vicious racist, a cruel misogynist, an arrogant bigot, an insecure braggart and a compulsive liar – altogether a very nasty piece of work. This awful man immediately became my muse. He inspired me. From his daily deranged utterings and appalling ways I produced drawing after drawing. It became a flood, a tsunami. It was the only way I could express the fear and horror I felt. How could it have happened? How irresponsible to put such a dangerous beast in the most powerful position in the world. One should never say 'never'. Now we have Prime Minister Boris – an ambitious, Machiavellian, foot-in-mouth clown.

Caricature comes as much from a study of the character. One could not portray Donald Trump as anything other than a raving idiot, a man who keeps losing it. It is not just a man with a big nose or big ears: a successful caricature should encompass the whole character. The way someone stands, walks, sits, talks and gesticulates can say a lot about who they are.

Do politicians hate being caricatured? Most of them love it. Swollen egos, thick skins and ambition. 'It's all a game,' Jeffrey Archer told me. Well, of course he is right. When a politician is caricatured in the national press it means he has arrived, he is now a person of note. Some object, though. Denis Healey once bore down upon me at the Labour Party Conference in Blackpool. 'Look!' he said, jabbing a finger in his mouth. 'My teeth are not – *not* – as big as you draw them!' They were. (Perhaps the iciest brush-off I've ever received came when I was sketching Prince Philip as he moved among invited guests at the Royal Geographical Society. As I glanced up from my sketch book an equerry blocked my view. 'You have incurred the Royal displeasure,' he hissed. I got the picture.)

I don't really want to meet the politicians I draw. I might dislike them personally, which should be irrelevant; I need to make drawings of them from a distance, which show what is wrong with their policies, or their personalities. Inevitably, on occasion paths have crossed. Invited to spend a week with some friends in Tuscany one year we found one of the other guests was David Blunkett, the former Labour Home Secretary. David is blind, so I found myself offering my arm and guiding the man I had unkindly caricatured so many times over the rocky Tuscan hillsides on walks. We chatted about this. He didn't seem upset by my drawings of him – but then he'd never seen them.

Whatever the subject, I have always drawn without reservation. They become objects, graphic puzzles that have to be captured on the paper. I don't mean that I have no feelings for them – on the contrary, at the time of drawing my feelings are usually running high – but the effort to capture it all on paper doesn't leave room for any worry as to what people will think. But after they are finished there are times when I would rather avoid my subjects.

One hot August afternoon in the mid 1990s I happened to be crossing the concourse at Victoria station when a small man in a crumpled mac walking towards me made me look again. Could it be? As he passed I stopped, turned and followed him out of curiosity. I overtook him, turned again and walked towards him once more. It was! Now I could see him clearly, I knew it was Ian Smith, the tyrant of Rhodesia. Out of context so ordinary and insignificant. I watched as he disappeared into the anonymity of the swirling crowds and was gone for ever.

I was always accused of being unfair to Ian Smith when I drew him for *Private Eye*. He had lost an eye as a Spitfire pilot in World War Two so it was thought unfair that I drew him with one eye. What else could I do, dammit? He only had one eye – to give him two would have been an insult.

While I was in Rhodesia during Smith's reign I was at a

barbecue and was surrounded by a group of men who took me to task about my drawings of him in *Private Eye*. One of them was very angry, asking me what I thought they should do about the African unrest. 'I would say you've had a good run,' I told him. 'Why don't you get out?'

'If you keep on like that,' he said chillingly, 'you'll find yourself swinging from a tree.'

I remember one event when Alan Coren and I dodged to one side, laughing together. While everyone else was trying to meet Princess Margaret, he and I were trying to avoid her. On another occasion I did come face to face with her when Jane and I were invited to dine at Kensington Palace. Seeing a young gardener at work at the house next door to ours (my garden was an untidy disgrace at the time), I called to him and asked if he could pop round later and give me a quote on putting it in order. The gardener turned out to be Roddy Llewellyn, at that time (in the seventies) Princess Margaret's 'boyfriend'. I accepted the quote and Roddy became a regular visitor to Cheyne Walk, turning up with forks, spades and plants, making the garden look trim. We got on well, and one day Roddy invited us to dinner with Her Royal Highness. He warned us to call her 'mam' like 'spam' not 'marm' like 'charm'.

On the appointed day Jane and I arrived at Kensington Palace in our car. The policeman at the gate knew nothing about us but spoke to someone on the telephone and then told us to drive on to the next checkpoint. Another policeman, another phone call. This time we were told to go up to the house and ring the bell. We parked in a silent, empty courtyard and approached the imposing front door. It was dark. Feeling apprehensive, we rang the bell. Silence. Dare not ring it again. Suddenly the door was flung open. There stood the Princess looking every bit like Lewis Carroll's Red Queen.

'Yes?'

Jane had met her before, so I pushed her ahead of me.

'Excuse me, ma'am, but we believe we were invited to dinner tonight?'

'What? No! That's tomorrow night!'

'Oh God! So sorry, ma'am, Roddy told us tonight.'

'Oh, Roddy is such a Noddy.'

Awkward silence. We weren't sure quite what to do.

'Oh well, since you're here you'd better come in for a drink,' said the Princess.

In we went. The room smelled slightly musty. She was obviously on her own and a tiny bit tipsy.

'Help yourself to a drink.' She indicated a table laden with enough booze to serve the British Army. 'And get me one too – gin and tonic.'

I poured her a large G&T and we chatted awkwardly.

We went back the following night for the planned dinner, this time with Roddy also present. It was an interesting but difficult evening. The Princess had a reputation for pulling rank. I felt a bit embarrassed as I had recently drawn her as a warthog.

Many years later Roddy asked me for a copy of another drawing I had made of Margaret in *Private Eye*, where the Princess clutched Roddy to her breast like a much-loved cuddly toy. Of course I sent it.

In my film *Scarfe on Scarfe*, I had filmed a drawing showing Rhodesian Premier Ian Smith hanging the Queen by the neck. Shortly afterwards we met Princess Anne at a charity event. 'I really enjoyed your TV programme,' she told me, 'but did I see Mummy hanging from a tree?' Bang went my knighthood on the spot.

I never met Mrs Thatcher, but she was my muse for a very long time. I could always draw her as something cutting, sharp, acerbic and cold. An axe, scissors, dagger. She didn't seem to understand those who could not fend for themselves. The only time I saw her cry was when she was toppled as prime minister. My favourite depiction of her was a drawing I called 'The Torydactyl'. She flies through a yellow primeval sky with her razor-sharp beak, her leathery wings beating the air, her gimlet eye picking out vulnerable prey below. If they can't take care of themselves they deserve to die, she thinks, and then, swiftly and mercilessly, she swoops with her blood-red talons extended.

Occasionally, even extreme caricatures seem to be admired by their subjects. Hugh Hefner bought a lithograph I had made of him masturbating with a rolled-up copy of *Playboy* in place of his penis. It hung behind his desk at the Playboy mansion in Chicago – I know because I saw it there during a visit to the house some time later. I didn't meet him but the house itself was remarkably small considering its reputation. He was said to keep his selective harem of Playboy bunnies there. #MeToo, where were you?

In the early seventies when I worked briefly for the girlie porn magazine *Oui*, which was part of the Playboy organisation, they put me up at the Playboy Hotel. It was so tacky, with stained plastic leopard-skin bed covers and mirrors on the ceiling, that I moved out immediately to another at my own expense.

Politicians love to have their fame captured in stone or marble but if I was going three-dimensional it seemed right to me to make these ambitious creatures in papier-mâché and cloth, as, like my newspaper cartoons, they were transitory materials. Here today, gone tomorrow. In the late sixties they said that John Lindsay, Mayor of New York, was destined for high office. He told the citizens there were too many cars in New York and they should take to cycling. I made a sculpture of him riding a real bicycle for my exhibition in New York. Unfortunately mice, beetles and time had their way with the sculpture. As for the real John Lindsay, I have not heard of him since but his bicycle was very useful – I rode it for years.

David Frost went the same way. I also made a life-sized

papier-mâché figure of him at his request which he thought would be amusing to have sitting at his desk on *The Frost Report*. (I once drew a portrait of Shirley Bassey showing her cleavage back and front live on Frost's show – much squealing from Shirley.) The idea was simply that my model should be sitting in the host's (David's) chair when the show opened. After the show the model was returned to my studio where it sat in a corner, dressed in his blazer and grey flannels. Some months later, working late into the night in my studio, my customary bottle of Jack Daniel's on my desk among my pens, brushes and inks, I heard a scuttling and scratching sound. Was I imagining it? Too much to drink? It was coming from my sculpture of David, and I realised, horror of horrors, that Frost had a nest of mice in his head. Poor David. I couldn't let them stay. The next evening I told my assistant Ed to take the whole life-size figure across the road to get rid of the mice. At twilight he left the house cradling David in his arms. After laying him on the pavement alongside the small park opposite, he started to wallop him with a broom. As the mice bolted, a taxi skidded to a halt in the middle of the road.

'Oi!' shouted the driver, leaning out of his window. 'Leave that old geezer alone!'

Sitting in the front row at the Conservative Party Conference I looked up to see Lord Carrington imitating my facial expressions. Somewhat like an impersonator I try to find an exaggerated version of the person I'm drawing so I can put down their main characteristics on to the paper. This often means mimicking to myself the way they move, laugh or speak as I draw – and Carrington had noticed my odd facial expressions as I muttered in what I thought were his plummy, upper class tones.

I I

The Greatest Train Set

The film director Michael Winner called to ask if I was free for dinner. He had a fan of mine staying with him who wanted to meet me, so the following week I made my way to Michael's splendid mansion on Melbury Road in Holland Park.

My fan was the actor Michael J. Pollard, who had asked to meet me and one other person, the actor David Warner, while on a visit to London. The only other guest at that dinner was Warren Beatty. There was good conversation, food and wine, and after too much of the latter I began to heckle Warren about his and Pollard's recent film, *Bonnie and Clyde*. I drunkenly accused him of glorifying violence and making gratuitous entertainment out of horror. What a pain in the arse I must have been. He was extremely patient and tolerant, answering my irritating tirade calmly like a man answering a child. I'm embarrassed when I think about it. What a prat! I had a preoccupation with violence. Michael Winner asked why, with my imagination, I didn't make films. He said it was very easy. Once you had the ideas and the vision it was simply a matter of hiring the right technicians. They would do the work.

In 1968 I was asked to make a documentary about my work by the BBC and I realised what he meant. A film director is like the conductor of an orchestra. Each musician knows his instrument and hopefully is professional enough to want to give a good performance. *I Think I See Violence All Around Me* was the world seen from my viewpoint; written and directed by me and John Irvin, it formed one of a series of BBC films called *One Pair of Eyes*, in which personalities explored their own life and thoughts. I took as my theme what I saw as the violent state of the world. I interspersed the live action with animation, drawn under a rostrum camera — the same method I later used to draw the titles for *Yes Minister*.

Traditional animation, conveying movement by filming thousands of individual, hand drawn and coloured pictures, is labour-intensive, skilled and expensive, not the sort of money BBC budgets can run to, so I had to use more economical animation methods. The BBC booked me several days in their rostrum camera unit and I spent hours making drawings and filming them as I added to them, line by line. The camera was fixed and pointed downwards towards the drawing board. I would make one or two pen strokes on my drawing, remove my hand and take two frames on old celluloid film. Then two more strokes, and two more frames, and so on. When the film was run at normal speed with no sign of my hand, the drawing appeared to be drawing itself, line by line. In one drawing I drew a skeleton in this manner and then gradually built up the muscles, sinews and flesh on top of his bones until he looked like a complete man. In a scene in the final film (about a nuclear explosion) I ran the film backwards and it appeared that my normal man was flayed alive, his flesh torn from his bones – all jolly stuff. On top of which stomachs split open. Entrails spilled out. Flowers grew from horrific monsters. President Johnson defecated bombs over Vietnam and napalm roasted the countryside. My self-portrait decomposed in five seconds flat, but the thing that upset the BBC most was Harold Wilson saying, 'Over the years many people have changed their position' – the problem being that he was saying it out of his bottom. John and I had a serious meeting about this with the heads of department at BBC Television Centre. Richard Cawston, head of documentaries, wanted it taken out. I refused. I was pleased with the animated anus lip-sync. Stalemate. Then compromise. Harold would appear with a small censored notice on his bottom. Honour all round. A small animated hand arose from the bottom of the screen and pulled down a notice headed 'Censored'. It looked funnier than ever. It's a strange business, making films. It is a corporate enterprise. Unlike writers, artists or composers, who need only a pen or pencil to express themselves, the director has to deal with a whole string of people before he can see a result. Communication is a big issue.

For example, in an effort to capture what he imagined was my lifestyle of E-Types and glamorous blondes in the 'swinging sixties', John had booked Alvaro's, the trendiest restaurant on the King's Road, Chelsea. The conceit was that I should be surrounded by the celebrity diners who came into lunch that day. The lights were set, sound was checked, and then we waited . . . and we waited. No diners appeared. One o'clock – surely they should be flocking in? One-thirty. No one. Surely someone wanted lunch that day? Something must be wrong.

'Where are the customers?' said John.

'No customers,' replied Alvaro. 'I've closed the restaurant to the public. No punters would want to come in while your cameras are here. I thought you just wanted the restaurant.'

The cameraman, who had spent a considerable amount of time lighting the room, exploded and turned in frustration on the director: 'You couldn't organise a fucking nail into a block of wood!'

'Come outside and say that!' said John.

They disappeared into the street. We all looked at one another. Fisticuffs? What now? I could see my film going down the drain. Half an hour later they came back the best of friends. They'd had a couple of pints in the Chelsea Potter. We all packed up and called it a day.

During the making of *I Think I See Violence All Around Me*, we decided to film in an abattoir. I was to sketch the scene. I have not forgotten that day. On a cold November morning a steady stream of cattle trucks packed with confused cows arrived at the abattoir. In the yard outside, the soft-eyed creatures were beaten off trucks with sticks down wooden ramps, slipping and sliding in their own excrement, and herded inside, nose to tail, down a narrow corridor between two iron fences. The animals became restless, jostling one another, showing the whites of their eyes, as they reached the end of their days. They knew it, they smelled it. The fear ran back through the chain and a terrible cacophony of lowing broke out. An iron head clamp encircled their necks and they were trapped, pinioned, they couldn't escape. Then a young lad with sweaty shoulder-length hair shot them through the temple with a bolt gun to the brain. These living, breathing, wonderful creatures collapsed on to the bloody wet concrete like giant sacks of coals. There they were skinned and decapitated. It was shocking. One minute alive, the next nothing. Chains were then attached to their hind legs and they were winched to the ceiling. Another butcher plunged a knife into their undersides and slit their stomachs from top to bottom. Bellies split, their innards – lungs, heart and intestines – spilled steaming on to the concrete. Rivulets of blood ran down the gullies. Another bloodied figure familiar with death sawed the empty rib cage down the spine until the two halves of the cow swung apart and hung separately. From living creature to those half carcasses we see hanging in a butcher's shop took about five minutes. Smithfield-like porters carried half a cow each away on their shoulders to be stacked for transportation to our plates.

I couldn't eat meat for many months after that day. However, over time many horrors fade and I am not a vegetarian today. Most of us have become immune to violence. We may sit eating our dinner and watching the most distressing scenes on the television news. Starving babies, soldiers in battle, refugee camps.

In 1969 the renowned film director Michael Powell asked me to art-direct the film he was going to make of Shakespeare's last great play, *The Tempest*. He had renamed it *The Magic Island* and cast James Mason as Prospero, Mia Farrow as Miranda and Topol as Caliban. This was a great opportunity and I was tremendously excited as Michael had a great track record of working in collaboration with artists on classic films he'd made with Emeric Pressburger: *The Red Shoes*, *The Life and Times of Colonel Blimp* and *A Matter of Life and Death*.

James, Michael and I met regularly in Cheyne Walk or at the Savile Club to discuss and work on the script. I made many production designs, some of which I still have today. I was a great James Mason fan and had admired many of his roles from Captain Nemo to Rommel. Not only a terrific actor, he was also charming and charismatic. To be working with him was an honour. But after many months of working on the script and designs the project collapsed when the backers withdrew the money. Many films never end up being made; it's a fickle, precarious business.

I didn't make another film for a few years, but in 1971 Norman Swallow, a well-respected producer at the BBC, thought I should direct a film about William Hogarth, the eighteenth-century satirical artist. 'I think we should make a film about Hogarth,' said Norman. 'Don't you?' There had been idle talk when I first came to prominence that I was the 'New Hogarth'. Flattering, but complete nonsense. He's a great hero of mine, but I couldn't compare myself to him.

Hogarth recorded life around him. His famous series – *A Rake's Progress*, *Marriage à la Mode* and *Industry and Idleness* – show the human race with all its fallibilities and pitfalls: lust, greed, drunkenness, gambling, pimping, prostitution, pious evil Churchmen and crippling poverty. These were all meticulously recorded in intimate detail in beautifully etched prints that could be bought by the eighteenth-century man in the street. The wonderful original paintings can currently be seen at the Sir John Soane's Museum at Lincoln's Inn in London. I would urge anyone to go to see them.

Norman was a very well-liked, gentle man, and he coaxed and coached me in every way. He introduced me to the Soane's Museum, suggested suitably eighteenth-century locations such as the Lamb & Flag pub and St Paul's Church in Covent Garden. He also suggested we use Handel's music. Then he handed the reins to me. It was to be my view of Hogarth.

On the first day of filming, in a fit of artistic endeavour, I ran out of the gentleman's lavatory in Covent Garden with a bucket of water and threw it over the pavement hoping it would look as though it had been raining. Five actors in eighteenth-century costume looked on.

'Do I shout "action"?' I asked Norman.

'If you like,' he said.

'Turn over,' said Mike, the cameraman.

'Action!' I shouted.

The five eighteenth-century gentlemen started leapfrogging among the colonnades of St Paul's Church, laughing and shouting. It was wonderful – I was directing actors for the first time. I felt happy. Such power.

A lorry full of twentieth-century vegetables backed across the scene. Covent Garden market was starting work. 'Cut!' I shouted in panic. This was not supposed to happen.

'No, don't cut,' said Norman. 'Get what you can while you can. You're not going to stop Covent Garden porters working.'

I wanted to shoot Hogarth's Peregrination, a journey he had taken with four friends from London to Rochester in Kent. It was my first attempt at filming drama. After dark I took the crew and the actors down to the foreshore of the Thames near Blackfriars Bridge and set them afloat in a wooden dinghy. I called 'action' and they rowed merrily into the centre of the river. The water seemed to be moving faster where they were. I called them back, but the tide quickened and the boat began to be carried away sideways on the racing water, off into the gloom and down-river. I truly began to panic. All five men were rowing with all their might, oars splashing and crashing through the murky, turbulent water, but some couldn't row well – they were actors after all – and they seemed to be making no headway. I ran alongside them on the muddy shore, slipping and sliding and helplessly shouting instructions. Luckily one of them was a burly Scotsman and I believe it was his strength that finally brought the boat to shore. I realised that as a director I had the ultimate responsibility for these actors. It isn't all fun.

I had the five actors, still dressed up, romping around the Kent countryside. Silly business. I put them in a field with some sheep.

'Action!'

'Just a minute,' they said. 'What shall we say?'

'Oh, anything you like – action!'

'But what shall we do?' they said.

'Just go over there and run about,' I said, getting irrita-ble. 'Action!'

I had my comeuppance when I got the rushes back to my cutting room in Ealing. They were almost unusable.

I changed tack. What would Hogarth be if he were alive today? An artist? A writer? A photographer? A television reporter? I set about exploring these possibilities in what I hoped were

Hogarthian contexts: I filmed in the gay Coleherne Arms pub in Earl's Court, bars, gambling establishments, the Playboy club. My cameraman and I managed to bluff our way into Boodle's Club in St James's by mentioning the name Hogarth (very acceptable) and filmed a private dinner given by members of the medical profession. Very jolly, very Hogarthian.

'May we offer you a brandy?' asked one member.

'No, thank you,' I said. 'I've just bought one myself.'

'Good God, bought one yourself?' he said. 'Must say, the standards of this club have gone down.'

Yes, very Hogarthian.

In the mid-eighties it was announced that my previous pictorial autobiography was to be turned into a TV film by the cutting-edge documentary and arts programme *Arena*, under the guidance of Alan Yentob, who was then head of Music and Arts at the BBC. My producer was Anthony Wall, whom I immediately liked. He was insistent that I should direct the film, which was terrific. The *Arena* office was open plan and the production team was legendary for being arty and crafty – and for its drunken Christmas parties where the floor was awash with beer.

The film, *Scarfe on Scarfe*, dealt with the two sides of my character – the repressed banker socialite versus my rebellious artistic nature. I began in black tie, delivering a typically BBC pompous po-faced diatribe about 'Art' to camera. Violently the door bursts open and my 'other self' – a paint-spattered artist – erupts into the room shouting 'Bollocks!' (Several correspondents later said this was the first time the word had been uttered on the BBC and wondered if it was now official policy? There has certainly been more bollocks on television since.)

Anthony said that my biography had a feeling of the Ealing comedy *Kind Hearts and Coronets* about it, and thought we should incorporate an element of that. I am a great fan of this witty film in which Dennis Price gradually murders his way up the family tree until he is in line for the family inheritance, but I could not see the connection. Instead I had a vision of painting pictures from my life like graffiti on the walls of a disused house with dramatic reconstructions interspersed. An enormous white four-walled set was built at Ealing Studios to be my room, and filming began. I spent an exhausting but enjoyable week painting my life on these four walls, talking to camera and playing all the parts – including one scene where my 'artistic self' drenched my black-tied socialite self in paint. Great fun.

I couldn't think how to end my film and day by day we were running out of time. On the last day I warned my brilliant cameraman, Chris Seager, about what I intended to do. I took a full bucket of red paint and threw it all over my painted walls, followed by another bucket of yellow, and obliterated all the work as some sort of statement. It seemed to mean something – I'm not quite sure what, but it was definitely an ending. One critic called it 'a "Whistlerean" comment'.

I was certain I wouldn't win when the film was nominated for a BAFTA Award. At the ceremony Alan Yentob sat next to me. I was still sure I wouldn't get the award, until the moment grew nearer and I began to think . . . maybe? Then I distantly heard the words 'And the winner is . . . Gerald Scarfe for his film *Scarfe on Scarfe*.' My mind floated away and outside of myself. I looked down as I rose to my feet. Jane kissed me. I found myself on the podium holding my award. Humphrey Burton, who presented it, asked if I would like to say a few words. A voice said, 'I want to thank my producer Anthony Wall . . . ' I stumbled. 'And my cameraman . . . ' My mind went blank. 'My cameraman without whom I could not have made this film . . . ' I heard distant laughter in the hall. 'You couldn't remember my name, could you?' said Chris when I met him afterwards. But I was lucky to have him. His beautiful images made the film look classy.

The house in La Bourboule, Auvergne, France, where I was sent for asthma treatment

Margaret Thatcher as the Torydactyl

Prototype drawing for the Marching Hammers from *Pink Floyd The Wall*

Location filming in Dorset with Alan Parker for *Pink Floyd The Wall*, 1981

I bought myself a nice leather jacket and some jeans and became rock and roll overnight

Me and Peter Hall during the production of *Born Again* at the Chichester Festival Theatre – an adaptation of Ionesco's *Rhinoceros*, 1990

Opening night of *Orpheus in the Underworld* at the English National Opera, 1985

Opening night of *The Magic Flute* at LA Opera, 1991

Filming *Scarfe on Scarfe* at Ealing Studios, 1986

At Walt Disney Studios in California with some of my designs for *Hercules*, during production in 1996

On *The Andrew Marr Show* with then leadership hopefuls David Cameron and David Davis, 2006

With Roger Waters in New York

My purpose-built studio at the top of the house in Cheyne Walk

With Jane

That BAFTA was a sea change. Suddenly I was an award-winning film director, and people began to offer me jobs. One such was Eddie Mirzoeff, the renowned film-maker who produced the well-regarded documentary programme *40 Minutes*. He invited me to write, direct and appear in a film about follies. Lucinda Lambton had been lined up to make it but it was snatched away by Eddie and offered to me. My star was rising in the television world.

As a concept for the programme I decided to build my own folly in a field and to travel around Britain getting ideas from existing follies. Follies can take any form but the most familiar ones are those built on the estates of eighteenth-century gentlemen. Those who wanted to improve the view from their drawing-room window would not only move the landscape around by having hundreds of men with shovels build hills and plant woods, they would also build in that landscape a mock Greek temple or old ruin to be reflected in the newly dug-out lake. They come in many forms, from pineapples to grottoes.

On my quest to discover more about follies I thought it would suit the folly of the programme if I travelled on the backs of various exotic animals. I thought an elephant would make a surreal sight if I rode it over a motorway bridge. So there I was, high above the thundering traffic of the A3, perched precariously on the back of my elephant. Startled motorists below swerved and honked their horns. I thought later that maybe I should have put the sound of a crash on the soundtrack – maybe too macabre. In another section of the film I rode a llama. Her owner said, instructionally and helpfully, 'Don't let her get her teeth into your leg. They point backwards and once they are in they are hard to get out.' I took care. Ivy the camel was the most difficult of animals to guide. I found out that camels tend to go where they wish, not necessarily in the direction you want them to. But she made an inspirational model and I constructed my folly in the shape of a camel. It still stands today, covered in ivy.

Any folly worth its salt should have a resident hermit, so to that end and for the purposes of the film we put an advertisement in *The Times*, 'Hermit Wanted for Live-in Folly', and filmed the interviews. Well, who should turn up and apply but my old friend Bob Geldof? His hair was already hermit-like so we stripped him to his underpants and gave him an old blanket to wrap around himself to keep out the chill night air, and off he went to his new home. There was no glass in the windows and no roof. In the conceit of the programme he liked the folly but said he thought it was 'a bit rough'.

'I thought you hermits liked it rough,' I said.

'Well,' Bob came back, 'there's rough and there's rough.'

My friend Terry Jones, of *Monty Python* fame, owed me a favour. I had illustrated his book of *Guardian* articles, *Attacks of Opinion*, so I roped him in to play Mad Jack Fuller for the film. Mad Jack was an eighteenth-century country landowner who loved a wager. Legend has it that one drunken evening when Mad Jack and his friends were at dinner he bet that one could see the spire of St Giles Church, Dallington, from the bedroom window of his house in Brightling, East Sussex. They all trooped upstairs to check. As it was getting dark no one could see, but he bet that the next day he would be proved correct. No one believed him, thinking that St Giles was too far away, so they took the wager. That night Jack had a false spire built on the horizon and cleaned them out! The other gamblers must still have been drunk to fall for such a simple trick. Also known as Fuller's Point, this folly is thirty-five-feet tall and still standing today, having been used as a cottage and a machine-gun post in the Second World War.

We dressed Terry, Jane and several other actors and crew in eighteenth-century garb from Berman's, the costume hire company. A make-up artist, as a favour, did the hair and gave the men whiskers. It was lit and filmed beautifully as ever by Chris Seager, all on a shoestring. We shot the dinner party scene with Terry making up the dialogue and Jane busking along.

I was also lucky to get a dear old actor called Robin Bailey, who had worked with Jane, to take part. I roped him in to play an eccentric who lived in the woods. For the film, Robin wore a foxtail hat and some pink pyjamas with circles on them – why I can't recall. Robin wasn't at all sure about the whole thing and I don't blame him. However, the scene I had devised was that Robin's character would meet a beautiful young girl, clothed only in a flimsy see-through robe, in the woods. He slips the diaphanous garment from her shoulders and she stands before him, naked. After I'd shot the scene Robin's doubts had disappeared and he seemed more cheerful. A little later he took me aside. 'Thank you, thank you so much, dear boy, I didn't think I'd ever see them again.'

Altogether it was a very peculiar film and intended to be so. But when I showed the rough cut to Eddie he clapped his hands in delight. 'It's like a soufflé,' he said. Excited and encouraged, I went back to the cutting room and added more jokes and much more film. At the next showing Eddie said, 'Oh no! What have you done? You've wrecked it. It was like a soufflé and now it's like a heavy suet pudding.' I learned the lesson once again that less is more. I went back to the cutting room and took out all the extra film that I had put in the day before. The soufflé rose again.

The head of documentaries, Will Wyatt, wrote me a very supportive letter and put out a directive to other BBC film makers to be more inventive in their interviewing techniques.

Discussing *Scarfe's Follies* on the TV programme *Late Night Line Up*, Jonathan Meades, who went on to make similar films himself, supported me. Spike Milligan, who didn't like the film, said it must have cost a fortune. It didn't – it came in on budget simply because no one got paid. Spike, not knowing this, remarked, 'Nice bloke, but back to the drawing board, Scarfe' – an economically worded reprimand that put me in mind of my appearance on the inaugural episode of *The South Bank Show* back in 1978, when I was interviewed by Melvyn Bragg alongside Germaine Greer.

Germaine and I had been to see several arts events, an exhibition, a show and a film. I was trying out my relatively new 'celebrity' and was very nervous. I had bought myself an expensive blue shirt for the occasion but it wasn't helping. I was overawed and tongue-tied. The programme was a nightmare for me. Later, the brilliant and funny Clive James wrote in the *Observer*, 'Melvyn's guest critics were fully up to the standards of glamour established by his prospectus. Germaine Greer had her hair in a frizz and Gerald Scarfe sported a blue open-neck Yves St Laurent shirt exactly matching his eyes. A touch of make-up ensured that his expanse of bare chest did not flare for the camera.' James went on, 'Gerald didn't think much of the movie, but somehow lacked the words to tell us why.' Years later I was invited back, to make a film about my time working with Disney.

After *Scarfe's Follies* I continued to make films with Eddie Mirzoeff. Ever since my bed-ridden radio-listening days as a child I'd been fascinated by music hall – the programme *Workers' Playtime* and stars in that tradition such as Russ Conway, Winifred Atwell, Arthur Askey, Archie Andrews and Vic Oliver. So when Eddie said he wanted to make a film about Max Miller I put myself forward. We called it *I Like the Girls Who Do* after Max's famous monologue.

Max notoriously had two sets of stories – clean ones in the 'white' book, rude ones in the 'blue' book. 'Which one would you like?' Max asked the audience. 'The blue book!' they would chorus. One of his jokes: Two girls were talking about a man they fancied. One girl observed, 'Such a gentleman, doesn't he dress nice?' 'Yes, and so quickly,' said the other.

Max worked in difficult times for 'blue' jokes. What was acceptable in the music hall was not accepted by the BBC. In the thirties an internal BBC directive banned all broadcasts of jokes about lavatories, effeminacy in men, chambermaids, fig leaves, prostitution, lodgers, commercial travellers, ladies underwear . . .

This meant that there was very little film of Max himself, so I knew I would have to come up with an idea to compensate. I decided to set the whole film on the stage of the Hackney Empire, an original music hall venue, and persuaded the stars of those days to tell their stories. I interviewed seasoned stars from music hall days: Mike and Bernie Winters, Tommy Trinder, Max Wall and Jean Kent. We had a unicyclist, a lady playing spoons, occasional reconstructions and outside locations in Brighton, where Max lived. I desperately wanted to interview Lonnie Donegan for the programme, being a great fan, and eventually he agreed. Lonnie was the king of skiffle, a style of music played on improvised instruments – washboards, tea chests, anything they could get their hands on. After the interview I asked him, nay begged him, to sing 'Rock Island Line', his famous hit. He said no – he had not done it for some time and was a bit rusty. I pleaded with him again and he reluctantly gave in. We filmed a couple of takes of 'Rock Island Line' with all his energetic movement and I thanked him heartily. But when I came to edit the programme I found I had so much very good material that there was no room for Lonnie. I had to write a difficult letter to him to explain that splendid though his performance was (and it was) there was simply no room for anything of that length, and to my great sadness he would not be appearing in the programme. I did start the letter by saying that as someone who had worked in the industry all his life he would understand my dilemma, but I'm not sure that he did – and it would still have hurt. I never heard from him again. That, as they say, is show business.

I was able to use some of Max's saucier stories. In one he was walking along a narrow mountainside path with a sheer drop to one side when he met a naked woman. There was no room to pass. 'I didn't know whether to block her passage or toss myself off,' said Max.

At one point during the filming of *I Like the Girls Who Do* I heard a confusion and looked up to see Roy Hudd (who was to take part in the reminiscences) storming down the centre aisle shouting 'Travesty! Travesty!' or some such. I was furious. I was in the middle of shooting six Max Miller impersonators in a line across the stage, saying things like 'Here, no listen' and 'Don't be filthy'. Roy had just arrived, seen six impersonators on the stage and thought how denigrating it was to the great Max Miller. He seemed to see himself as the self-appointed keeper of Max's dignity. Calming him down, I explained that the idea was to show that so great was Max, all these years later he was still revered and impersonated by a younger generation.

I always adored the movies, and telling stories in picture and dialogue was completely up my street. My mother's observation still rang in my ears: 'Pictures, pictures, that's all you think about.' And the BAFTA kept on opening doors for me; it meant I was seen as a film-maker and director. A delightful producer, Katie Lander, asked me to direct three episodes of a series with a comedian I'd never heard of, Rowland Rivron, for Jonathan Ross's production company Channel X. The other three were to be directed by John Stroud, the director of *Spitting Image*. It gave me the opportunity to direct drama which I dearly wanted to move towards. Jonathan invited me to his house in Kentish Town, where I met his wife and his extraordinary, dynamic mother – clearly the driving force of the family. I liked them all and I liked Katie very much. I'd never directed comedy before and there it was on a plate – so yes, I said, of course I'd do it.

The series, *Set of Six*, was devised by Katie and Rivron in a mock-documentary style with moving cameras, as though the film had been made 'on the hoof', on the spur of the moment. Although they were scripted, the dialogue would be improvised. In one episode, Rivron played the part of a tramp down on his luck on the streets of London. The make-up and costume departments made him look a very convincing down-and-out with long dirty hair and beard, wearing torn and grimy clothes. We were filming with him in this get-up just off Piccadilly in Jermyn Street when a real down-and-out stormed up effing and blinding. 'What the fuck do you think you're doing? Isn't there enough fucking misery in the world without you fucking making it up!' He was right. I felt ashamed, but by this time he was wrestling with the cameraman who was trying to protect his camera which the man was determined to destroy. Eventually the guy wandered off, still effing and blinding. An unpleasant episode that really made me think how – and if – we should make films about other people's misfortunes.

I didn't like Rowland Rivron very much and didn't think he was funny, so you might say accepting the job was a mistake – and, well, so it was. Early in the shooting at a boozy company dinner, Rivron thought I had made fun of him and put him down. He asked me to come outside for a fight. I refused. The thought of me, the director, rolling around in an undignified drunken heap on the ground in front of the entire company didn't appeal. I should have got out then – but I felt I should be professional and not let Katie down. Katie had a strong word with Rivron, telling him any more of that nonsense and there would be no series. The filming continued, and thereafter he did what he was told, and we pretended to get on.

I went on to make two further episodes, with Rivron playing a boxer and then a photographer. Katie also asked me to make a series with Jo Brand, who was not universally known at that point. After my experience with Rowland I declined. Then Katie suggested I make a series with Ruby Wax. Ruby and I met and got on well but I wasn't sure I wanted to go on making films, much as I liked the obvious power and the fun of collaboration. They took so bloody long to come to fruition and, after all, I was an artist. How was it that I was making films? But then Alan Yentob, who had been overall producer of my *Scarfe on Scarfe* film and was now controller of BBC Two, offered me a series of my own. I felt I couldn't refuse that.

A little later I met Ruby at a BBC party.

'What happened?' she said. 'You never got back to me.'

'Sorry, Ruby, but Alan gave me a series of my own.'

Ruby was quite rightly peeved. Sorry, Ruby.

Following the success of *Scarfe on Scarfe*, the new series followed the same format, all beginning with *Scarfe on* . . . I tried to take an off-beat approach and make visually quirky films with wit and humour. I am understandably a visual director, very much concerned with what you see, whereas most BBC documentary directors, with academic backgrounds, appeared to me to be more concerned with the words.

In the early 1990s the art world went mad again. The Japanese were paying insane amounts for impressionists, and I think it is fair to say that it was a case of the emperor's new clothes. As an artist I was to give some insight into this madness in *Scarfe on Art*. In some instances art is purely a commodity, an investment. Many of the buyers would not hang their Monets over the mantelpiece – they were far too valuable – they would pop them into a vault immediately and hang a copy over the mantelpiece. I interviewed Suzie, whose job it was to make copies of old masters. She seemed to be able to turn her talent to being a legally licensed forger. She could copy any masterpiece to decorate your home, whether or not you had the original secured in your safe.

I thought it would be fun to hang a Picasso on a railing on the Bayswater Road among all the other paintings regularly displayed there and offered for sale, and jokingly asked the art dealer Leslie Waddington if I could borrow a Picasso. To my amazement he said yes and generously lent me a portrait about a foot square. He said it was worth about half a million and to please take care of it. It was hung alongside seascapes and sticky technicolour sunsets and we filmed people's reactions to see whether they recognised the Picasso as priceless, 'important' art or not. Not surprisingly, no one did. I also displayed an abstract I had painted, *Gauguin's*

Mother, and another canvas I'd created by sitting naked in a large pool of blue oil paint and then sitting down on a blank canvas. I called the resulting picture *Blue Moons*. None of them sold. At the end of the project I'm ashamed to say I forgot about the Picasso and left it in the boot of my car for the best part of a week before guiltily returning it to Leslie without mentioning where it had spent the past few days.

When the next film went out, my local butcher told me he'd never seen anything like it. I certainly had a great time directing it, and although writing the script with Patrick Barlow was challenging and I never felt entirely happy with it, *Scarfe on Sex* was one of the most enjoyable films I've made. I had a terrific team around me, including Vanessa Courtney who had the amazing ability to find, on a small BBC budget, pretty much anything I asked for – a stripper, a zebra, a tube train. The incredibly well-organised Sally George was my producer – she was great fun. Everyone had a terrific sense of humour. The premise of the film was that I would sally forth to discover the parameters of sex. I had my libido personified in the form of a 'cheeky' snake which I wore like a sleeve on my right arm and operated like a puppet, moving his mouth from inside with my hand. It was voiced by Martin Jarvis. I also used the rhino with two actors inside it that I had designed for Peter Hall's production of *Born Again* in Chichester. The rhinoceros represented full-blooded lust, and there was an awkward incident when we were stopped by the police on Westminster Bridge at two a.m. and asked what we were doing with a rhino. Hard to explain really. But as soon as I said the word 'film' the policeman nodded wearily. He said we must get the rhino off the street immediately. The strange sight of the policemen escorting a lumbering rhinoceros over Westminster Bridge made me smile but I felt sorry for the poor actor who was the back half of our pantomime-horse rhino walking bent double over the other actor's backside.

I hired two actresses and told them they had been lucky enough to land the roles of 'tarts' – streetwalkers – in my film. They didn't seem thrilled but agreed to do it, such is the actor's desperation to work on screen. The idea was that in my examination of sex I should be accosted on a dark Soho street by two prostitutes. I called 'action' and the two women sidled up to me making lewd gestures and asking me whether I 'would like a good time, dearie'. At that very moment three real Soho sex workers erupted from a club doorway and told our two frightened thespians in no uncertain manner to 'piss off'; our ladies were on their 'bleedin' pitch' and I was *their* customer. I then showed them the camera and explained what we were doing, thanked them, and declined their kind offer as my sex life was well served, thank you.

In pursuit of the truth I stayed at an S&M bed and breakfast where one could get a full English plus bondage and *The Times* delivered to your room with morning tea. (For those of you who are interested, I'm sorry to tell you that this particular hotel is no longer in business.) It was there I found myself being turned on a spit wrapped in cling film. It wasn't my sort of thing but amusing for others to watch I suppose. Alan Yentob said he enjoyed it.

I was asked by an independent company to make a film about the brilliant German photographer Horst P. Horst. We filmed an interview with Horst in Oyster Bay, New York. He had met and photographed everyone of note in the twenties and thirties – Salvador Dalí, Picasso, Jean Cocteau, Greta Garbo. He was a gay man who loved women and photographed them erotically in delicious black and white for French *Vogue*. (During that trip, on my way through the New York *Vogue* office to interview Condé Nast editorial director Alexander Lieberman, who had known Horst in his *Vogue* days, I saw Anna Wintour's name on an open door. I went in and introduced myself. I discovered immediately, without a shadow of doubt, that you do not pop into Anna Wintour's office unannounced. She looked startled and outraged. When I mentioned that I knew her dad, Charles Wintour – whom I had met on several social occasions – and why I was there, she softened a bit and I backed out, as one would do with the Queen. After that interview with Horst, the producer Nicky and I flew to Paris to speak to those who had known him over the years: Jean Cocteau's lover, Jean Marais; a charming Paloma Picasso, Pablo's daughter; and a less charming Karl Lagerfeld, who kept me and the crew waiting many hours past the agreed interview time in *Vogue*'s Paris office. Eventually he swept in surrounded by an entourage of arse-lickers and toadies, and made some small sketches for me and the camera which he later tore to shreds. I know the feeling – when I am filmed I also destroy any drawing made during the filming. Otherwise people ask if they can have them.

We had booked ourselves into a small hotel in Montmartre. On my way to get a coffee and a croissant one morning, walking across the tiny reception area, the street door burst open and two bulky men in motorcycle gear and visored helmets burst in. I was the only person there except for the hotel manager and cashier behind the desk. One of the men pushed me against the reception desk, thrust a gun into my stomach and said in French, 'Don't move! Be quiet!' No doubt about it, I was scared. I experienced the same feeling of 'suspended reality' I'd had when held at gunpoint by the IRA in 1971. If those robbers were prepared to go this far, how much further would they go? The second man, also holding a gun, leapt over the reception desk, took the manager by the throat and pushed him violently against the wall. I felt as if I were in a film. He threw several black plastic bin bags at the cashier and told her to fill them fast. She did this without quibbling. I was staring fixedly at the wooden grain pattern on the top of the reception desk. I just wanted it to end, to go away. After what seemed like twenty minutes but which was probably only three, they left, mounted a motorbike and roared away through the Paris streets.

As they went out, Nicky came in through the revolving door from the street. 'Hi!' she said. 'How are you doing?'

'We've just been robbed!' I blurted out.

I later used this story with actors to start my film on the afterlife, *Scarfe in Paradise*, where in the same incident I was shot and died and thereafter went to examine what various religions thought happened after death.

I wrote, directed and appeared in most of my films – the ultimate ego trip. In stepping out in front of the camera, I may have thought I was entering Jane's world of acting, although she once said of my screen appearances, 'I don't know what it is you do, but it's not acting, it's something else.' Jealous, I suppose. I should have told her I had internalised my performance rather like Daniel Day-Lewis and distilled it into pure silver-screen magic.

Scarfe in Paradise was set in the departure hall of Stansted Airport, where different check-in desks represented various destinations in the next world – for Catholics, Jews, Buddhists; there was even an empty one for atheists with a 'desk closed' sign. In the background, the muzak of Mantovani's 'Charmaine' lamented our having to wait. I interviewed the Abbot of Dartmoor on a wild, rocky hillside in teeming rain. 'For God's sake get on with it!' he snapped, understandably calling on his maker. The fact that I had forgotten what I had brought him there for didn't help. The wind and rain were very disconcerting. I had to go back down the slippery hillside to ask my producer, Sally George, who was heavily pregnant and waiting in the car, what it was I'd forgotten to ask my interviewee. The Abbot was still alive when I got back, but only just. We brought in several genuine 'experts' – rabbis, priests and so forth – to see if they had any idea what happened next. They all thought they did, but I wasn't convinced.

Perhaps the most surreal moment I arranged was the arrival of Buddhist Flight 109, which was terrific fun. As I stood at the arrivals gate various Buddhists arrived back as zebras, llamas and camels.

There had been talk of a brilliant writer at the BBC called Richard Curtis. Eddie asked me if I would like to work with him, and I was very glad that I said yes: Richard was terrific to work with – funny and professional. I already had the film shot and edited on tape so Richard had to write the script to fit it. He said the most difficult part was running back and forth over the existing tape of the edited film, stopping it and writing appropriate dialogue to fit exactly into that space. But he did it brilliantly, and not only did his dialogue fit perfectly but he exactly caught my method of speech – it was very easy to read, and sounded like me. One of his lines was 'One of the great moments in life is death'.

I made several films with Richard until he moved on to bigger and better films: *Four Weddings and a Funeral* and *Notting Hill*. Meeting him later, I asked why he had abandoned me. 'Because you didn't pay me properly,' he said. I'm not sure he was joking.

I certainly was embarrassed by the meanness of BBC salaries. They paid peanuts. Martin Jarvis, who had been wonderful as the voice of my libidinous snake in *Scarfe on Sex*, was so angry that he refused his derisory fee and said he would rather do it for nothing. Which he did. Actors who appeared in my other films – including Ian McKellen, John Bird and Terry Jones – all performed for me out of kindness or because they were friends. I felt uncomfortable about this but these films were such passions of mine, and I could see no other way of accomplishing what I wanted. Ironically, it was thought that I had spent a huge amount of BBC cash hiring these stars. Not so.

By the time I was making my fifth film with Eddie, *Scarfe on Class*, his attitude had changed towards me. When I'd first arrived after winning the BAFTA he was all over me; I could do no wrong. 'Once in a lifetime a director like Gerald comes along,' he said on seeing my *Scarfe on Sex* rushes. But now he seemed irritated by me, and therefore me with him.

Eddie had warned me that British class was a tricky subject

to approach. Others had fallen at this fence, and I certainly was finding the editing very difficult.

Also, a new head of department was in place, an acclaimed documentary maker, Paul Hamann. I think Eddie was worried – he had got on with Will Wyatt, but would this new appointment destroy his little fiefdom? There were certainly those in the documentary department who felt my light and jokey films didn't fit. They believed, not unreasonably, that documentaries should be serious examinations. I thought that there ought still to be room for fun. Perhaps I was in the wrong department. These worries were set against John Birt's climate of cost-cutting and sacking. Fear ran like a river of fire through the BBC in the early nineties and certainly through the nervous documentary department, where the question was always, who would be sacked next? I wasn't too anxious, having another job to go to, but I feel Eddie feared that in Paul's new department he was backing the wrong horse.

Paul came to see me in my office one afternoon. 'What is it with you and Eddie? Why is he destroying his kingdom? I thought you two were good friends.'

I said I believed he was just watching his back and he thought my light-hearted work might not meet with Paul's approval.

'Oh, we're a very broad church,' said Paul – but I'm not convinced they were.

With Eddie's rather unpleasant chivvying visits to my cutting room I began to feel unhappy and lost my confidence. Although Eddie could be very charming if he wanted to, the other side of his coin was that his attitude could be rather petty and childish. I thought he was behaving like a pompous little Napoleon, wielding his power in his tiny empire. A small fish in a small pond. It was the first time I had experienced anything like it at the BBC. Having been freelance for so many years I didn't understand the hierarchy that existed within the corporation and I realised how lucky I had been not to have to answer to a boss most of my working life. Suddenly I felt all 'doco-ed' out. It had been great fun but it wasn't any more.

Eddie seemed puzzled by my departure: 'What more could you ask for? You've got your own TV series with your name on it.'

But although the BBC books department had proposed a *Scarfe on* . . . book I felt I'd had enough and wanted to get out. It wasn't worth it with all the anxiety and misery. And all the time I was making films I was neglecting my drawing and painting. So I got out, which may have been a mistake. I always hoped I would move on to make a movie, maybe a comedy. My agent asked me afterwards what I would like to do next. I replied, 'A movie in the manner of Jacques Tati, my hero.' He found that strange. I never did make that film.

The trouble with producing TV films is that it takes at least six months of one's life – three months' preparation and three months' shooting, editing, dubbing and tweaking. I increasingly began to think that making films was my 'mistress' and that drawing and painting were my 'wife'. I eventually decided to abandon the mistress and return to my wife. I miss the life, though, especially the 'best train set in the world' aspect, which is how Orson Welles described film-making.

Ever since those early Disney experiences in the Odeon Swiss Cottage I had been fascinated with animation. The pure magic of being able to give a character life, the illusion of movement. Animation is simply a series of still pictures run one after another that bring those still pictures to life. Every second of animation we watch contains a minimum of twelve individual drawings, sometimes double that number. The more pictures, the smoother the animation.

I created one of my most enduring works in this genre in the eighties, the title sequence for the hugely popular BBC television series *Yes Minister*, written by Antony Jay and Jonathan Lynn, and the subsequent *Yes, Prime Minister*. The producer asked me to attend rehearsals and sketch the actors: Paul Eddington, Nigel Hawthorne and Derek Fowlds. He wanted the three characters to be animated for the title sequence, but animation is expensive and this programme didn't have the budget for that, which is why I revived the rostrum camera trick I'd used for *I Think I See Violence All Around Me*. When the drawing was finished we could run the film through and it looked like the drawing was happening live. Then we'd end the sequence with the title of each episode super-imposed on a facsimile of an edition of the *House of Commons Weekly Information Bulletin*. The titles became quite iconic and, thanks to the scripts and the actors, the show has not dated at all. I had no idea at the time that it would be popular worldwide with viewers for so long. I still regularly receive emails, some from people as far away as Hong Kong, about the series as it is often repeated and has been available online.

Back in the early seventies, the BBC sent me to Los Angeles to create a new film on the theme of America using a so-called magical new animation system – the De Joux system, which filled in missing frames. Up until that point animation had been a very labour-intensive process. For instance, for a man rising from a chair, the principal artist would draw three of the neces-sary twelve drawings – the man seated, the man rising halfway up from the chair, the man standing. Then it would be passed to another animator, called an in-betweener, whose job it was to fill in the missing drawings. Could a machine fill in those missing drawings instead? I was fascinated by the prospect, so Jane and I packed our toothbrushes and arrived in LA.

I was once again excited and seduced by the horrific glamour of Los Angeles. The sprawling, seemingly unplanned awfulness, the haphazard architectural wreckage of billboards, gas stations, diners, neon signs and stop lights that line the streets and highways in random chaos. In the distance the blue-grey silhouettes of the mountains through the smoggy yellow haze, and at night strings of glowing white and red corpuscles on eight-lane arteries racing bumper to bumper to their doom, rattling over the concrete slabs at breakneck speed, peeling off at exits with magical names – Sunset Boulevard, Ventura, Venice Beach, Sunset Strip – swooping up and over the freeway to merge with another road to hell. I love it.

Well, hey, guess what? The De Joux system wasn't a magic system at all: it simply mixed or dissolved between one frame and another instead of sharply cutting – a disappointment. But while I was there I decided to make the best of it, to draw everything I could think of about America at the time – John Wayne, Indians, Coca-Cola, Mickey Mouse on drugs, Frank Sinatra, Black Power, freeways, Playboy girls, billboards, astronauts, the Empire State Building and the American obsession with money. In the film that resulted from this, *Long Drawn-Out Trip*, I had that emotional line of John Wayne's, 'The word America brings a tear to the eye and choke in the throat, like the first time you hear a new-born baby cry' – all the while shooting an American Indian in the face. I realised I had never questioned Hopalong Cassidy's continual slaughtering of American Indians at the Odeon Swiss Cottage. Finchley Road was awash with innocent blood.

'The Movable Feast Lady is here' announced the Tannoy. I had just finished turning Donald Duck into a hot dog. The Movable Feast Lady sold avocado and prawn sandwiches, chocolate brownies and coffee – home-made wares – from a large wicker basket which she carried over her arm from office to office. After having completed over a hundred drawings that day I was peckish. I was working in an air-conditioned office in downtown Burbank, making my first animated film and doing the hundreds of drawings by myself.

This was my first experience of a fully animated film. The surreal creatures and worlds one could create and give life to were endless. I couldn't draw fast enough to see what happened next, and my drawings became a stream of consciousness. I found while working on the film that I could introduce a character in frame one, entering from the side of the picture. I could then, say, make him turn a cartwheel, and very soon I found that the character was dictating to me what he could or could not do: he had taken on a life of his own, and I was just helping him to act out whatever he wished to do. He had taken charge. The puppet had come to life. There were some exhilarating moments.

But in practice it could be a rather tedious business. I drew every frame myself directly on to 70mm film, in a frame area of two or three inches; when drawing cartoons I tend to work much, much larger on A1 cartridge paper. The first frame I drew would be projected underneath the next empty frame so that I could trace and slightly alter the image. That would in turn be projected under the next empty frame, and so on. I was supposed to be there for ten days but stayed for six weeks – hence the title of the film. And because it was very much the drug era it was also another kind of trip: a sort of hallucinatory journey. Some days and nights I drew three or four hundred drawings, hour after hour, before Jane and I would finally drive home in the early hours of the morning to my brother-in-law Peter's house in Beverly Hills where we were staying. During the day Jane planned the shooting sequences of the coloured cells, and she and two other women painted all the drawings with brightly coloured inks. It was a period of intense concentration broken only by the Movable Feast Lady and the occasional dip in Peter's swimming pool.

Mickey Mouse on drugs had shock value – even years later when I was production designer on Walt Disney's *Hercules*. During one of my lectures in the squeaky-clean Disney studios I projected Mickey freaking out on my laptop presentation. A gasp ran around the room. Our Mickey? Clean-living Mickey? Mickey on drugs – unthinkable! How dare you?

In 1974 the BBC entered *Long Drawn-Out Trip* into the Zagreb
Animation Festival in what was then Yugoslavia. They asked me
to attend. I flew to the communist country on the edge of the Iron
Curtain. Eastern Europe was at that time a hot-bed of experimen-
tal animation. Butterflies of freedom fluttered on damaged wings.
Birds sang in barbed-wire cages. Zagreb was grey: streets were
grey, buildings were grey and the sky and people were grey. I felt
grey too. It was catching. The main building where the awards
were to be presented was a bleak municipal mausoleum. In the
centre of the gigantic exhibition hall stood a glass case, and in that
case stood the awards. The awards were little cartoon wooden
heads on wheels. They didn't look like awards, they were like
wooden toys. I was aghast. I supposed it was some sort of Eastern
bloc/Soviet joke. I had imagined something like an Oscar or a
large silver cup especially engraved so I walked away from the hall
in disappointment. But three days later, as the award ceremony
approached, the ambition to win took over and I oh so desperately
wanted one of those little wooden heads on wheels. They were
the most desired object in my lonely Eastern bloc universe. I won
the Best Newcomer award, and eventually gave it to Katie, my
newly born daughter, to pull around when she was old enough.
Not as useless as I had thought.

While in California making *Long Drawn-Out Trip* I took the
controls of a private plane as it flew over Palm Springs. 'Yeah, I
used to be a cartoonist,' said the pilot and owner. 'Mug's game.
Listen, you don't want to waste those brilliant ideas of yours on
paper, you want to put them into harness. I marketed mine. I
patented a remote-control camera that films operations. I sell
them to medical schools as instructional films. I'm a millionaire
several times over now. Keep the nose up.'

12

It was *Long Drawn-Out Trip* that led to my association with Pink Floyd and changed my life. Nick Mason had seen the film on the BBC and rang Roger Waters to say, 'You have to check this guy out.' Roger did, and called Nick back – 'We definitely have to get him involved, he's fucking mad.'

Nick contacted me to ask if I would consider working with the band. I was uneasy and uncertain. Although I had heard of Pink Floyd, I was by no means a fan. But Nick is a gentle, witty soul who was very careful to treat me with respect. He paid me great compliments about the BBC film and urged me simply to 'work with us, maybe to do some animation. Whatever you like.' The band was well known for pioneering aural and visual effects. I really didn't know how to react, how to go about it, or exactly what they wanted. I was also working on many other commissions at the time. Nick asked me to come to his house in Kentish Town to talk over the project and meet the others.

I walked into his sitting room and there they all were. It was a slightly uneasy meeting because I knew so little about them. I was surprised how reserved and middle class they were, not at all like my clichéd preconception of rock stars. Nick and Roger did most of the talking while David smiled and Rick said nothing. They all seemed very pleasant. We chatted awkwardly for a while and they gave me their albums so that I could become familiar with their work.

That was early in 1972, and they then invited me to the Rainbow Theatre in Finsbury Park to watch them perform *Dark Side of the Moon*. It was that evening that truly changed my attitude towards them: their show was spectacular. One particular effect had me hooked. As I and the rest of the audience were focused on the band on stage, a very large model of a Stuka (a Second World War German dive bomber) flew on fire over my head from the upper circle behind me as I sat in the stalls, and crashed in smoke and flames on the stage, exploding with a horrendous noise. Real, exciting theatre. I hadn't expected anything to come from behind and it startled and surprised me. I've always liked the grand gesture and at that moment I decided working in this kind of environment was the place for me. A fantastic opportunity not to be missed. So I bought myself a nice leather jacket and some jeans and became rock and roll overnight – just like that.

The band suggested I do some animation for the upcoming *Wish You Were Here* tour. 'Just go ahead and do something.'

'What sort of thing?'

'Just do what you feel like.'

'OK,' I said.

I really didn't know what I felt like but I started work. I suggested that I start work in my house in Cheyne Walk. We moved in half a dozen desks and some animation equipment, and employed two brilliant animators – Mike Stuart and his girlfriend Jill Brooks. I drew a man who walked slowly towards the camera, stopped, and eroded like sand in the blowing wind. A metal monster stomped across the landscape to the song 'Welcome to the Machine'. A sea of blood appeared over the horizon, raced towards us and engulfed two shining, circular, metal towers; the blood turned into groping hands, praying to metal monoliths. A leaf tumbled through the sky and slowly turned into a naked man who, still tumbling, smashed through the sky as though it were made of glass. All very surreal images.

Over the next few years the band and I continued to work together. In the spring of 1978 Roger came to my studio in Chelsea carrying the raw demo tapes of *The Wall*. We sat together in my studio and listened to them right through in silence, Roger singing into a synthesiser. Finally it ended. Roger looked at me expectantly. There was an awkward silence. It's quite difficult to find the words to do justice to such a huge amount of work.

'Great,' I said inadequately, then fell silent again. 'Very good,' I added.

Roger shifted uneasily. 'I feel as though I've just pulled down my pants and taken a shit in front of you,' he said.

I know that feeling of vulnerability only too well, having for years presented my own work to bewildered eyes.

Roger was very clear from the beginning that he saw this project as a record, a show and a film. I set about designing the main characters in the story – Pink, the vulnerable, shell-less prawn of a creature; The Wife, who becomes a Praying Mantis; The Teacher, as a monster with bulging eyes; and the overprotective smothering Mother clasping Pink to her bosom. These characters would become huge inflatables for the live shows.

Some weeks later I flew to the south of France to meet Roger and work on the album cover. Roger had a strong idea that it should be all of my characters crouched in holes in a wall. Part of the wall would be missing and we would see the Judge and the Marching Hammers beyond.

Roger had hired the German actor Curt Jurgens's splendid ski lodge, and we'd go out skiing on the mountains. Roger would carve an almost perfect turn in the glistening Alpine snow. He has to do everything perfectly. He is a perfectionist. When we played snooker it had to be strictly by the rules, even among friends. If a ball was accidentally touched by a cue that was a four-point penalty. 'What's the point of games having rules,' he would say, 'if you don't stick to them?' Well, he did have a point, but . . . come on! However, it is Roger's perfectionism and determination that make him what he is.

We stood on our skis, resting on our poles in the warm January sunshine, gazing at the distant jagged Alps, the only sound the squeaky crunch of the snow as we shifted our feet.

'Oh, it's great to be rich,' said Rog, as we turned to go into Curt's lodge for lunch. I suggested that he could perhaps let me have a bit. 'Do you know, Gerry,' he replied, 'one never seems to have enough.' Ain't that the truth. Nick had told me the band could all live like princes for the rest of their lives.

'I'm just popping to the toilet,' said Rog at one point during the meal.

'Oh, Roger,' said his wife, Carolyne, 'don't keep calling it the toilet. It's so common.'

'Sorry,' he said. 'I'm just popping to the shithouse.' I always enjoyed Roger's sense of humour.

The Wall stage show is without doubt one of the most ambitious theatrical events ever attempted. Initially, Roger talked to me about the idea of doing the show in a giant inflatable tent that would be large enough to act as a vast auditorium and hold thousands of people as well as the stage area, and the gigantic wall would be built across it. The tent was to be shaped like a worm that would be easy to inflate and then deflate, ready to be moved to the next venue. It was an exciting idea – Roger thinks big – a grand concept on a tremendous scale. I made several drawings and designs for this, showing the possible shape of the tent and how it could be constructed and transported by helicopter from one location to another. Wonderful though the idea was, it proved too ambitious to be achieved at the time, and eventually, sadly, was abandoned.

As for designing the characters: who knows what comes out subliminally? I suppose you could say the Mother is loosely based on my own mother – the protective arms smothering and molly-coddling at the same time. 'Mama's going to put all her fears into you.' The Teacher I based on Mr King, the head teacher who caned me for the horrendous crime of playing tag in the lavatories. My wife was not the inspiration for The Wife in *The Wall*. She is definitely based on someone else's wife, but whose I'm not prepared to say.

I set about creating a storyboard for the show on the walls of my studio, pinning up drawings to show the characters and sequences of action. I found it wonderfully liberating. This was so much more creative than drawing stuffy, boring politicians and their self-important little lives over and over again. It was creating something from beginning to end. Something completely new, that hadn't existed until we made it so. Then Mark Fisher, the wonderful production designer, produced highly technical architectural drawings to show the band how it could all be achieved and made to work practically. The scale was spectacular: building a wall across the whole arena during the concert was a huge undertaking. My inflatable puppets would be thirty feet high and would move across the stage as if by magic, inflated by fans: it was a long way from the puppets I had made on my sick bed as a six-year-old.

The helicopter took off from beside the Hudson River, wheeled right and flew dangerously and illegally under the Triborough

Bridge. 'I do that once in a while,' said the pilot, 'to liven things up.' It was the first night of *The Wall* in New York, and Roger, David and I were bumping our way over the silver evening map of Queens to Nassau Coliseum. We landed and jumped out, ducked under the rotor blades and into waiting black limos. It was a short ride to the big grey-blue silhouette of the arena which stood out against the yellow and orange sky. We drove up the ramp and into the mouth of the monster building. A huge steel shutter slid down behind us.

Outside, thousands pressed against the turnstiles, patiently filing to their seats. Excitement mounted. Stalls sold T-shirts, programmes, souvenirs, badges, sweatshirts, posters, postcards, buttons, hamburgers, frankfurters, soft drinks, beer, sandwiches – anything. It amused me to see the pirated T-shirts with their weird approximations of my text and drawings.

We were backstage in a vast, dry, dusty cavern of concrete pillars, filled with giant travelling boxes, a mass of electronic equipment, cables, wires, ropes, a giant circular cinema screen, guitars, keyboards and empty beer cans. Roadies with ID badges stepped back as their bread and butter whispered by. Steel barriers and heavy heavies guarded the band's area. The limos pulled up in an area of pretend civilisation, a large AstroTurfed square, sided by four trailer caravans, café chairs and café tables with parasols – very tasteful, very nice. To amuse the band there were pinball machines. Each caravan was loaded with drink and food. Here the band would rest. All appeared calm as the occasional roadie ran past with a piece of equipment to the stage, but there was also a feeling of nervous anticipation.

The arena filled and the noise increased. The crowd undulated and swayed in the half light. A tense atmosphere of expectancy electrified the air. A swell of emotional violence was about to erupt. The stage was dark. There was an ominous, brooding silence, and then a nuclear explosion of ear-bursting sound and eye-bursting lights. A swelling thunderous roar from the crowd, now on their feet. The show is on. Sixteen thousand punters swaying and waving their arms, singing the lyrics. There is nothing like the feeling of the crowd's appreciation in these vast arenas: it's the most exhilarating sound. It's no wonder rock stars go slightly mad with self-importance.

Backstage and on stage, all is business: people each with their allocated tasks busying themselves building a huge alienating wall across the front of the stage, spanning the whole arena, gradually cutting the audience off from the band. The giant puppets I designed stalk the stage like great ghosts and three of my animated films are projected in 3D on to the huge wall and synchronised with the live band. It all worked like a dream.

It always amazes me to see the end result of what started as a few scribbles on a piece of paper. Roger and I had sat for hours planning and designing the show in detail in my studio in Cheyne Walk, and here it was, a reality, a gigantic Roman circus. The film-maker Nicholas Roeg called me the 'fifth' member of the band, the Sir Francis Drake at the court of Elizabeth I.

After the show the band returned to their safe green AstroTurfed world looking tense but relieved. The sidewalk café tables were peopled now with grinning, free-loading hangers-on. One night I saw Mick Jagger crouched on the steps that led up to the front of the stage being shooed away by a very large female security guard. 'He's OK,' I said. 'Let him be.'

True to all rock and roll legends, there was a certain amount of 'substance' around backstage, and during those days with the entourage I sniffed a line or two occasionally. The effect was invigorating. If I had felt tired I would feel wide awake, as though I could go on all night – and I often did, ready for anything. But I didn't try it often: because of my asthmatic childhood when I had relied on prescription drugs to keep me going, drugs had a scary connotation so backstage drugs held little attraction.

After the adrenalin of the show and after-show party we drove back to Manhattan in a black limo, bottles of drink clinking gently as we sped over the concrete slabs on the expressway. Roger, a hunched figure in a racoon coat, sat in the middle of the black leather seat clutching a beer can. I sat opposite him. Although we were doing sixty miles an hour a bearded figure appeared, staring in at the window. 'Hey, Roger! Will you sign my album?' The lunatic leaned further out of his driving seat causing his car to bounce and sway, offering the album for signature in the middle of the expressway. It felt like a disaster to me. Bonnet to bonnet, the cars sped down the New York expressway at dizzying speed – it was truly frightening. Somehow, with driving skills worthy of Lewis Hamilton, our driver got away and expertly took a slip road into the city, jumping lights and doubling around blocks. He lost the fans. We dropped to a normal speed and with only the noise of the tyres clunking rhythmically over the uneven road surfaces of New York City made our way to the hotel.

As we stepped from the car the two fans from the expressway reappeared.

'Hey Roger, will you sign my album?' said the lunatic driver.

'Listen, man,' Rog said, 'I've done my job. Can you give me some peace? I need to relax.'

'Yeah, sure, but will you sign my album first?'

It can feel dangerous standing eye to eye on level ground with your audience. You don't quite know what they will do. Paradoxically, they may love you so much they may want to kill you.

When John Lennon was murdered later that year, Roger hired a bodyguard, a huge fellow who never spoke. His shoulders and neck were so gigantically thick that when I sat behind him in the limo the view of the road ahead was completely blocked. Luckily he was never needed.

The final part of Roger's original ambition for *The Wall* was a feature film. As I knew well, the movie business is a fantasy world that often evaporates. Given the several abortive attempts to make feature films I'd experienced, I was overjoyed when Roger's plan was finally realised. After a struggle, the money was forthcoming and we started work with MGM. But before we reached that point there were to be many changes of direction and personnel.

First we needed a script and we began to look around for someone to write it. I suggested Roald Dahl, being a fan. I travelled to Gipsy House, Dahl's home at Great Missenden in Buckinghamshire, to ask if he would be interested in writing the screenplay. He was very polite and gave Jane and our three-year-old daughter Katie a guided tour, including the shed where, famously, he worked surrounded by strange objects – a large ball of silver paper saved from his much-loved chocolate bars, the bone taken from his hip during an operation, and so forth. I remember it all vividly because when we were having tea together in the main house later, Katie knocked a priceless Minoan sculpture off a side table on to the floor and the head came off. Dahl was very charming about it and said not to worry – it had happened before and been glued back once already. He didn't seem terribly interested in our project, saying that he didn't need the money as he'd recently signed a lucrative deal with Penguin Books, but would think about it. He did eventually send me a script he had written for another unrealised project, but Roger and I rejected it.

So Roger and I worked together on the project throughout the autumn of 1980, discussing ideas in my house in Cheyne Walk. I made notes as we talked and, thinking it would be a good idea to write it into some semblance of a script, had my secretary transcribe my notes, titling it *The Wall – Screenplay by Roger Waters and Gerald Scarfe*. We had another week of spasmodic script meetings. This time Roger had it transcribed, and when it arrived I noticed my name had disappeared and it now said *The Wall by Roger Waters, Copyright Roger Waters*. Fair enough.

We went through a list of possible directors for the film, including Ridley Scott. Ridley and I shared an agent at the time. He later said he didn't get *The Wall* and thought it a load of crap. It was probably for the best he didn't sign up. But Roger saw hiring a director as no different to hiring a cleaner. I think he wanted the much-respected Alan Parker, partly because he was British and would understand the aftermath of the Second World War and all its connotations.

Storm Thorgerson, the long-established Pink Floyd album cover designer, renowned for the complicated sets he created, had flown to Cairo to shoot the famous *Dark Side of the Moon* cover. Apparently it cost a king's ransom. I did the final artwork for *The Wall* album on our kitchen table and didn't charge a penny for it; I hadn't quite got the drift of things. One of my difficulties was that I thought of Roger as a friend and always found it embarrassing to ask for payment once we seemed to be working on an artistic project together. Don't get me wrong, I did receive payment, but Alan Parker thought it wasn't enough. During an early meeting while setting up the film, Alan said, 'Are you paying Gerry? Well, you should be – no one works for nothing.' Good old Alan.

When I first met Alan, I liked him as much as one can on a first meeting. He was very matey – arm around your shoulder, a friendly guy. He was also an amateur cartoonist and was extremely complimentary about my work. He said the animated flower sequence was one of the reasons he was interested in the project. I was flattered. Alan stated in an article that I had 'a wonderfully strange brain which is upside down when other people's brains are the other way around' and that my drawings had a weird psychopathic quality which coaxed viewers into dark corridors they might not normally have comfortably explored on their own (Come with me, Alan – you'll be quite safe!).

At that stage Alan wasn't sure he could direct the film; he was also finishing another project. He suggested to Roger that in order

to get my vision on to the screen I should co-direct with his cameraman, Michael Seresin, and that he, Alan, would be producer. I
was surprised and flattered to be offered the directorship but had
nagging doubts as to whether I could handle such a huge project.
Seresin was a pleasant New Zealander who had worked as Alan's
cinematographer on many films. Having been pushed together
into a strange coalition, an arranged marriage, we got on OK, but
it didn't work out. Eventually Alan took over as director. Maybe
that was his plan all along.

The evening before Alan's first day of filming, a few of us went
out for dinner. Two of those at the table were friends of mine.
Apparently Alan had at one time lived near them and it transpired
he felt the wife was a snob who didn't want to know him. Alan
started effing and blinding and I then became incensed by this
attack on my friends. 'Shut up! Shut the fuck up!' I screamed,
banging my fist on the table, knocking bottles of claret flying
and spilling the wine everywhere. Not a good start to our relationship. Later, Alan told me I was the only person who had ever
told him to shut up. I'm not sure about that unlikely claim, but it
brought our awkward relationship into the open. I turned up at
filming the next day, but things were never quite the same. Roger
said he was glad he hadn't come to dinner that night. He had a
feeling something like that might happen.

As the film progressed and Alan sought to exert his directorial
control, things became more fraught. With the passing of time I
have become much more sympathetic to him than I was during
the latter stages of filming *Pink Floyd – The Wall*. I can see now
that, as director, he naturally wanted to control the film, and
that Roger and I as authors, having invested several years of our
time, were not about to give that away. I was furious. I stormed
into Alan's office at Pinewood. 'The only credit I've got is director of animation. Come on, Alan, you know how much I've put
into this. I'm much more than that. I've worked on this for three

years – worked on the script, designed live action sequences. Director of animation doesn't do it – be generous. What difference does it make to you?'

'Be generous,' mused Alan, as though that was a new concept in the film world.

There I'd be, some beautiful sunny morning, driving to Pinewood with a bottle of Jack Daniel's on the passenger seat next to me. I'm not a heavy drinker, but I sometimes felt I had to have a slug before I could face the tension to come. I had always wanted to make a movie and work on a huge screen and reach all those people: be careful what you wish for. My wish had come true, and I was miserable. I had imagined that a collaboration between three people would be fruitful – in our case it was hell. What else do you expect when you put three megalomaniacs in a room together? they said.

'We don't usually allow writers into the rushes,' said Alan Marshall, Parker's omnipresent producer. 'We have to get on with our work.' 'Yes,' said Roger. 'But you've got to have something to get on *with* haven't you?'

As the tension mounted between us all, there was one day when, as we entered the screening room at Pinewood to look at the rushes, we found that Roger had had a large notice about twenty feet long stuck to the wall under the screen reading, in letters made of gaffer tape a foot high, IT'S ONLY A FUCKING FILM.

I felt very alone in the middle of this warring group. Parker had Alan Marshall to back him; Roger had Pink Floyd's manager Steve O'Rourke as his champion, although he was more than able to handle any situations himself. I had no one to back me except Roger, and I occasionally appealed to him. I once talked to David and Nick while we were at Pinewood because I felt sidelined by Alan and said I might have to quit, it really wasn't worth it. David said he thought that would be a big mistake and persuaded me to carry on.

Eventually, after all the bloodletting and angst, the film was finished and we attended the premieres. I made some notes: 'Sunshine glints on the silver bucket cooling my champagne in my suite at the Carlton, overlooking the sunny, sparkling Mediterranean. A gentle breeze blows through the open window causing the curtains to billow. Down for the Cannes Film Festival. This is more like it. This is the film world I've read about. I knew it was there somewhere.'

After the crowds, lights and applause of the European premieres it was straight on to Concorde. Travelling at twice the speed of sound at 57,000 feet I ate *noisettes de chevreuil aux cerises amères* and drank a glass or two of Bordeaux – Château la Dominique 1973 (I still have the menu). Bob Geldof and I swapped our life stories as the plane roared its way noisily to New York. We were on our way to promote the film and attend the New York premiere. There was champagne in my suite off Park Avenue, then interviews, interviews, interviews. Big black limo two blocks long to the movie theatre. On the opening night Roger, Bob and I dutifully sat in our seats as the lights went down. Then, after a decent five-minute interval, we rose silently, stole out of the cinema and went to a bar down the street to play pool. Having worked on the film for over a year we had seen enough to keep us going for a while. Then to Hollywood – the West Coast premiere. More champagne in my Beverly Wilshire suite. A white limo three blocks long this time. Bob and I retold each other our life stories as we flew to Toronto for more interviews.

Sadly, it was while making the film of *Pink Floyd – The Wall* that the band itself finally split up. The end of an era. The band famously played together one last time at Bob Geldof's 2005 Make Poverty History concert in Hyde Park, and three years later Rick Wright died.

We revived the stage version of *The Wall* for a one-off show in Berlin in 1990 as the Berlin Wall had recently been breached and brought down. I had watched it on television – people on top of the wall, smashing it. I had thought they were going to be in trouble, but no, everybody seemed to be joining in, and the wall slowly came down. It was an echo of *The Wall*, but of course much more important. Our concert there with its relatively tiny, pretend wall coming down on the stage felt like a homage to this great moment in history. I had a tremendous sense of jubilation.

I had visited Berlin soon after the wall went up and made some drawings for *Esquire* magazine, including one of the grave of Peter Fechter, a boy who had climbed over the wall and been shot. Inhumanely, he was left, injured and bleeding, at the base of the the wall for many hours until he bled to death. There was another boy who had been shot in the leg, and I sketched him in hospital. I visited Checkpoint Charlie and talked to the American soldiers as I drew three or four of them. I felt I ought to go to the other side of the wall to see what was happening, and when I went through I was shocked: it was such a wasteland compared with prosperous West Berlin. In East Berlin there were few shops open and those that were had little in their windows – a toaster or a hairdryer, a book, anything they could find to sell. The windows were dusty and dirty. It was very run down, and I felt sorry for the East Germans. I have recently held three exhibitions in Germany and I'm glad to say things are now very different there.

By the time I got back there in 1990 the wall was already down and they were selling bits of brick and concrete from tables. I bought a piece, not a very expensive piece. You could get big pieces with pictures on them, so I suppose the wall itself became an art form, and there were several pieces with graffiti on them. Jane took a photograph of me in front of the wall with my two daughters, which is a really good souvenir of the time.

In 1990, Roger Waters hired an aeroplane for him and his friends and their families to go over to Berlin for the concert, and the seats were covered with the crossed-hammer motif. As

I said before, my drawings are about the misuse of power, how the ordinary man is crushed by politics and by armies, tyrants and power-mad monsters; the Berlin Wall coming down was a celebration of the people having beaten the powers-that-be.

I received an email from a fan of *The Wall* recently. It said, 'I had posters of the Hammers and Judge and also the Teacher and the Mincer. The former I had on my wall while at boarding school, the latter made a massive (and somewhat disturbing!) impression on me as a five-year-old when the song was in the charts in the late 70s. I would like the opportunity once again to get your artwork on my walls and perhaps make an impression on my own kids.'

Various people have asked my permission to have my *Wall* designs tattooed on to their bodies. I always give it, saying, 'It's your body, if you want to mess it up it's your choice.' Although, personally, I wouldn't. A tough American veteran sent me a video message on a DVD – 'Mr Scarfe, I want to thank you for getting me through the Gulf War'. He had originally written to ask if he could have my signature emailed and would I mind if he had it tattooed on to his arm, which he had already covered with some of my drawings. I sent him my signature and told him to go ahead. Now, as the tattooist mopped up the trickling blood his sharp needle had produced, I found it difficult to understand how my disturbing images had helped him in such a horrific environment, but I was pleased that they had. He ended his video message saying that as a mark of his appreciation he was going to send me his Gulf War medal, which he later did. I was touched but returned it to him with a letter saying that he was the hero, not me. But it does indicate how extraordinarily potent images and music are in affecting one's psyche.

Rock and roll brought me a new kind of worldwide audience, and it was truly an exciting time. But the intense lifestyle was having a disturbing effect as this note I wrote during *The Wall* tour makes clear: 'PS: Small last-night party somewhere in New York.

Went on too long. I had to catch my plane. What was the time? My God, seven o'clock in the morning. Straight to the airport. Flew to London. Only took an hour. Surprising. I felt awful. Had to go home and do the *Sunday Times* cartoon. When I looked at it later in the paper I had no memory of doing it, or worse, of what it was about. I'm not sure it's good for you, rock and roll.'

13

Drawing in the Dark

'An alien, Byronic figure struggled through the scenery and half fell in the orchestra – it was Gerald Scarfe,' wrote the *Sunday Times* theatre critic Alan Brien in a 'behind-the-scenes' feature.

I must have taken a wrong turning, for from the darkness of backstage I suddenly found myself on stage in blinding spotlights and in the middle of a dress rehearsal with Tommy Steele. In embarrassment I jumped into the darkened orchestra pit. It's a long way down. A miracle I didn't break my legs.

One of the pleasures during my tenure at the *Sunday Times* was to be given a good pair of seats in the stalls on first nights. I was sent weekly to make caricatures of actors in plays the paper wanted to review. It was, as you might expect, very difficult drawing in a darkened theatre but I learned to scribble on my sketch book without taking my eyes off the stage. These notes, although disjointed and rambling, would conjure up the actor's face and manner from my retentive memory and enable me to make the final caricature back in my studio. There was inevitably a problem with the sound of my pencil scratching over the surface of my sketch pad, and I would receive irritated frowns and angry glances over the shoulders of the theatregoers in front of me. Usually I feel very much at home in the theatre, drawing actors and musicians. Dave Brubeck, the jazz pianist, allowed me to sit and sketch him on stage while he played to his sell-out Festival Hall audience. I think he rather enjoyed the spectacle and importance of being drawn before an audience. When I drew the American pianist Murray Perahia in a rehearsal, he asked, 'What would you like me to play?'

'Whatever you please,' I replied.

The joy of being personally played for by a brilliant musician made me feel like a prince. On other occasions I sat among the orchestras as Stravinsky and Leonard Bernstein conducted.

The conductor Riccardo Muti was the only subject who actually asked to vet my sketches. He made this a stipulation when I drew him during rehearsals. I was summoned before the 'great man' as he sat in the stalls going through his notes. I stood awkwardly in the aisle for some time, sketches in hand, before he looked up and gave me an Italianate jerk of his head. He went through the drawings silently and then handed them back without a word.

Another conductor, Giuseppe Sinopoli, was convinced the *Sunday Times* had it in for him when he saw my caricature in the paper.

Nicol Williamson was most definitely not pleased with the portrait I had drawn of him. He thumbed through my sketch pad and heckled me. 'Hey, hey, I'm a good-looking boy. Have you been drinking again, Rembrandt? Whose dog is this supposed to be? This one must either be Alastair Sim or Aleister Crowley, or perhaps the young Shelley Winters. What about this eyeless guru? There's only one word to describe you, Gerald, and that's "moribund". You see nothing but death, and the desecration of the flesh – like me.' Of course I have upset people. Caricature is not a kind art and many people don't like seeing their faces pulled apart.

Food critic Clement Freud reacted badly after I made a drawing of him for *Private Eye*. He confronted me at a drinks party and told me in no uncertain manner that he did not like it. In fact, many years later Jane and I were at a dinner and found ourselves seated at the same table as Clement. I attempted to make conversation with him but he cut me dead. Jane asked him why he would not acknowledge me. He said, 'Mr Scarfe will know why.' The drawing, by the way, showed him as a roasted suckling pig on a plate with an apple in his mouth.

In 1985 I, Alan Price and Braham Murray, the director of the Royal Exchange Theatre in Manchester, created a musical based on Hogarth's *Rake's Progress* called *Who's a Lucky Boy*. Alan wrote the music and lyrics, I designed the set and costumes, Braham directed. In our story Tom Rakewell wins a fortune on the lottery and proceeds like Hogarth's rake to squander the money on wine, women and song. I travelled up to Manchester several mornings a week in the Pullman to see how the building of the sets and making of the costumes were progressing. I liked the Pullman because I could pass the time eating a very large English breakfast.

A proscenium-arch theatre demands designs that work within a box. No one has to see the back or the sides of them. But the Royal Exchange, a theatre in the round, allows the audience to see what is going on from every angle. The set must be recognisable from all around, and furniture must not obscure anyone's view. Because I could not use much scenery I covered the floorcloth with my version of Hogarth's rake. I enjoyed the whole exercise, but for one reason I was glad when it was over – those breakfasts were killing me.

Because of my reputation as a 'second Hogarth', in 1973 my name had been put forward as designer for the Glyndebourne production of *The Rake's Progress* by Stravinsky, but John Cox, the director, thought my worked lacked humanity, so David Hockney got the commission, making a terrific job of it, and I had to wait ten years before another chance at designing an opera came up. I thought back nostalgically to the days of the *Eagle* comic when I'd come first.

Just prior to my work on the Alan Price musical I had been approached by the director of the English National Opera, David Pountney, who had admired a drawing I made in the *Sunday Times* of his production of *The Valkyrie*. He invited me to design their new production of Jacques Offenbach's *Orpheus in the Underworld*. I had never before designed an opera and jumped at the chance. There were to be twelve months before it opened in September 1984, but the majority of the work would have to be produced in six – a very tight schedule.

David and I began meetings with the writer Snoo Wilson and it soon emerged that this was to be a very light-hearted production of the comic opera. We decided to use painted backcloths as scenery, and there would need to be a large number of them. Very much in the tradition of Victorian theatre. I started work on my designs. I felt that first and foremost it should be fun. Not too many messages about life, just entertainment.

There seems to be a convention in the opera world of moving stories from their original time periods and updating them. In this case David wanted it to take place in a Victorian lunatic asylum. I was unconvinced by the idea but decided that if that was what was wanted I would do my best. I wanted to create a world entirely my own, so the asylum conceit hampered me and threw me off course. I made many designs, but nothing seemed to gel and they felt very conventional and dull. I found it difficult to translate my visual language to the opera stage. By the spring of 1984, with just six months to go and costs mounting, panic set in. I knew this was a wonderful opportunity to develop my work in another field but just couldn't find the key.

I shared my worries with David and Mark Elder, the conductor, and they were very concerned. By April it was a nightmare – my own personal asylum. I received a visit to my studio from David and Lord Harewood, the managing director of the ENO. I showed them the designs and stumbled through a sketchy scenario that I knew was not convincing. They looked and listened silently. I had a feeling of imminent doom, but they said nothing. I watched as they left my house in Cheyne Walk and paused at the gate, deep in conversation. It didn't feel good. Sure enough, a couple of hours later the technical director, Noel Staunton, telephoned me to say they had cancelled the production. I was distraught. All of the excitement, expectation and many hours of work dashed away in a phone call.

I got over my disappointment and decided to try to rescue what was for me an exciting and wonderful project. I telephoned David and said I was not a quitter and I would like to try again, if he could give me some hope that it would be possible to revive the project. He reluctantly agreed, more out of pity perhaps than conviction. My new approach kept the Victorian theme but dropped the bloody asylum idea. Immediately I felt free to do what I was good at, and ideas began to flow.

Orpheus is set on Earth, in Heaven and in Hell – great scope for set invention. But more difficult than it seems. What does Heaven look like? Does it have golden clouds with people playing harps? I wanted something more inventive, funnier. Offenbach's written direction says 'the Gods are asleep', so I set about designing individual beds for them. Mars had one that was made of fierce weaponry, fashioned out of swords and spears. But where would these beds go? I knew they would look insignificant dotted around the vast Coliseum stage. I jacked them up on long legs. I suspended them from the ceiling. But nothing seemed to work.

Suddenly it came to me. Instead of individual beds, why not have all the gods in one bed, with an eiderdown that looked like clouds? I could put the whole chorus of forty singers in one bed and that would certainly fill the stage – one huge bed in the middle; no need to worry about any environment, just give it a sky backdrop. Next problem: how to construct the bed. It could be a gigantic inflatable, but with the multiple quick scene changes how would they get it off the stage in time for the next scene? It had to be light and movable. The chorus could carry it off, but how would they get it through the narrow gaps between the scenery at either side of the stage? It would have to be constructed in pieces. Why not make a series of flat segments that would slide easily into the wings, painted pieces of portable scenery which would give the illusion of a bed, with Jupiter in pyjamas and Juno in nightgown, nightcap and curlers sitting up in bed painted on the cloth backdrop? That was it!

The next scene was to be of the gods rising, showering and washing. So it quickly followed that the bed should turn into a bath. I thought it would be wonderful if it transformed before our very eyes. I designed the end of the bed as a flat painted piece, hinged horizontally in the centre, that would flap down and turn into a bath in five seconds flat. A bathroom backcloth with tiles and taps would fly in, the chorus would cheerfully strip off their nightgowns and appear naked but for towels in the bath, and a large sponge would walk on followed by soap. I thought this could work brilliantly.

When I returned to see David with the new designs it was that scene that convinced him I could do it. 'My God, you've done it!' *Orpheus* was back on.

As it was to be a co-production with Houston Opera, the director flew in from Texas to approve the designs, and I presented a model box of the show's designs to him. He didn't mind the naked Victorians in sexual clinches. He didn't mind Pluto making his entrance through a giant hellish backside or John Styx (Pluto's servant) in a red leather S&M corset, fishnet stockings and carrying a whip. But the last scenery consisted of six enormous fat Victorian gourmets. They were composed of food themselves in the manner of Arcimboldo. 'That's grotesque,' he said. I thought it was a bit late to introduce the word. 'Oh, no, it's disgusting. We wouldn't tolerate that in Houston.' So I produced a new design. Six fat Victorians in top hats eating, but not composed of, food, which he approved.

One of the themes in our quirky interpretation of the opera was that the gods in their 'Heaven' were bored stiff and sick to their back teeth of the continual flow of ambrosia. They longed for real food. Bangers and mash. Steak and kidney pud. A food revolution began and off they all went to Hell for a jolly good blow-out.

The gods were to appear at the back of the stage through a gigantic, grotesque gourmet's mouth. An aeroplane escape slide would then drop down and inflate, like a glistening wet tongue, and the gods would slide down to their slap-up dinner on stage. It looked great and the singers had an uproarious time sliding down the tongue. The only problem was that the roar of the slide inflating completely drowned out the orchestra and Offenbach's music. We dropped that. Back to the drawing board.

It was an intensely complex show with countless scene changes and an enormous amount of design work: the costumes alone took months. Public Opinion was a character, personified in our production by a large figure of Margaret Thatcher (PM at the time). I designed her as an enormous movable piece on wheels with six singers hidden in her huge bustle. At a given moment, the bustle flew open and revealed four members of the chorus, singing lustily. Jupiter inflated into a spectacular fly that literally flew. Garden hedges were composed of painted and costumed chorus members. Bonny Bottone as Mercury, the messenger of the gods, was dismayed when he first saw that I'd dressed him in nothing but sequinned running shorts and vest, with a delivery boy's pillbox hat on his head, but on his tap-dancing entrance on the first night he brought the house down and realised the huge potential of his simple spangled costume. Councillors were like fat balloons, Venus was a cross between de Milo and de Mille, lambs danced, little girls in frilly knickers played violins, the Hounds of Hell sang, Mars was an apparition eight feet tall. Jupiter was psychoanalysed for his womanising problems on a couch that looked like a naked black woman. I had many singers and dancers dressed as items of food – sausages and mash, cauliflowers, tarts (jam and blackcurrant), eggs and bacon, tomato sandwiches, bananas, pineapples and so on. I really had the time of my life.

A few years ago, the celebrated actor Damian Lewis sidled up to me at a party. 'I was your banana,' he confided. He had apparently begun his theatrical career in the chorus of *Orpheus*, and was indeed my banana. A terrific start to a distinguished career.

Rehearsals were incredibly enjoyable, with my props arriving daily from the workshop; my costumes were fitted in various rooms as and when we could steal the singers from rehearsals. The first day I was introduced to the chorus they were kneeling uncomfortably, supposedly naked, in the communal bath that I had designed. 'Sorry,' I said. No one had told the poor singer, the celebrated Richard Angas who played Jupiter, that he was to sing and dance in elephant's trousers. During the fitting he looked bemused and worried. I explained that because of Jupiter's habit of changing into animals in order to seduce his victims, I had given him a dressing-up trunk full of animals' feet, tails and horns to wear for his disguises. 'Oh, I see.' He smiled wanly. 'It's just that I didn't understand.' He warmed to it later, when he realised the potential of a cheap laugh.

The theatre for which it was designed, the Coliseum, has an enormous stage (at one time they held chariot races there). This meant my backcloths would need to be vast, and, because of the pressure of time, this entailed the services of fifteen scenery makers and their painting teams working flat out on paint frames, all in different locations. It was an exciting time, much of which I spent driving from Hammersmith to Wapping, from the Elephant & Castle to West Hampstead, and to Watford via the Theatre Royal Drury Lane and the Old Vic to check on progress. It was stressful – a report at the time said I was 'extremely thin with dark circles around my eyes' – but I thrived on it.

One of my favourite scenery painters was Rita: some do their job with interpreting genius, others much less so, and she was clearly one of the former. Her job was to transfer my designs, which I had painted on paper three by five feet, on to the gigantic 150-foot-wide, 30-foot-tall backcloths. She would draw a grid of one-inch squares over my design in the traditional way and the skilful part was in copying and enlarging these small squares by hand on to the three-foot squares on the backcloth.

Rita was working on what I called the applause cloth. At one point in the opera Orpheus stands centre stage and plays his violin. As a finale, he rips off his costume to reveal his boxer shorts and a T-shirt on which is written 'Orpheus in the Underwear'. It was that sort of production. I gave him a backdrop of enthusiastically applauding opera fans – inspired by Daumier's drawing of the French assembly 'Legislative Belly'. Rita loved to discuss the individual characters and had given them all names. She told me that when she went to bed at night she thought about them and invented stories for them all. She was so in love with the cloth and was taking so much trouble over it that as the first night drew near I began to worry whether she would finish it in time. One afternoon I called in to see how she was getting on. I was met by a distressed Rita.

'Your master drawing has disappeared!' she said.

'Disappeared where?'

'Well, the light was so bad in here I put it on a chair on the balcony to see the colour better and when I came back from lunch it had gone. I think a strong wind blew it away.'

I was devastated as time was short and just the idea of starting the drawing all over again and matching it to the last one exhausted me. However, I went home and made a start.

The next day Rita called me. 'I've found it!' she said.

'Where?'

'A workman brought it in – he found it in a builder's skip.'

'Thank goodness – what did he say?'

'Oh, he thought it was very good.'

Finally, everything was painted and set up on the Coliseum stage. The night before we opened, seeing it on the stage I felt unhappy about the scene of the gourmets which, owing to Houston's prudery, had been changed from my original food-embodied characters to primly dressed Victorians. I once again felt strongly that I wanted them to be composed of food. Jane said I should follow my instinct and, with my painters, we set about altering the fat Victorians. We painted furiously. We gave them poached-egg eyes, strawberry noses and carrot lips. We painted until about five o'clock in the morning. It was a bit rough and ready, but I at least felt I had done what I wanted. No one seemed to notice, and there never was a managerial protest in Houston. We had lift-off.

During previews it was still a work in progress. I was frequently painting, touching up some detail on stage, shortly before the curtain went up. I thought I might get caught on stage with a paint pot and be obliged to sing an aria. I would make late additions to the set throughout these early previews, adding details even during the day on press night as long as they were high enough for the wet paint not to smear the actors' costumes.

On that opening night of *Orpheus* I was anxious and tense. My feelings, sitting in the audience as the overture began, were unbearable. Over a year's work waiting to be judged. The lights went down and my tension increased. After the overture, the curtain rose to reveal the first scene. A respectable Victorian street of six houses, three on each side of the stage, with neat gardens and trimmed privet hedges. The houses were flat cut-outs, sixteen foot high, and although in house-shape they were at the same time painted to represent respectable, upstanding, top-hatted and bonneted members of Victorian bourgeois society. At a given moment in the music these huge Victorian 'houses' would revolve and show on their reverse sides the same Victorian men and women, but now half dressed, in sexual clinches and up to all sorts of fun and games – the other side of two-faced Victorian society. Apparently prim and proper on the outside but prone to all manner of shenanigans behind closed doors. There was a stunned silence from the audience, and then applause. Lovely, lovely applause. It was all worth it.

At the end of the opening night the director, David Pountney, the writer, Snoo Wilson, and the conductor, Mark Elder, all went on stage to take the many rapturous curtain calls. David left me in the audience. 'You should be up there,' said audience members near me, but I hadn't been invited. I was disappointed.

Some critics felt I had upstaged the show. 'Don't work with children, animals or Gerald Scarfe,' said the *Telegraph*. Yet *Orpheus* played to capacity houses before travelling to Detroit in September 1986 and to Houston in November before returning home to the Coliseum for a further season and then on to Los Angeles.

Opera is supported by very wealthy patrons, particularly in the US. Some of them buy boxes at the theatre for a year or more because it makes them seem intelligent and better people, intellectuals even. The then director of LA Opera, Peter Hemmings, told me that some buy the box for a season but don't turn up or ever use it. It sits empty, every performance. At one meeting he asked these rich patrons what they would really like to see on next season's schedule. 'Longer intervals' they said, after some thought. They like extended intervals to allow them more time to show off and admire one another's jewellery between acts. But *Orpheus* brought a new audience to the Coliseum. Even some Pink Floyd fans turned up, I'm told. Roger Waters himself came, invited by the actor Michael Gough. He said he thought my designs terrific but Offenbach crap.

One sad day many years later the telephone rang and I was told that *Orpheus* had come to the end of its long, successful run and that the scenery would be broken up and the costumes destroyed as they would no longer be needed. They asked if I would like to keep anything in particular but I had nowhere to store it. I'm glad to say that the Victoria & Albert Museum took Pluto's costume for its collection and it is occasionally on display.

On the celebration of his retirement as managing director in 1985, the ENO held a special gala for Lord Harewood. I designed the backdrop, which featured gigantic cut-out figures in the shape of birds – the Grey Gowrie bird (Lord Gowrie, who was then Arts Minister), the Lesser-Spotted Rees-Mogg (William Rees-Mogg, chairman of the Arts Council) and the Whitehouse Bird (campaigner and self-styled keeper of the public morals, Mary Whitehouse). The birds were being shot at by a large cut-out figure of Lord Harewood wearing his sporting tweeds, which I had to copy. In order for me to be able to draw the distinctively personal bright yellow check design accurately, and because it was a surprise for him, Lady Harewood had secretly stolen her husband's tweed trousers from his wardrobe while he was out, and had them chauffeured round to my studio where I quickly made my drawing before chauffeuring them back to his lordship's wardrobe before he could notice their absence. (She told me they'd been freshly laundered.)

Sir Peter Hall, a towering genius of the theatre, told me once he still occasionally had the feeling he would be found out and denounced as a fraud. I first met Peter in 1965 when the *Sunday Times* sent me to make a drawing of him. He was directing *Hamlet* at Stratford-upon-Avon. I remember being slightly unnerved when Hamlet, played by David Warner, began haring around the stage like a damaged rabbit. We didn't meet again until 1990, when we were invited to share a box at the BBC Proms in the Albert Hall. 'I've been meaning to contact you,' he said. 'I think we should work together on a new project I have in mind. I'll ring you tomorrow.'

Oh yes, I thought, I've heard that one before. But the next day he did telephone and described a new musical he intended to produce at Chichester Theatre, based on Eugene Ionesco's play *Rhinoceros*, in which members of the public one by one become brutalised and metamorphose into rhinos. He wanted me to design the set – a shopping mall – two full-size rhinoceros and twelve two-legged upright dancing rhinoceros. The actor José Ferrer was in it. I'd always admired him – he had been a splendid Toulouse-Lautrec in *Moulin Rouge* – but it made me reflect how the mighty can fall when Peter had him shuffling around the stage in my rhino costume. Rather like those RADA-trained actors who feel the world is waiting for their Hamlet but end up in a teddy bear suit on children's television.

I have always thought rhinos wonderful beasts, but they are approximately twelve feet from horn to tail and seven feet high at the shoulder, so no small order. I made some designs and decided that the full-size version should be constructed like a pantomime horse, with one actor in the front half and another in the rear. I contacted Vin Burnham, a brilliant designer who had made sculptures for me before. I knew she would have some thoughts on how to build these animals. We needed something that would look and act like rhino hide. Immediately she recommended tripe:

the stomach lining of a cow has the mottled look of rhino skin. Vin made a mould from some tripe she got from a butcher and used it to imprint on to a thick lightweight plastic that would be suitable to build the rhino body from and not too heavy for the actors to wear. Painted a muddy brown, our rhinos looked pretty real and menacing.

There was one *coup de théâtre* that I was very pleased with: midnight in the mall, and a glass-and-steel elevator rises through the centre of the stage, bearing the full-size rhino. The rhino smashes the sides of the glass elevator and, crunching over the shattered glass, advances on the audience. For several seconds it looked so real that I thought the first few rows of blue-rinsed Chichester ladies were going to have heart attacks. A proud moment.

Although *Born Again*, as the musical was called, didn't make Broadway, the rhino costumes didn't go to waste. One was the lusty star of *Scarfe on Sex* who was questioned by officers on Westminster Bridge, one climbed Mount Kilimanjaro in Tanzania to raise money for the Save the Rhino campaign, and each year in the New York, Los Angeles, Tokyo and London marathons they run to raise money for the charity. So in a way the play did run and run.

A year after *Born Again* I was working in my garden when the phone rang. It was Peter asking if I would be interested in designing *Die Zauberflöte*. It was to be produced at Los Angeles Opera, where *Orpheus* had played. Peter wrote me a wonderful and detailed letter explaining what he felt *The Magic Flute* was about. 'I want an eighteenth-century Gerald Scarfe,' he told me.

Because of the Masonic and Egyptian themes of the opera, my main design feature was a giant pyramid that dominated the stage in the first act. On seeing my designs, Peter decided that the pyramid motif should be deployed throughout all acts – that it should be omnipresent and transform itself into a temple, a mountain and a crypt. So the pyramid was designed to split in half and become hillside stairs, rocks, temples, whatever the scene demanded. As the pyramid moved around the stage apparently under its own steam it looked very computerised. But, in fact, three men lived in it for the whole three-hour performance, including the intervals, and it was their job to push it around. They had a cosy little set-up in there, though – hammocks, TV and a tea-making machine. The technical rehearsals were among the funniest I have ever attended. The pyramid lurched across the stage as its drivers inside tried to find their marks with stage hands screaming whenever it headed for the orchestra pit. Hilarious.

Backgrounds were not painted backcloths but projected paintings of mine, meaning that I could change the mood of the sky – blue-washed morning melted into blood-red and black thunderous skies, and back again to moonlit mists.

Most fun of all were the animals that Tamino tempts and enchants out of the forest with his magic flute. These I made half one animal and half another: Tigoon was half tiger, half baboon, and there was a Crocoguin, a Giraffstrich (on stilts) and a Zebkey.

Sitting next to Peter at a rehearsal of *The Magic Flute* after lunch one afternoon in the stalls of the Dorothy Chandler Pavilion in downtown Los Angeles, I thought I heard him snore. Surely not? There, on stage, the singers were giving it their all. Peter couldn't be snoozing, could he? There it was again – a gentle snore. I stole a sidelong glance at him as he sat beside me. Well, he certainly had his eyes closed – better to concentrate on the music, I suppose. I learnt later that he was infamous for snoozing during rehearsals.

The *Flute* proved very popular and has played on for many years, and as this book is published it is about to open again in Dallas, Texas. When I go back to see a production after some time, it's like visiting my children. It's good to see them again and find out how they are faring. They are usually a bit dog-eared and need freshening up

Peter embodied the word 'workaholic'. He always had several

productions on the road and in the West End, plus many more in the pipeline. As a consequence, this led to some frustration among actors – Peter was frequently absent from rehearsals and would have a deputy rehearsing for him. Once, after he had been missing for some time, he turned up and I was sitting with him in the stalls watching a rehearsal at the Theatre Royal Bath when a well known actor stepped to the front of the stage and, shading his eyes from the glare of the footlights, bellowed into the darkness of the theatre, 'Peter, if you're out there, can you please tell us what the fuck's going on?' Peter had many tales about difficult performers. He was once directing the Spanish soprano Montserrat Caballé in Puccini's *Tosca*. The dramatic climax requires Tosca to throw herself from the battlements to a certain death below. The designer's battlements were at the back of the stage the other side of which were numerous mattresses to cushion her fall. Peter told me she refused point blank to throw herself over the ramparts (she was a short but very large lady). Instead, at the dramatic climax, with the music rising in a crescendo, she strode off into the wings. Not quite the same dramatic effect, but a diva to the last.

Peter also told me that he was seated next to another diva, Margaret Thatcher, in the stalls on the opening night in 1979 of Peter Schaffer's *Amadeus*, which he had directed at the National. At the drinks party after the curtain came down he asked the Prime Minister if she had enjoyed the show. She said it was wonderful apart from one fault: she really didn't like the vile swearing of the young Mozart. It was disturbing and unnecessary.

'But,' said Peter, 'that was the language Mozart did in fact use. There are many contemporary references and accounts. The young Mozart swore like a trooper.'

'Oh no, I'm sure he didn't,' said Mrs T. The oracle had spoken. Matter closed.

I learned a great lesson from Peter, a lesson about theatre and life, I guess. If you want something, ask for something more than you want so that you will look gracious when you accept what you wanted in the first place. Peter wanted three child singers in the production of *The Magic Flute*. He knew if he approached Peter Hemmings, the LA Opera director, about it he would be told 'out of the question. Far too expensive. We're already over budget.' So Hall asked Hemmings for a complete chorus of children. Children are expensive because they can only work so many hours and it means hiring three to play the part of one, meaning Peter needed nine in this case. He knew this would freak the other Peter out. Which it did. During an acrimonious meeting in the director's office Peter Hall threatened to quit, and walked out leaving Peter Hemmings to stew. So Machiavellian was Hall, he also insisted he and I sit at a different lunch table to poor Hemmings, who kept glancing across in a troubled, insecure way, wondering if Hall would quit. Needless to say, Peter Hall got his children.

One of my fondest memories of this giant of the theatre was seeing him standing in the stalls silhouetted against the lit stage munching a Magnum ice-cream. He did like a choc-ice during rehearsals.

I will forever be grateful to Peter – he took a risk and backed me as a stage designer. He was a great communicator. I complimented him on his ability to explain situations, plots and concepts simply. A great gift. He smiled and said wearily, 'Yes, it's years of talking to actors.' He called me 'a great colourist', but did one day confide in me that 'Most actors are pretty uninterested in costumes and scenery. They just want to wear jeans and sit on a stool.'

In 1994 Peter asked me to design a stage play – a Feydeau farce, *Le Dindon* (*An Absolute Turkey*) – to be performed at London's Globe Theatre (now the Gielgud Theatre). I was nominated for an Olivier award for my work. Before the winner was announced, our producer, Bill Kenwright, joked, 'It's all fixed, I'm on the jury.' When I won, the other regular designers comforted themselves, saying, 'That's weird. Never mind, it will all be back to normal by next year.'

A couple of years later I worked with the ebullient Bill Kenwright again on the West End production of *Mind Millie for Me*. I tried to get Bill to spend more money than originally budgeted to allow me to produce a better set, a concept he seemed unhappy and unfamiliar with. However, he eventually did come up with a bit more and I did my usual thing of improving the set during rehearsals wherever I could.

I returned to the Los Angeles Opera in 1998, when Peter Hemmings asked me to design the costumes and scenery for Roald Dahl's *Fantastic Mr Fox*, a new opera by Tobias Picker. The production was directed by Donald Sturrock. Donald suggested a set which revolved to show the foxes' den, the house where the wicked farmers Boggis, Bunce and Bean lived, and then the destroyed den. I wanted the singers to wear masks, as ears and whiskers stuck on to the human face would look feeble, and I wanted children to see the full animal. Opera singers detest having anything around their throats and ears, so I designed the costumes to leave those areas free. The masks were not very popular, but they wore them with cheerful fortitude. Gerald Finley set the mark by not complaining one bit and creating a dashing Mr Fox. We also had a handsome porcupine, a drunken rat called Rita and a singing farm tractor called Mavis.

As in film, theatrical projects don't always work out. Agents for Jim Steinman let me know he was a fan of my work for Pink Floyd, and flew me to his weird, dark, black Gothic lair in a white clapboard house in Connecticut so I could work with him on a script for his musical *Bat Out of Hell*, based on the famous album he wrote with Meat Loaf. He spent several days describing the show but I struggled to understand what he was talking about and what was in his mind. Although Jane and I were there for a week, our collaboration didn't go much further, and I was left knowing I had completely wasted my time.

My first ballet, *The Nutcracker* for the English National Ballet in 2002, was, I reasoned, for children as well as for ballet fans. I thought that if I could make it entertaining for my five-year-old granddaughter Ella I would have achieved success on at least one level. I made it colourful and fun, hoping to introduce a young audience to the world of ballet. I had soldiers landing by parachute, snowflakes jumping out of a fridge, Grandpa dancing with his Zimmer frame, and terrorist mice that lived in a giant fruit cake.

Unlike actors, ballet stars have to exercise and practise every day to keep themselves fit, otherwise they very soon get rusty. The apparently effortless beauty and grace with which they almost float around the stage requires immense strength. I watched from the wings many times, and when they come off stage their chests are heaving and they are gasping for air. I discovered ballet dancers smoke like chimneys. Maybe it's an effort to keep slim? There was a smoking room, through the window of which one could dimly define shadowy figures.

After I had designed the tutus, the head of costume posed a question I had never been confronted with before: 'Now, I have to ask you, what colour will the girls' knickers be?' The designer designs everything.

I think it fair to say there is a certain amount of vanity in the ballet world. Some male dancers, who thought of themselves as Greek gods, hated the bald caps I gave them to wear as older characters. I was shocked when, on the first night, they were wearing them badly on purpose, wrinkled and puckered, in the hope that I would drop them. I didn't. Outrageous behaviour.

When the production was due to open, the *Independent* newspaper ran an article headlined 'Outrage as Gerald Scarfe Turns *The Nutcracker* into a Tale of Terrorism'. The article read:

The children's ballet, *The Nutcracker*, has been given a controversial makeover by the caricaturist Gerald Scarfe – featuring
an attack by 'terrorist' mice armed with Kalashnikov rifles.
The reworking is causing outrage before it has even been
staged. A spokesman for ENB denied that the new production would frighten children, pointing out that the guns were
clearly plastic and loaded with nothing more sinister than
champagne corks.

Ballet fans hated it – what had I done to their darling
Tchaikovsky? But I found I wasn't particularly upset by the reaction. Perhaps there was a side to me that enjoyed shaking up their
precious establishment.

A year or so later Cameron Mackintosh rang me out of the
blue, asking me to animate a sequence for the touring production
of *Miss Saigon*. He knew about my work in Vietnam during the war
and thought I would understand the show. Cameron explained
that the famous scene where the helicopter appears on stage was
too difficult to travel and present in other countries due to the
scale. He wanted me to design and direct a piece of animation to
fill that spot, and to illustrate the song 'The American Dream', in
which the main character is a Saigon pimp who dreams of going
to the United States, believing that all things there are bigger and
better – bigger dollars, bigger tits, better everything. Cameron
was exploding with enthusiasm and ideas when he came to my
house to discuss the project

The theatre is magical – a world that reflects our world but
is not real; it can often be an escape for those who cannot face
reality. The logistics are infinitely more complex than drawing a
cartoon in my studio, but I have enjoyed these opportunities to
bring my wildest thoughts to theatrical life.

14

Hollywood and the Mouse

In Los Angeles in 1970 I thought I'd try my luck and explore whether I could interest Disney in my work, so I made an appointment to see a Disney executive. The answer was *Absolutely not*! My work was too caustic etc. No interest. He sent me packing. I was smarting as I left and walked into his outer office. 'I know I'll be working on a Disney film some day,' I felt impelled to tell the secretary. She looked a tiny bit scared, but I had a very strong premonition that I would indeed work with Disney at some point.

Most of my work has arrived through serendipity. I have never had an agent for my artwork. My partnership with Peter Hall came about through that chance meeting at the Albert Hall, my opera work through a drawing I made of Wagner's *The Valkyrie* for the *Sunday Times*, and it ended up being a similar process that led to my working with Disney.

In 1993 a Disney animator, Rick Maki, said that as a fan of my work he'd like to visit my studio while in London. I agreed and he enthused about everything he saw. Rick asked if I would like to work with Disney if given the chance. I said yes it would be exciting, but didn't realise at the time that he was testing me out, scouting for Disney, and in particular for a director who had me in mind, John Musker. Several months later John himself contacted me, asking if I would be interested in working on their new full-length animated feature film, *Hercules*. I was thrilled.

This glorious offer had been prompted by the two producers of the film, John Musker himself and Ron Clements. John told me he had been a fan of my work for many years, having seen my exhibition at the Sears Vincent Price Gallery in 1969 when he was at school in Chicago. Both John and Ron had seen my designs for *The Magic Flute* in Los Angeles and had been impressed. John was now a very successful director at Walt Disney Studios. He thought I could put some off-beat life into his *Hercules*. I was on the next plane to Hollywood where a limo picked me up and took me to meet John. He gave me a brief outline of what they wanted and a copy of the script. I returned to London to start work.

John later showed me a scrapbook he had made in Chicago when he was about fourteen. He had pasted in copies of my work cut from American newspapers and magazines, and he told me he particularly remembered my lithograph of Jackie and Aristotle Onassis which was published in the *Chicago Tribune* and which showed Jackie clutched in the leathery tentacles of a lecherous old octopus (Onassis). Its half-hooded lustful eyes loll on muscular stalks. Its blubbery suckered tentacles squirm and writhe as they possessively clutch the scantily clad widow of the assassinated President Kennedy around her tiny waist. And her uplifted leg

kicks the American eagle fairly and squarely up the backside.
Jackie Kennedy had shocked America by marrying Onassis, the
Greek shipping multi-millionaire, soon after her husband had
been shot. She was America's princess. She and Jack Kennedy
were America's golden couple. How could she have done such a
thing? As I said earlier, it got me into a spot of bother on a chat
show I was on to publicise my exhibition at the Sears Vincent
Price Gallery. Little did I know then how that drawing would
one day get me through Disney's doors.

Back in London I got to work. I immediately warmed to the
subject and once again the ideas began to flow. I made a design
for every character in the movie, from Hercules himself to the
humblest pot-seller in the market – roughly four hundred character and setting concepts – – an enormous amount of work, but
also an enormous amount of fun. Once again I felt I was creating
a whole world. I tried to give the drawings a feeling of movement
in order that the animators could see their potential. Day after
day I worked non-stop producing hundreds of brightly coloured
designs, intermittently sending them by courier to the directors
in downtown Burbank. They were always received with such
enthusiasm that I ultimately produced a prodigious number.

The Executive Vice President of Walt Disney Animation,
Thomas Schumacher, paid a visit to my studio in Chelsea a few
months later to have a look at what I'd done. Here is his memory
of the occasion in *The Art of Hercules*, a book about the production
of the film:

> I had the great fortune on a trip to London to climb the four
> or five flights of stairs in Gerald's home to his top-floor studio.
> I walked in and thought I was going to fall over. From floor to
> very high ceiling, a wall of enormous-scaled drawings looked
> down on you that had such motion, such beauty, such colour
> and line, it was like an ocean wave just smacking you. We

pulled all the artwork off the wall, I loaded it into a portfolio and flew it right back to Los Angeles.

As well as using couriers, on and off for many months I flew back and forth to the Disney studios carrying new designs with me. Then, when all my designs were complete and the senior key animators had been hired and allocated their characters, we were invited to a 'retreat' with the object of nailing down character design. On 18 July 1995 I travelled to Santa Barbara, a beautiful Californian seaside resort, to meet them all and show them my designs for the first time. I was tremendously nervous. I can see the conference room at the Four Seasons Hotel now: thirty or so senior key animators and the directors clustered around a gigantic boardroom table. Apprehensively I spread my drawings, each on my usual five feet by three feet paper, before them. I felt incredibly vulnerable. After all, they were the cream of the Disney team. What would they say to this interloper from Britain? I was the first outside designer to work with Disney since Walt asked Salvador Dalí for some input in the 1930s, but that film was never made. I heard rumours that Dalí's drawings were somewhere in the vault but despite asking several times I never saw them.

But as soon as the team crowded around enthusiastically and we began to discuss what would and wouldn't work, I realised I had nothing to fear. After the weekend I was cheered by everybody's positive attitude and returned to London full of renewed excitement about the project. I admired the way these animators could, with a series of still sketches, create the emotions of jealousy, anger, unrequited love and so on through their skill with a pencil. They had their house style, which tends towards the cute, of course, yet paradoxically their villains are often very frightening.

The centrepiece over the main entrance to the Disney building in downtown Burbank is a huge pointed conical hat painted with stars and moons to resemble the iconic magician's hat that Mickey Mouse wore as the sorcerer's apprentice in *Fantasia*. Inside that hat was the office of Roy Disney, Walt's nephew, who was running the company when I worked there. (Later I learned that it was not really Roy's office; it was only for publicity's sake. He had a huge office elsewhere.) I met Roy and we had a polite conversation. He was the only person allowed to smoke in the non-smoking building. Everything at Disney was squeaky clean: not a cigarette butt, not a scrap of paper, not a chocolate wrapper or an old Coke can to be seen in the whole spick-and-span place. It was anodyne; everything was workmanlike.

I had an office in the building and worked there during my long stays in LA, visiting the animators and explaining how I saw my characters and what they might do. In the Disney building the animators work in an open-plan studio partitioned into tiny cubicles, in which they weld themselves like bees in a honeycomb. Some practically seal up their doorways with drawings and 'stuff', which almost says 'keep out'. My approach to these very brilliant animators was simply, 'Listen, I'm not saying that my way is the best. It's just my way. I'm only trying to help you.' The animators, who couldn't have been more gracious, kept saying, 'Don't apologise. We're used to having our work criticised.' I prised my way into their domains and looked over their shoulders rather like a schoolteacher, pointing out that 'this nose is too long' and 'these feet are too big', just as the editor of *Punch* had done to me long ago.

My job was to try to keep my style on track. When I was back in London I'd receive a weekly FedEx package full of samples of the latest animation work, which it was my job to alter into my flowing line and style, by tracing over their drawings. I would then send back dozens of my versions to show what I wanted. It was an enormous effort trying to keep the animators following my style from a distance. Some of them warmed to this and adapted very quickly, others never quite managed it during the whole period. But there was no bad feeling at all, so I was surprised when Disney later published a book about the project to find the animators saying how difficult they had found it to adapt to my style of animation.

In the book Andreas Deja, who was lead animator for Hercules, wrote,

> It was groundbreaking for such a well known artist to be brought in as a production designer for a Disney movie. We were afraid of Gerald. Before I met him, images would come to me of an eccentric artist who would tear up all our drawings, going 'No! No! No!' The reality was different. In Santa Barbara we all put our drawings up on the walls and Gerald made comments. It was never about 'This is not a good drawing, you are not a good artist.' It was about making the drawings fit the world that Gerald was helping the directors create. I remember colleagues back at the studio looking sceptically at our designs and model sheets, saying 'that looks so odd'. But it was the shock of the new, because it doesn't look like the Disney we have come to know over the years. I think even Gerald wondered whether the characters would just come out looking Disney-fied in the end, but he was surprised to find us very receptive to his style. We wanted to go as far out as we could.

Various illustrated sheets of instructions were issued to be pinned above the animators' desks. They showed how to achieve the 'Neo-Greco-Disney-Scarfian Style', entitled: 'Mixin' Disney-n-Scarfe.'

'Gerald Scarfe is the artist the directors have chosen to be the main influence on our style. His energetic sweeping line pushes his caricature – often distorting technical anatomy and perspective in order to express his point clearly.'

I was very flattered by all these sheets of close analysis and learnt quite a lot about myself. It was my job during the following months to try to keep the animators to my style, an almost impossible task. Some made the transition but most reverted to their comfort zone, the Disney house style. Sue Nichols, Production Stylist, wrote, 'The puzzling questions were how do you keep it Greek and how do you keep it Gerald, and how do you keep it Disney? People started having mental breakdowns trying to figure out how to do it.'

Andy Gaskill, the Art Director, wrote: 'The animators would step up to Gerald's style, go away to work and wind up doing it the way they always did. Ron and John kept pushing it, turning the animators right back around and saying, "Look at Scarfe again."'

Also in the book, the animator of the little goat-like figure of Phil, Eric Goldberg, has the Phil character saying, 'I dunno, kid . . . this Scarfe stuff is giving me a Hades-uva headache.' So I patently caused problems.

There were nine hundred people working at Disney and one Scarfe. Who do you think won?

At Disney, each major character is animated throughout the whole film by one key animator, as an actor would take one part in a movie, but supported by his or her team. So, for example, the main movements of Hercules would be drawn by the key animator with his own team of 'in-betweeners'. There are at least twelve drawings per second but if you want the action to give the effect of slow motion you increase the number. In the old days, these drawings were drawn on to celluloid and inked by hand. The 'cel' was then passed to the paint department, turned face down and coloured with inks and paints on the reverse, matt, side. This was then filmed. Today, Disney animators draw directly into a computer system. Although one can buy Disney cels, they are separately produced for sale.

When I am drawing a character, you always know when he or she has arrived. Various characters come in and audition on my drawing board, but they don't look quite right. Suddenly one materialises and I think, 'That's him. That's the guy'; I almost say to him, 'I've been waiting for you. Where have you been?' Hercules was the most difficult – the good-looking ones always are. It was suggested early on that Hercules could be modelled on the young Elvis Presley or Paul Newman but I wandered away from that concept and, using pictures of Greek gods, I designed him as a handsome hunk who is not the brightest guy in the world. I do everything instinctively. What does this character look like? What does he feel like? I almost become the character, rather as the animators do. I want to feel what that character feels without working it out too intellectually. The brilliant Andreas Deja 'Disneyfied' and adapted my Hercules into the figure you see in the film.

Heroes are always harder for me to realise than the villains: we all seem to enjoy the baddies best. In a Disney film, as in pantomime, the entry of the villain is eagerly awaited. With Hades, I reasoned that as he lived in an underworld of fire and darkness he should be a saturnine, sardonic creature capable of bursting into flame at any moment. He was the element of fire himself, able to rise from a smouldering ember into a blazing inferno. I designed him with his hair always gently afire, and with tiny blue flames flickering along his fingertips. I'm drawn to Hades. It's human nature, but evil is certainly attractive. The baddies are the best ones to draw. Think Hades, think Trump. I was particularly pleased when I realised that Hades could express himself through fire. While he was being merely sarcastic the little blue flames could flicker around his person but when he lost his temper he would burst into fire.

When I was a child, the queen in *Snow White* scared me out of my wits. One of my tasks on *Hercules* was to make our menacing characters truly wicked and frightening, as in the Centaur who became a Hell's Angel. We all know that in Disney movies good will win and that all the villains will get their comeuppance in the end, but while the wicked characters are there, let's have fun with them. I was told that people would find it difficult to imagine my work, with its darkness, adapting itself to Disney. Disney is cute – but Disney can be dark too.

Hercules was effectively Disney's last film to be hand-drawn. With the advent and growth of computer-generated imagery in films such as *Toy Story* and *Shrek*, hand-drawn animation has almost died out. Young animators were no longer learning that skill. Animators who worked in the old Walt Disney method, who were commanding huge salaries and were being told that they would live like princes for the rest of their lives, were suddenly out of work. It was adapt or die, learn the new method or get out: CGI was king. Some adapted, but many got out, and sadly the great art of hand-drawn animation is not being passed on to the new generation – although I'm glad to hear talk of a resurgence.

When the film was finished, producer Alice Dewey asked me to help with the publicity, together with her, John Musker and Ron Clements. Disney had converted an ice rink in New York into a venue for the two-day press junket. The ice itself had been covered with wooden boarding, small canvas cubicles were fitted with two chairs and two video cameras, and as the film's production designer my two days were spent sitting in one of these cubicles answering journalists' questions non-stop. Most of the questions were the same – 'Hercules was a hero. Who would be your hero?' Me: 'Nelson Mandela.' After the first twenty interviews it all became a surreal blur; I couldn't remember what I had already said to a particular journalist and what I hadn't. Each journalist was given fifteen minutes and at the end of the session they were handed two videos to take away, one of them asking the questions and another one of me answering them. They could then edit the footage as they wished. It was an incredibly intense production line and I had never been part of anything like it before.

The premiere was held in New York in June 1997 at the New Amsterdam Theater. It was accompanied by a parade of electrified floats beginning outside the building and then travelling through the streets of New York. It was a huge event. I had been allocated a seat in stands specially set up to watch the floats glide by. A crew from *The South Bank Show*, who were making a film about my work with Disney, had set up ready to film me taking my place for the parade. I was about to sit down when a grim-faced and determined man plonked himself in my seat clutching a child to his chest as protection. I told him I was the designer of the film and that he was in my seat, and there was a film crew set up to film me. I realised he wasn't going to move without a fight, so Jane and I moved on and the film crew collected their gear and scrambled after us. I noticed the same thing had happened to the directors – their seats had also been stolen, and we all trooped down the stands that lined the street looking for somewhere to perch.

The opening night party was held in the Chelsea Piers complex. I still have the vision of a spotlit Michael Bolton, who sang the pop version of the song 'Go the Distance' from our film, standing with his arms outstretched, long hair blowing in the wind that blew off the Hudson River.

Hollywood has a terrible reputation for chewing people up and spitting them out. From Scott Fitzgerald and before, writers and scriptwriters have had their work altered, bastardised until they can stand it no more and they take their name off the project. I was worried the same would happen to me, but I had a wonderful time at Disney. They treated me extremely well. Together with Tina Brown and the *New Yorker*, they threw a party in my honour in New York. All the great and good attended. They also organised two exhibitions of my Disney work: one in New York, the other in Los Angeles. When the film was finished there was the promotional tour. I travelled in style, with my family, to the Far East, Japan, Taiwan and Hong Kong. First-class planes, hotel suites, restaurants and limos. In Japan an exclusive eight-seat restaurant was recommended to us, found in a back street through an archway. We sat at a bar on stools while the chef cooked each prawn individually and placed it deliberately before us so that it was fresh and piping hot. It was the favourite eating place of a famous sumo wrestler, the owner told us, and the archway had to be taken down to allow his huge body through.

The only fly in the ointment was that while my family visited many temples and shrines, I would sit in the hotel suite giving interviews to an endless stream of Asian showbiz reporters. But overall it was the Hollywood lifestyle as we like to imagine it – the nearest I'll ever get to being Tom Cruise. When it was all over, I suffered from severe limo-withdrawal symptoms.

In 2018 I was in Los Angeles to give a lecture at an animation convention and I went back to Disney with Jane. We had lunch at the iconic Walt Disney building which has the seven dwarfs on a pediment above the main entrance. Afterwards we visited Walt's old office. It's still there. When he died they just locked the door, closed it up and left it as it was: a time capsule. Recently they have opened the office to visitors. All of Walt's belongings are there. His desk, pens, paper, notes and briefcases have all been assembled to match the photographs taken at the time. Even the books in the bookcase are in the same order that photographs show he had in his day. It was an eerie feeling for me – this hero of mine who had influenced my early life had actually worked here.

15

My Mother would have loved it.

The Millennium Dome was an impressive construction, designed by Richard Rogers, built in a curve of the River Thames to celebrate the New Millennium. Impressive, but empty. The general consensus at the time was that it was a great-looking building, but no one knew what to put in it. My friend Harvey Goldsmith was the impresario who produced the Pink Floyd live shows. At a party I was talking to him about the Dome.

'I smell onions!' Harvey said.

'What, Harvey?'

'I smell onions! Onions, hamburgers, frankfurters, chips, milkshakes and fizzy drinks. Money to be made.'

Harvey saw money. Everything I read about the Dome said public money would be lost.

One day the journalist and Millenium Commissioner Simon

Jenkins asked me if I would be interested in making some sculptures for the Dome. Well, I had been completely against the project: it seemed like a huge waste of money to me, and I thought it had the smell of failure about it from the start. However, when Simon introduced me to Jennie Page, the chief executive of the New Millennium Experience Company, who had been given the task of filling the void, and she offered me a job, unsurprisingly I saw it differently. Oh well, I thought, maybe it's not that bad . . . I was to create a series of sculptures to give a true picture of who we, the British, are for the Self-Portrait Zone. The brilliant designer Thomas Heatherwick was to design the area in which my sculptures would be placed. The artist David Mach would decorate the walls with his collages. It was all going to be terrific. Everybody enthused – yet the enthusiasm somehow felt forced.

Jennie told me she felt that the Self-Portrait Zone was becoming rather self-congratulatory, bearing messages about what wonderful sportsmen we, the British, were, how impressively multi-racial we were, and so on. I was to produce the antidote to this: it would be my job to show the other side of the coin. Where it said we were great, I would say, 'Hang on, we have our problems too.'

In an interview in the *Sunday Times*, Jennie said: 'What we needed was something nasty in the woodshed – a mordant look at national characteristics.' And she added to me, 'You smile while the knife goes in. That's your style, Gerald.'

For Sport, I made a beer-bellied, boot-headed football hooligan clad in white leather. I sprayed him with graffiti. The vicious looking studs on his boots were steel icing nozzles from Jane's cake shop. I showed us as couch potatoes, watching a vomiting television, clutching a remote control and beer can, while we became part of the fabric of our armchairs. British Comedy, which I consider to be very scatological and prurient, was a laughing lavatory, with boob eyes and a condom hat, lavatory brush in one hand, sausage in the other and, naturally, trousers down with a tap for a willy. Thomas's floor itself, upon which my sculptures were to stand, rolled itself up at certain points like a wave, to form a bench upon which the public could rest and look at my sculptures. I loved it. We had many enthusiastic meetings and it was all going to be too, too marvellous.

And then we found out, almost incidentally, that there was not enough money to pay for it. Thomas's floor design was dropped – too expensive to build. You may ask why pay large amounts of public money for an expensive, top professional to design an expensive environment when it was clear the budget was so tight it would not be possible to have it built. I found the whole exercise symbolic of the farce that was Tony Blair's signature Dome.

John Sorrell, Baroness Tessa Blackstone, Thomas Heatherwick and I had weekly meetings, chaired by Tessa's son Ben. He was a nice guy but not a natural leader. Most meetings ended without resolution, just with another date for a meeting in a week's time. A week! What? We were thundering towards the opening night and we had very little planning in place.

On the evening of the Millennium party all was chaos. Again, it felt very symbolic. Many of the invited great and good who had travelled to the Dome on the Jubilee Line, packed tight into stifling hot tube trains, with endless waits at each station, found themselves still squeezed into unmoving queues at the other end at North Greenwich station, because most of the security machines had broken down and only one was working. It was hilarious to see outraged celebrities trying to prove that they had a special case and should be allowed through. It's always good to see the high and mighty made to stand in line in the cold night air. I believe it's very good for them.

Once we finally got inside the Dome we were all given little boxes of unappetising food and designated our party area – which is when I became a bit high and mighty myself. I was miffed not to be in the main party upstairs – after all, I had filled a whole zone with my sculptures at short notice, and there I was down with the hoi-polloi. I never felt I received much praise for the enterprise.

Jennie Page rang me a couple of weeks after the Dome opened. 'It's absolutely ghastly,' she said. 'British Comedy burned down in the night.' I learned that when Special Branch was checking the Dome for bombs before the arrival of the then Prime Minister Tony Blair at the Millennium Eve party, one of them had peered into British Comedy's lavatory-pan mouth and dislodged the seat, creating an electrical fault. During the night, this short caused the laughing lavatory to burst into flames. 'It's terrible,' Jennie went on. 'It's been taken away to be repaired, so . . . have you got another sculpture to put in its place? It's too embarrassing to have a gaping space in the Self-Portrait Zone.'

'Well,' I said, after some thought, 'I have got a rhino . . . '

'Splendid!' she said. 'Can we have it?'

'But what,' I asked, 'has a rhino got to do with the British character?'

'Never mind about that. We can't have an empty space.'

And so, there my faithful full-size Chichester rhino stood for the following month. When I was in there one day, a respectable lady visitor asked me what it was doing there, and I told her the story. 'Oh,' she said. 'I thought it meant that we, the British, are thick-skinned and horny.'

When I was approached about doing my book *Drawing Blood*, I felt I needed a literary agent to help me with the negotiations. I was advised to get in touch with Ed Victor. Ed was from a New York Jewish background. I loved him. Lunches with Ed were great fun. A gigantic, legendary name-dropper, his fund of stories was fabulous. He had made a great deal of money as a literary agent and was an unabashed boaster about his success. He lived some of the time in a Tudor barn that he'd taken apart, packed into a container and reassembled in upstate New York.

Here I must steal a story I heard Andrew Marr tell at Ed's wake. Andrew had been appearing at the Hay Festival, and after his performance Ed (who was also Andrew's agent) offered him a lift home. Andrew got into the passenger seat of Ed's Bentley Continental, and they sped off towards London. After some miles Andrew wondered if he might venture a question that was turning in his mind.

'Ed,' he said, 'how is it that I as the author drive a Skoda and you as my agent drive a Bentley Continental?'

Unabashed, Ed replied, 'I have two Bentley Continentals, one for each seaboard.'

Drawing Blood was printed in China, and I travelled there to oversee the printing. The factory in Shenzhen used a state-of-the-art press that ran off high-quality pages at an incredible speed. They would set the inks by computer and allow me to check to see if I approved of the result. If so, they would print sixteen pages at a time for the twenty thousand copies my publishers Little, Brown had ordered. The machine ran all night, and every half an hour I would be called to check the colours. I had a small bedroom at the printing works and the telephone would ring at half-hourly intervals. It was torture: I understood how the Stasi and KGB got confessions, correct or otherwise, from their prisoners by depriving them of sleep. At first I checked every drawing but as the night went on and the phone kept summoning me I grew more and more tired, until finally I thought, Sod it. I don't care what they look like, and slept on.

It obviously stemmed from the authorities, but the Chinese printers objected to a photo of my sculpture of Chairman Mao and the drawings I'd made of him. Although Mao was long dead they were still worried about the regime closing down their works. They also apparently objected to some of my drawings of males with very long willies. I asked them what was wrong with that. After some inscrutable Chinese murmuring, they said, 'Ah . . . too big!'

'Well, that's the way we are in Britain,' I told them.

The offending pages had to be printed separately in Hong Kong (although Hong Kong is still in China it is much more liberal). However, on printing *Scarfe*, the new and updated version of *Drawing Blood*, I find that I have been banned totally in China and we're printing in Italy. As Confucius says, 'Enough is enough!'

My next official state communication was more cheering. In 2008 an official brown envelope arrived through the post from the Cabinet Office. The letter inside informed me that my name had been put forward as a candidate to receive the CBE. I had absolutely no idea who lobbied for it. It certainly wasn't me. How is it that I, reportedly known as a 'scourge of the establishment', could receive an honour from the establishment? And why would I accept it? Well, this was very much to do with the acknowledge-ment of my work, however lowly – an attestation that I had made a mark. The Queen will be relieved to know that I have never wanted to do her any harm. In my younger days I did see the Royal Family as the head of the hierarchical class system we are plagued with in Britain, and although I think this has improved, it has not gone away.

In 1966 I drew the Queen in her familiar headscarf, riding a clapped-out old nag. Inside the rotting horse one could see Harold Wilson-like worms and grubs at work. The horse represented Britain and the stuffing was coming out. The Duke of Edinburgh clung to the animal's decaying backside. The Queen, with a wind-up key in her back, sported a sweater bearing the message 'Britain for Sale'.

Now, here she was, standing before me on a dais. Small, as they say, but very friendly. I bowed awkwardly. After she had put the medallion around my neck she stepped back and by way of polite conversation said words to the effect of 'are you still at it?' – by which I assumed she meant my art. I replied that I was, that there were still so many frightful characters left to draw – the ghastly gun-toting Sarah Palin, Republican Party nominee for vice president, for instance. With a polite flicker of a smile she let me know without any shadow of doubt that this was not a suitable subject and our meeting was over. I stepped backwards – three tricky paces. Exit left. My mother would have loved it.

16

Still So Fucking Angry

In January 2013 I was on board the cruise ship *Queen Elizabeth 2*, just off the coast of Mexico, giving a lecture about my work. As I returned to my stateroom, the phone rang. An irate passenger launched into an attack, telling me I was 'disgusting' and 'anti-Semitic' and asking, 'did I not understand the significance of the blood libel?' At that point I had no idea what he was talking about, but it soon became clear.

I'd always had an arrangement with the *Sunday Times* that, when I was away, I would leave a selection of drawings to cover my absence, and on this occasion I had left, among others, a drawing of Israel's Prime Minister Benjamin Netanyahu building a wall which was trapping and squashing some Palestinians. This represented my objection to Netanyahu building on agreed Palestinian settlements. To improve the look of the drawing graphically and to increase the apparent violence – and for no other symbolic reason – I coloured the grouting red to look like blood. As that particular week would include the Israeli elections I sent the drawing by email to the editor, Martin Ivens, and suggested it might be a possible subject. Martin printed it.

Unfortunately, what I hadn't been aware of when I submitted it was that the day it would appear would be International Holocaust Remembrance Day, and it seemed that my editor had also either been unaware of this or had considered it irrelevant. I asked him later if he had known what that Sunday was commemorating, 'Do you understand this business about the blood libel? Did you understand the connection the drawing might appear to have had to it?' Apparently not . . .

He initially defended the cartoon and the *Sunday Times* released a statement: 'This is a typically robust cartoon by Gerald Scarfe. It is aimed squarely at Mr Netanyahu and his policies, not at Israel, let alone at Jewish people. It appeared yesterday because Mr Netanyahu won the Israeli election last week.' But later the same day, Rupert Murdoch put out a tweet: 'Gerald Scarfe has never reflected the opinions of the *Sunday Times*. Nevertheless, we owe major apology for grotesque, offensive cartoon.' The next day Martin announced I had 'crossed a line'. He said, 'On behalf of the paper I'd like to apologise unreservedly for the offence we clearly caused. This was a terrible mistake.'

I have often depicted blood in my work, and I hadn't held back on using it in a drawing of Syria's President Assad that had been published just a couple of weeks earlier, in which he was holding the severed head of a child. In the Netanyahu drawing I was not trying to symbolise the blood libel (of which I was entirely igno-rant), nor making any anti-Semitic comment, but it caused a huge protest. I was called anti-Semitic in newspapers in England and around the world; my assistant, Julie, received a flood of angry, abusive and threatening emails that were sent to our office. The gentleman who had phoned me in my cabin had timed his call to within twenty-five minutes of my going on stage to address an audience of eight hundred people, and he warned me that he would be there watching me. Somehow I managed to get through that routine lecture, but the following days were horribly tense and unpleasant, as I didn't know who was on board or what they might want to do to me, considering the violence of the reaction to my drawing.

I had no chance to defend myself, being afloat on the Pacific Ocean for several weeks. My fellow cartoonist Steve Bell spoke up for me on the *Today* programme, pointing out that no one had objected to my recent Assad drawing. Various Jewish friends and acquaintances wrote to say what better day to make this point than Holocaust Day, that being the day to remember how the Jews themselves had suffered. There was also a supportive letter in *Private Eye*:

> Sir,
>
> Re. Meyers Culpa (*Eye* 1450). There was no anti-Semitism in pointing out that Israel has abused the people of Palestine for many years. (Channel 4 News has made the same point in far more robust terms.) It was daft (of the *Sunday Times*) to publish the cartoon so close to the Holocaust Memorial Day for the sake of underlining Israel's deliberate obfuscating of the religious and political issues. Rupert Murdoch must have been very pleased to be presented with the opportunity to prostrate himself before Netanyahu.
>
> HOWARD THOMPSON

About a week later I took part in a public question-and-answer session on board the ship, and the first question from the floor was, as one might have expected, about the drawing. I explained how its publication had come about and that I had attacked

Netanyahu because of his misuse of power – one of my constant themes. But I absolutely denied that the drawing – or I – was anti-Semitic.

It was very upsetting to be accused of anti-Semitism and being forced to prove that I wasn't. After years of crying out through my drawings against injustice and prejudice, I was being accused of the very thing I abhorred. I clearly, inadvertently, offended some in the Jewish community, and to them I deeply apologise – it is the last thing I would want or would ever have done intentionally.

When Martin Ivens, my editor at the *Sunday Times*, invited me for a drink at the Savoy in 2017, I assumed it might be news of plans to celebrate my long association with the paper. It was in fact my dismissal. It came out of the blue, as my contract had recently been renewed. I wrote Martin a letter:

Dear Martin,

As you can imagine, after our meeting the other week I was left deeply shocked. I am puzzled in the extreme as to the events that have led up to your – apparently overnight – decision to sack me after fifty years on the paper. Five days later I am still reeling and confused, and I think the least I deserve is a fuller explanation of the reasons that are behind it. Your explanation that you just needed a change seems too superficial and cavalier.

At the Christmas party I remember you telling me that I would be 'very pleased' that you were redesigning the paper and that I would be given a larger space at the top of the leader page. And that indeed took place: in the 'new look' of the paper that followed not only was I given a much better position and size but I was asked to provide extra drawings which were used in other parts of the paper. (Indeed, it's not that long ago that my drawing of Cameron over the roulette wheel was used as a full wrap-around front cover, and was specifically mentioned at the recent Press awards: 'Another great year for an accomplished talent, Scarfe's striking cover illustration for the historic referendum issue set the *Sunday Times* apart from its competitors, and helped the title achieve a substantial rise in circulation'.) I seem to have been more appreciated in the last few months than at any time previously under your editorship: when I came to the Savoy I was expecting news of some sort of acknowledgement or celebration of my fifty years' service.

So to be told that it is due to the 'new look' of the paper that you have decided to dispense with me doesn't make any sense. I was clearly an important and ongoing part of this 'new look' which has already taken place, and received the signed terms of the renewal of my contract only a few weeks ago. I'm sure you can see why I cannot understand the logic of my peremptory firing. I would be grateful if you could explain fully the truth of what is behind this. However unpalatable the facts might be, I would like to know exactly what has happened over the short time between my being given higher prominence in the new-look paper and my sacking.

The fifty years I have devoted to the *Sunday Times* covers the vast majority of my working life and it is unforgivable that I have been treated in this way.

What a reward for my half century of political cartooning dedicated to the paper: I am particularly devastated that you, Martin, should be the one to give it to me.

Best, Gerry

I received no reply. I telephoned Robert Hands, the finance manager, and explained how upset I was and that Martin hadn't replied to my letter. I needed a rational explanation as to why this had happened overnight when everything seemed to have been going swimmingly. He asked me to send him my letter and said he would talk to Martin.

Robert phoned me back to say that the only explanation he could get was that Martin felt he wanted to get away from the paper that John Witherow, the previous editor, had created – to get away from Witherow's shadow.

In my effort to get some sympathy I rang my friends Simon Jenkins, Andrew Marr and Geordie Greig, then editor of the *Mail on Sunday*. Simon immediately said he would come to see me, which he did, and we talked it over.

Geordie told me, 'Remember you are not Gerald Scarfe of the *Sunday Times*, you are Gerald Scarfe.'

My final cartoon for the paper showed Theresa May being peed on by a dog-like Jeremy Corbyn. They ran a short tribute in the editorial which Martin wrote:

Today, after a remarkable fifty years, we say goodbye to Gerald Scarfe. For half a century his superb weekly *Sunday Times* cartoons have lacerated generations of British political leaders from Harold Wilson to Theresa May.

He has cheerfully courted controversy all the way. In 1964 *The Times* commissioned the twenty-eight-year-old Scarfe to sketch Sir Winston Churchill on his last day in Parliament, but rejected in horror his brutally honest drawing of a shambling old man.

We know Gerry, who is leaving us but continuing his career, as the kindest of men. His targets are the powerful, never the weak. His magnificent valedictory cartoon for us last week – depicting Jeremy Corbyn as a dog relieving itself on a slumped, splay-legged Mrs May – drew a final burst of praise and obloquy.

To this day I have had no letter of regrets or explanation from Martin Ivens. On 30 June 2017, this piece appeared in the 'Street of Shame' column in *Private Eye*:

'Today, after a remarkable fifty years, we say goodbye to Gerald Scarfe,' a brief *Sunday Times* editorial announced two weeks ago. 'He has cheerfully courted controversy all the way.'

It omitted to add that editor Martin Ivens was rather less cheerful about his cartoonist's appetite for controversy. His relationship with Scarfe never recovered from the row caused by a cartoon in January 2013 showing Benjamin Netanyahu building a wall containing the blood of Palestinians. Ivens scarcely gave the cartoon a glance before it went in – and failed to notice that it would be appearing on Holocaust Memorial Day.

Amid international uproar accusing Gerald Scarfe of repeating an old anti-Semitic blood libel, the Dirty Digger humiliated his editor by issuing a public apology for the 'grotesque, offensive' image Ivens had seen fit to print. 'From then on,' a colleague says, 'Gerry was a marked man.'

I asked Andrew Marr if there was a possibility of me drawing cartoons on his Sunday morning programme. He said signs weren't good as they had recently tightened up on their budgets. However, the following week George Osborne was a guest on the programme: he praised my final *Sunday Times* cartoon and called me the Gillray *de nos jours*. I thanked him for this by email and he immediately asked me to join the *Evening Standard*, saying it would be a great coup for me and them. So I once again joined the *Evening Standard*, where I had begun sixty years ago.

I was alone backstage in a dimly lit, grubby dressing room before one of my talks. I was calm enough and I could hear the audience coming into the auditorium – a comforting sound. I had that lovely relaxed feeling that one has before the curtain goes up, one of expectation and excitement.

'Ladies and gentlemen, the performance will commence in three minutes,' came over the Tannoy, and suddenly it struck me, and an icy-cold feeling hit me in the pit of my stomach: 'Fuck! I *am* the performance!'

I have given many talks over the years but in the final moments before walking on stage that relaxed feeling always subsides and mild terror takes over. The relationship between a performer and his audience must be established in the first few minutes. I always try to start in an easy-going, chatty way, with a joke or an aside to let them know that this is not going to be a po-faced lecture on art, this is supposed to be fun. My wife has told me, 'Remember all of these people have paid because they want to see and hear you. They are already on your side.' I'm not so sure, but I try to bear that in mind.

Stepping on stage for a lecture on the *Queen Elizabeth 2* liner I had that legendary moment that is the stuff of dreams and nightmares – I hesitated and couldn't remember what I had to say, or almost why I was there. I stood awkwardly for several moments before I managed to kick-start myself, and then I was up and running. The silence of three hundred people waiting for you to speak is unbearable.

After one of my talks, washing my hands in the gents, I looked up and saw in the mirror a man using the urinal and looking at me.

'Are you Gerald Scarfe?' he asked. 'Wow, it's such a privilege to meet you.' Zipping himself up and coming forward, he held out his hand. 'Can I shake your hand?'

'Not just at the moment,' I said. 'Maybe you could wash your hands first?'

Matthias Roeke, the managing director of Rosewood, London – a newly opened hotel in Holborn – asked if they could name their new bar after me. Strange, I thought, am I a renowned drunkard with a reputation for putting it away?

Rosewood is the 'sister' hotel to the Carlyle in New York, which was a famous gathering place for celebrities and an integral part of the city's history. And that hotel's famous bar and well-known meeting place is named after an artist of the 1930s called Ludwig Bemelmans. The story goes that Bemelmans, the Austrian-born artist and illustrator who created the *Madeline* books, frequented this bar and covered the walls with his whimsical drawings in payment for a year and a half's accommodation for him and his family. Now Rosewood had the idea to create a similar bar in London – Scarfes Bar (with no apostrophe) – with my paintings on the walls. So I went to check out the hotel – would it be some dive with expensive hookers perched on leopard-skin stools around a mirrored bar? But I discovered the Rosewood company had renovated the old Pearl Assurance building on High Holborn and had turned it into a high-end luxury hotel. The bar itself reminded me of a comfy New York haunt with deep leather sofas and a roaring fire, bookshelves and a plush carpet – very clubby. I didn't hesitate long – 'Look, if the Prince of Wales can have pubs named after him, why can't I have a bar?' During my speech at the opening party I was able to say something I'd always wanted to: 'Ladies and gentlemen, the drinks are on me.'

'If ever there was a marriage that should be made,' said Geordie Greig, 'it's you and Adrian – you are meant for each other.' Geordie, who was editor of *Tatler* at the time, was convinced that the writer and columnist A. A. Gill and I should work together, and maybe write and draw something for *Tatler*.

Adrian and I met and talked.

'Maybe it would be a good idea for you to draw something first and then—'

'No,' I countered. 'Surely it's better for you to write something first.'

Neither of us seemed to want to go first. Lack of ideas? Laziness? Both?

We collaborated on a piece for the *Sunday Times* colour supplement about the Crufts dog show, which wasn't really earth-shattering. Later, Adrian asked me to join him in a life-drawing class for a piece he was working on. He had been an art student and was convinced that life drawing – figures drawn from a live model – was essential and the basis of becoming a true artist. He had booked the Naked Rambler to pose for us. The Naked Rambler was an interesting guy who insisted on walking about the streets with no clothes on whatsoever, except his boots. It was a protest about freedom. We artists assembled, then the news came through that the Rambler had been arrested again while letting it all swing free. So no model. Adrian tried to book a professional stripper but she said she was 'too shy' to pose in front of artists. Eventually a very well-endowed gentleman arrived and we sharpened our pencils.

On the train to Birmingham for the Crufts assignment, Adrian and I had exchanged brief histories. He didn't drink as he was an alcoholic and knew that just one drink would set him back on the road to ruin again. He was dyslexic, and dictated everything he wrote – he remarked it was surprising when he talked to his transcribers how little they knew of people and things in the world, not knowing even who Margaret Thatcher was. I do have an email typed by him which shows his difficulty with writing.

He kindly agreed to write a couple of pieces for the book I was preparing for the National Portrait Gallery called *Heroes & Villains* showing two opposing opinions of well-known people. I had asked him to contribute one piece praising the Beckhams, the other denigrating Sir Isaac Newton, but when the time came for the book to be delivered, I had nothing from Adrian. Then came the final deadline: still nothing. At that point I thought I should make other plans. Only then did Adrian call and dictate his final copy over the phone to my editor, Celia Joicey. She told me that although he was composing it as he spoke, it was absolutely perfect.

Ed Victor was the agent for both Adrian and me and he was determined we should do a book together. Adrian came to my studio and we talked enthusiastically about the project for several hours. There was some half-arsed talk about Hogarth's *Rake's Progress*, but I still couldn't see a really good idea. One thing that has stayed in my mind from what turned out to be our final meeting was Adrian saying, 'The one certain thing about us is that we are still so fucking angry!' He died several weeks later.

Get to it! It's later than you think.

Farewell to My Studio

Considering where I began – as a sickly, bedridden child, with minimal schooling – I've been lucky. Thanks to my ability to draw, I've had an entertaining, comfortable and fulfilling life. I've met interesting people, from presidents to coalminers, travelled widely, lived extremely high on the hog, and had tremendous fun mocking the high and mighty: exploring caricature, sketching and pulling faces to screaming point.

I've never been psychoanalysed but I once found myself at a party enjoying a glass of wine with the wife of a well-known politician and Dr Anthony Clare, a psychiatrist who presented a popular programme on television called *In the Psychiatrist's Chair*, in which people in the public eye offered themselves up to be analysed by him.

'Ah, Gerald,' said Anthony, 'I'd really like to interview you.'

'I can't imagine anything worse.' I said, fearing he might uncover something I didn't really want to know.

'Oh, I'll do it,' said the politician's wife. 'I'd love to.'

'No, I don't want you,' said Anthony bluntly.

Now, in spite of myself, I have ended up invading my own privacy. I have revealed more in this book than I would have done in the past. My publisher told me that readers would want to know what in my background made me the way I was. I'm not sure I have answered this, because I don't know the answer myself. As I have told you, I have horrific hospital memories: I can still picture a poor man in pyjamas, out of bed and gasping at the window, trying to open the bottom sash to gulp more air. He collapsed and died soon afterwards. But however grim this kind of experience was, there must be countless people who had similarly blighted childhoods who haven't ended up with the 'bitter, grotesque and cruel' outlook that people see in my work. There is no doubt that in my case some childhood experiences have stayed throughout my life. As a wartime child, I still today tend to go around the house turning off lights that have been unnecessarily left on.

There are, however, certain causes and effects that are clear to me. Being constantly behind the others in class at school made me feel that I was a late starter and so I had to push hard to catch up. It's made me a person who is guilty of impatience. Some years ago, my family and I were on holiday in St Lucia. I hired a small boat with an outboard motor to take us to sea. Sharky, the boatman, was a cool, handsome guy, wearing only tattered denim shorts and mirrored sunglasses. He seemed to be taking a long time to get things ready for us to leave and after a while I became agitated.

'How much longer will we be?' I demanded.

'Cool it, man,' said Sharky. He slowly straightened up and looked at me over the top of his shades, 'You ain't goin' nowhere.'

He was clearly right: why was I so impatient?

*

I have also been lucky to have had the freedom of being freelance. Apart from my early years at Scarfe's Studios, I have avoided a 9–5 job and all that goes with it. Naturally, being a freelance brings with it some stress but mostly, more interestingly, the excitement and tension of not knowing what is coming next. The pressure of the deadline, having to whip myself into action: an uncertain way of life.

Of course, I wonder what would have happened if, here and there, I had taken a different fork in the road, but that applies to us all. I am proud to have been known, correctly, as a cartoonist, but have endeavoured to expand and explore, to push my art into other areas of expression like film, theatre, animation, musicals and opera.

I was lucky to find myself the right person at the right place at the right time. My dark, sarcastic view of the world coincided with the age of satire – *Private Eye*, *That Was the Week That Was* and *Spitting Image*. I just seemed to slot in as though it were meant to be.

If I had taken another turning maybe I would have been an architect, a garden landscape designer – or a down-and-out. I would never have made a banker or a politician.

It's interesting to see how others view me. When I went to draw my friend Auberon Waugh, one of the *Private Eye* regulars, for a group portrait, he later wrote in his amusing *Private Eye* diary:

Tuesday:

This morning is spent sitting for my portrait by Gerald Scarfe, the cartoonist. This may seem a curious thing to do but I am persuaded that it is one's duty to leave for posterity such a memorial, showing warts and all.

Scarfe's problem is one which has confronted all the caricaturists who have ever faced the task of making something ugly or grotesque out of my bland, symmetrical features: there are simply no warts to show.

As I watch Scarfe wrestling with the problem of finding ugliness where there is only refinement, stupidity out of high intelligence, spite out of good humour, affectation out of manliness, a strange transformation comes over him.

First, I notice a wild, frustrated look in his eyes, then his lip begins to curl like a cabbage leaf, ending up like a sort of jam and chocolate Swiss Roll. Next his tongue elongates like a snake, until it lies ten feet long, red and glistening on my carpet. His eyes pop out on curious antennae, and his penis . . . but then, perhaps I had better not say what happens to his penis, as this is a family magazine read by many impressionable young people.

I have made a large part of my living caricaturing politicians. They are not all double-dealing, back-stabbing liars, but it will be blindingly evident that in general I don't like them. I don't trust them.

In 2003 the then editor of the *Spectator*, Boris Johnson, telephoned me out of the blue. I did not know him and had never met him, but he spoke to me as if I were an old acquaintance.

'Look,' he said, 'I'm in a bit of a hole. The guy who was going to draw the magazine cover has let me down. Could you possibly help me out – I need it tomorrow morning?'

'I'm sorry,' I said, 'I'm completely snowed under with work and I just don't have the time.'

Boris persisted. 'It's just a simple drawing of George Bush as Superman, flying away with the head of Saddam Hussein (Saddam had just been captured by the Americans in Iraq). I apologised again. For one thing, the deadline seemed impossible to achieve.

'Look,' he said again, 'I know it's a bit tight, but I'm desperate. I'll promise you this: if you do it, I will publicise your next book. We'll review it in the magazine. How about that?'

Well, I relented, stayed up late, made and delivered the drawing the next morning. And I have to tell you . . . no mention or review of my book ever appeared in the *Spectator*. Just one personal experience of our Prime Minister. Beware!

Many, many times I have drawn Boris as a creepy, Machiavellian clown with his foot in his mouth, or in his revolting running shorts mouthing his awful gaffes about 'letter boxes' and 'watermelon smiles'. It shows what little effect cartoons have. Many years ago, when my daughter Katie was at junior school, I was asked to draw the school's magazine cover. I satirised the selfish mothers who, collecting their children each day, double parked and blocked the narrow street outside the school while commuters and tradesmen were brought to a standstill. After the magazine was published one mother approached me outside the school as I waited for Katie to emerge. 'Oh, Mr Scarfe, I loved your cartoon. I haven't laughed so much in ages,' she gushed, as she got into her double-parked car.

I have always pushed the parameters of taste, taking a delight in seeing what I could get away with. Some drawings have been censored and others have caused offence. I came across an old *Daily Mirror* headline following an exhibition I had in Grimsby: 'FURY AT NUDE MAGGIE STATUE'.

On a different level, I feel I was unnecessarily badly treated after my fifty years at the *Sunday Times*. A tremendous wrench. But – I tell myself to get over it! I was saved for a year or so by George Osborne and his offer to give me a page to myself in the *Evening Standard*. George, who as Chancellor of the Exchequer some say ruined the economy, certainly saved my bacon. Good old George. Maybe I should have apologised for all those rude drawings I had previously made of him in the *Sunday Times*.

One of the most traumatic experiences, they say, is moving house, especially leaving a home you have lived in for a long

time. Despite having a studio in my house at number 10 Cheyne
Walk for over fifty years, Cadogan Estates would not grant me an
extension to my lease and we couldn't afford the freehold. So, as I
write this autobiography we have been embroiled in the business
of moving to a new home. I was very sorry and upset to leave my
studio. Working in it for all those years had built up an ambience,
making it a very reassuring, familiar domain. I could walk into it
and immediately feel in work mood.

An artist's relationship with his studio is very intimate. I am a
fairly tidy worker but nevertheless my studio became filled over
the years with layer upon layer of 'stuff', and in the end burgeoned
and bulged with past work and work in progress. I knew where
everything was – approximately – it was my environment and I
felt very, very comfortable in it.

Just before beginning the sad task of packing it all up, I sat
looking around, facing the window at my large drawing table with
its ready-for-work stack of large cartridge paper waiting expectantly and dauntingly for images. I have frequently upset my black
ink with disastrous results, and there were nine jars of brushes,
pencils, pens, water-pots, palettes, pans of water colour, bottles
of ink and tubes of white dotted around, all spattered with ink.
And Ronald Searle's doorbell.

Gazing at my detritus I could see that it sort of represented a
history of the last sixty years of my working life. In one corner
was a model of *Cuspicephalus scarfi*, the pterosaur named after me
when the palaeontologist who discovered it saw a resemblance
to my drawings of Mrs Thatcher. In another, a life-size copy of
the head of the exhausted horse from the Parthenon frieze that
I bought as a model for Pegasus to help my designs for *Hercules*.
Elsewhere a collection of awards – a BAFTA, an Olivier, cartoon
awards going back to the *What the Papers Say* award of 1966, a
lifetime-achievement award and so on. There were statues of
my Pink Floyd characters, a model of me made for Scarfes Bar, a

large oil painting I made of The Teacher and a second one of six flowers from *The Wall*, as well as posters from German and Czech exhibitions. I loved my studio.

Francis Bacon worked in a studio in South Kensington – a small, grotty room where his life and work grew around him until eventually he was cocooned in what to anyone else would have been a hell-hole, encrusted with paint, newspaper and magazine cuttings, photographs, pages from books, many that he had used for paintings. His work was not only on the canvas but on the walls and floor of his studio. He lived in one of his paintings. When Bacon became famous and rich he bought a much bigger apartment in South Kensington but found he couldn't work there. He couldn't work away from what was familiar, so he left and went back to the hell-hole. That studio has now been taken in its entirety to a museum in his hometown, Dublin. Mine has disappeared now, although it was recreated in a small way for the Tate Britain show *Rude Britannia*, and Sotheby's filmed it for posterity.

I have tried working in other places but with no real success, finding it difficult to get up to speed. In the space which is to be my new studio will the same thing happen; or will it bring about a new phase of my work?

I suppose many of the people I have drawn will have been offended by my caricatures of them, but most think it beneath their dignity to show any reaction. Many politicians are flattered to have been chosen to be drawn because any kind of publicity is better than none. But not all.

In my line of work I have never known what exactly will happen next, which is part of the fun. As I write this, I'm looking forward to listening to the sublime music of Mozart when the production of *The Magic Flute* that Peter Hall directed and I designed is remounted in Dallas, Texas. I am also putting together a complete archive and potential show of my Pink Floyd work from first scribble to full-blown epic, telling step-by-step the journey we took to make *The Wall*. I'm hoping a museum will take the (huge) remaining body of my work, both political and theatrical, and house it as a permanent collection.

At the same time as writing this autobiography I have enjoyed putting together a companion book, a large 'coffee-table' collection called *Scarfe: Sixty Years of Being Rude*. It contains a comprehensive review of my work from my teenage years to date with a running commentary to accompany the many, many pictures. My editor, David, tells me these are the only books he can remember having publicity articles written in both *Heavy Metal* magazine and *Saga* magazine. I'm proud of that.

I've had a rollicking good time and I intend to go on being rude as long as I can. I've enjoyed writing this, but reluctantly I must let go and get on with the rest of my life. Even at my advanced age I still have enough energy and drive to keep producing ideas and works. I draw all the time – I need to draw – and can't imagine ever wanting to stop.

There comes a point with a drawing when I feel it is finished. Go on beyond that point and the drawing could be ruined. Maybe the same applies to this autobiography, but I feel as though I could go on refining and adding new stories ad infinitum. However, my publishers tell me that cannot be. There is a schedule and I should keep to it. They are desperate for the manuscript and must have it today.

But, one last thing, I must tell you. While I was in Angkor Wat— oh, hang on . . . that's them at the door now . . .

Acknowledgements

I would like to thank the following:

My wife, Jane Scarfe, for her enormous support and advice during the writing of this book.

My assistant, Julie Davies, for patiently typing the manuscript and alterations from my hand-written scrawl.

My editors, Tim Whiting and David Bamford, and the following people at Little, Brown, without whom this book would not have been possible: Daniel Balado and Viv Lipski, Clara Diaz, Abby Marshall, Nico Taylor, Linda Silverman, Emily Moran, Sarah Shrubb, Louise Newton, Mike Young, and Sian Rance for her work on the inside cover.

sixty years of being rude

In the stunning retrospective *Scarfe*, which expands on
2005's *Drawing Blood* in every way, Gerald Scarfe's work is presented
as no book has presented it before. This fully illustrated, 576-page
volume reveals the truth of sixty years of politics and culture, packed
with images that have defined not only one artist's career, but also
twentieth and twenty-first century British life. A showcase of Scarfe's
glittering career in design, reportage and showbusiness, *Scarfe* presents
drawings, sculptures and photographs alongside witty and poignant
captions and stories. Scarfe's muses: Thatcher, Clinton, Blair, May and
Trump, as well as many other titanic figures of our times are all
here, revealed as they really are by Scarfe's cutting pen. Carefully
curated by the artist himself, this monumental book is the
definitive guide to the career of a national treasure.

Exclusive editions available at
www.scarfebook.com

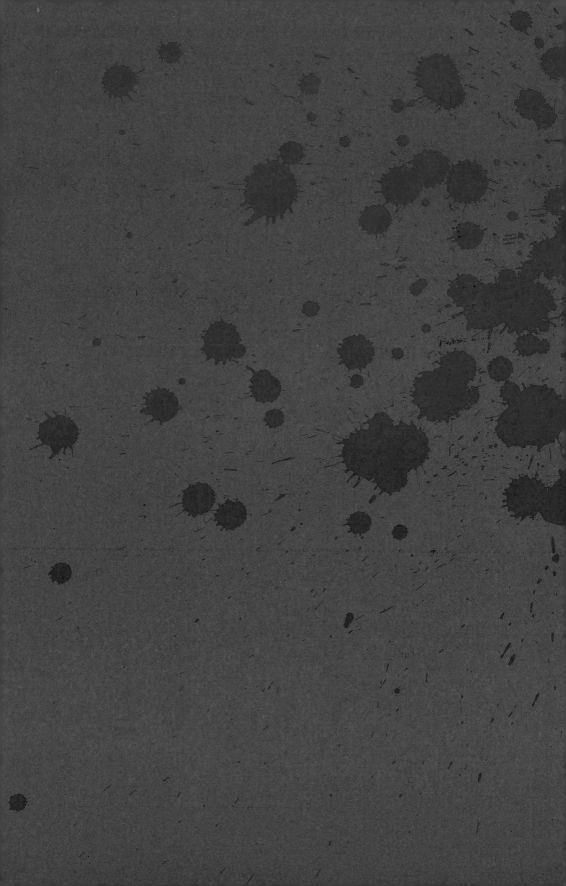